PROFESSIONAL HECKLER

THIRSTY OR HUNGRY?

McGill-Queen's University Press
Montreal and Kingston | London | Chicago

PROFESSIONAL HECKLER

The Life and Art of DUNCAN MACPHERSON

TERRY MOSHER

Foreword by John Honderich

ISBN 978-0-2280-0212-3 (cloth)
ISBN 978-0-2280-0156-0 (paper)

Legal deposit second quarter 2020
Bibliothèque nationale du Québec

Printed in Canada on acid-free paper

Funded by the Government of Canada | Financé par le gouvernement du Canada | Canada

Canada Council for the Arts | Conseil des arts du Canada

We acknowledge the support of the Canada Council for the Arts.

Nous remercions le Conseil des arts du Canada de son soutien.

Library and Archives Canada Cataloguing in Publication

Title: Professional heckler : the life and art of Duncan MacPherson / Terry Mosher ; foreword by John Honderich.

Names: Mosher, Terry, 1942– author. | Honderich, John, 1946– writer of foreword. | Container (of work): Macpherson, Duncan, 1924–1993. Works. Selections.

Identifiers: Canadiana 20190232714 | ISBN 9780228002123 (hardcover) | ISBN 9780228001560 (softcover)

Subjects: LCSH: Macpherson, Duncan, 1924–1993. | LCSH: Editorial cartoonists–Canada–Biography. | LCGFT: Biographies.

Classification: LCC NC1449.M3 M68 2020 | DDC 741.5/6971–dc23

Set in 11/14 Bulmer by Sayre Street Books
Book design by Garet Markvoort, zijn digital

This book is dedicated to the memory of Bob Ross,

who got it right – at least twice.

CONTENTS

FOREWORD

Cartooning, at its finest, is a rare art. Its practitioners are many, its giants are few. To be a giant is to have not one but two fundamental skills.

The first is to be able to survey the landscape and then deftly grab out of the ether an absurdity, an irony, a scandal, or a point of humour that will resonate. The second is to be able to translate that idea into an image – and draw it brilliantly.

How else to describe Duncan Macpherson's famous cartoon about Prime Minister John Diefenbaker's contentious decision to scrap the RCAF's AVRO Arrow program? The controversy was explicit. The outrage over the loss of more than fourteen thousand jobs was palpable. Yet how to capture the essence of that dramatic moment? To Macpherson, the answer came in a centuries-old offhand remark from the last French queen, Marie Antoinette. When told the peasants of her country had no bread, she reportedly sniped, "Let them eat cake." The cartoonist's idea came to life in his dazzling drawing of Diefenbaker in the plumes, jewels, and feathers of a French queen of the eighteenth century.

Voila! A cartooning masterpiece.

To sum up Duncan Macpherson by saying that he lived a raucous yet immensely creative existence would be a gross simplification. The story of his life is a tale best told by someone who knew and appreciated the man and his art, and who thoroughly understands the world of political caricature. Who better, then, to chronicle Duncan Macpherson's memorable personal journey than another Canadian cartooning giant, Terry Mosher, known nationally as Aislin? Although he continues to draw for the *Montreal*

Gazette, Mosher has also devoted a great deal of his energy to ensuring that Canadians never forget their great cartoonists.

It was Mosher's inspiration, and his alone, to write Macpherson's story. From the family, he secured full access to the man's personal journals and photos. He also spent countless hours poring through old Macpherson cartoons in forgotten corners of the *Toronto Star*, in the vaults of Library and Archives Canada in Ottawa, and in the collection held by Montreal's McCord Museum. He interviewed a host of former Macpherson colleagues, friends, and acquaintances to learn their stories – and debunk a few myths.

In his narrative, Mosher takes us back to Duncan Macpherson's early days as an illustrator at the *Montreal Standard* and *Maclean's* before tracing his path to the *Toronto Star* in 1958.

It was a golden age at the newspaper. My father, Beland Honderich, then the *Star*'s publisher, had brought together such journalistic stars as Pierre Berton, Ron Haggart, Milt Dunnell, Val Sears, and the caped Nathan Cohen – and he also hired Duncan Macpherson. The cartoonist and the publisher formed a unique and lasting bond that survived many a tumult. It also led to Macpherson winning the right to control copyright of his work, the first Canadian cartoonist ever to do so.

During his thirty-five-year career at the *Star*, Macpherson developed a highly personalized style that often ventured from the humorous to the wicked. His one-time colleague Gary Lautens once characterized his work as a combination of "Mary Poppins, Mark Twain, and Attila the Hun." In the craggy wrinkles of former prime minister John Diefenbaker, Macpherson found the perfect foil, and Mosher takes particular delight in leading the reader through this fascinating era when Macpherson first won his fame.

The yarns Mosher has unearthed about Duncan Macpherson's life – and his adventures along the way – make for fascinating reading. But Mosher always intended this book to be principally about Macpherson's art, so he takes readers on a journey through a collection of the cartoons and illustrations he feels are the best and most representative of his friend's career, with context provided by the text.

Aislin's objective in undertaking this project was always to reacquaint Canadians with the genius of Duncan Macpherson and to firmly establish the artist's reputation as the best editorial cartoonist Canada has ever had. With this engrossing book, he has surely succeeded.

John Honderich
Chairman of the *Toronto Star*'s Board of Directors
30 June 2019

PROFESSIONAL HECKLER

A LITTLE SELF-RESTRAINT, S'IL VOUS PLAIT!

When Duncan Macpherson worked as the *Toronto Star*'s political cartoonist from the late 1950s to the early 1990s, he had a myriad devoted followers, all of whom had their own favourite Macpherson caricature. In his time, "Dunc" was the most celebrated political cartoonist in Canadian history.

At the end of my twelve months becoming reacquainted with Macpherson's body of work, I was able to confirm that cartoons I had loved when they were first printed were as good as I had remembered. One standout, which Duncan and I had actually discussed at the time, is a caricature he drew for the *Star* in 1975: Prime Minister Pierre Trudeau is living the high life, drinking champagne and tripping the light fantastic, as he boots a humble Joe Citizen out of the way. Macpherson used text very sparingly in order to focus attention on the drawing. The cutline simply reads, "A little self-restraint, s'il vous plaît!"

In this cartoon, Duncan shows his mastery of costume detail, as well as his uncommon ability to suggest movement within a static image – just look at Trudeau's protruding foot and the little man flying through the air, toes spread wide in anticipation of a rough landing. Trudeau's apparent arrogance and disdain are captured with just a few simple lines in the face.

Lots of people knew Duncan Macpherson, so what qualifies me to write a book about him, other than the fact that I admired him and am still standing? Well, no one else seems to be doing it. People are starting to forget about Duncan and his art, and that doesn't seem right to me. In my

There was so much I wanted to see!
Putting my head down to draw
meant I might miss something.

DUNCAN MACPHERSON

1

THE DUNCAN I KNEW

Ian Macpherson, Duncan's son, sits in front of a display of his father's originals at the *Toronto Star*.

not always humble opinion, Macpherson drew as well, if not better, than any other Canadian artist who comes to mind. He combined that talent with a diamond-drill wit. This book is therefore my personal contribution to keeping the memory of Duncan Macpherson alive.

The idea of writing this has been simmering in the back of my mind for years. Although Macpherson had published nineteen books of his own – mostly annual collections – no one had ever done an in-depth look at the person: his childhood, his wartime experiences, his training, his career as a cartoonist, and how he felt about it all. He inspired me and a generation (or two) of others working in the same field. For that reason, I was not interested in simply selecting several hundred of his cartoons, adding a few explanatory notes, and publishing a deluxe, boxed edition for your coffee table.

Macpherson's family, friends, and colleagues – even a few politicians – have been extremely generous about sharing their stories with me. Macpherson's wife, Dorothy, and their son, Ian, lent me the private journals Duncan wrote in 1984 and trusted me to make respectful use of them. Despite the occasional head-scratcher (the late-night writing may sometimes have been inspired by a bottle of Scotch), these fascinating journals have offered essential insight into Macpherson's memories, interests, and pet complaints, and provided the jump-off point for the narrative.

In preparing to write this book, I spent many a happy hour poking in archives and reading books and articles from decades ago. From all this research, I selected my favourite Duncan Macpherson paintings, illustrations, and caricatures in the hope of expanding every reader's list of best-loved Macpherson pieces. I have also revisited my personal memories of the man in order to explain the immense impact he had on my life and career.

Duncan Macpherson and I first met in early 1971. We both happened to be doing courtroom sketches during the Front de Libération du Québec (FLQ) trials, he for the *Toronto Star* and I for the *Montreal Star*.

At the close of each day's proceedings, there was a chaotic scene at the taxi rank, as reporters and courtroom artists rushed off to meet their filing deadlines. One afternoon, five of us piled

Macpherson's sketches of brothers Paul and Jacques Rose, on trial in Montreal in 1971 following the FLQ crisis.

into a cab that was headed downtown. *Montreal Star* crime reporter Paul Dubois turned to Macpherson, who was sitting in the back seat. "Duncan," said Paul, with a twinkle in his eye, "I'd like you to meet our new guy, Aislin."

"Well, well, well," said Macpherson in that surprisingly high-pitched, crackly voice of his. "Can I buy you a drink?" A number of brandies later at the Montreal Press Club – well, I really don't remember too much after that, but we did agree to get together when I was next in Toronto.

Of course, I had admired Macpherson's work for decades before we actually met. When I was a boy, our family lived for some years in Toronto. As my father was a freelance writer, he and my mother were friends with many of the prominent journalists of the day. We subscribed to both the *Toronto Star* and *Maclean's* magazine, which is where I was first exposed to Duncan Macpherson's art. Although I greatly admired his cartoons and illustrations, it never occurred to me then that I could follow a similar career path.

As a teenager, I did develop some drawing ability, but I assumed that one needed a degree in political science to be an editorial cartoonist. Since I was always being thrown out of school for one reason or another, that degree seemed an unlikely prospect.

In 1962 my parents sent me to Toronto's Central Technical School, where I studied life drawing under an elderly professor by the name of Bob Ross. Under his tutelage, something clicked: I began to understand line, shadow, and the dramatic use of form and layout. It was only when I started my research for this book that I

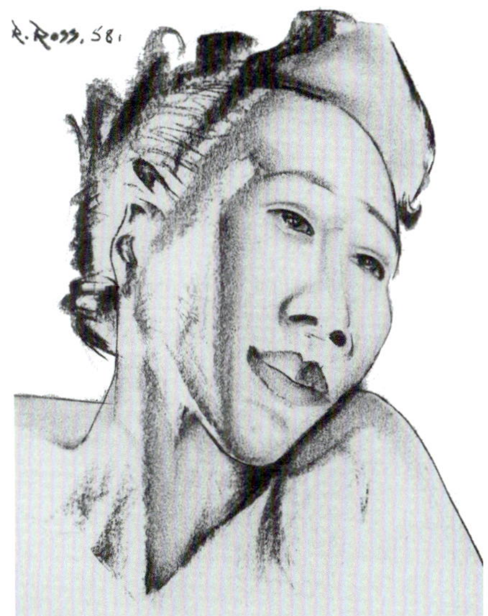

Bob Ross's 1958 drawing of his favourite model (name unknown).

An original Macpherson cartoon, given to Ian McLaren, producer of *The Hecklers* for the National Film Board.

learned that Macpherson had also studied briefly at Central Tech in 1940. In his journals, he credits the development of his ability to draw the human figure to a young teacher named Bob Ross. It was immediately obvious to me that this book should be dedicated to our teacher's memory.

When I met Macpherson, I had just begun to establish myself as a cartoonist, working for the *Montreal Star* and freelancing for a number of other Canadian publications. I came up with the idea of doing some work in Europe, and wanted to take my young family along.

The *Montreal Star* and others agreed to fund an extended sketching tour of the Continent, and I got a $4,000 Canada Council grant to study cartooning in Europe. Over the eight-month trip, I talked to as many cartoonists and visited as many libraries, museums, and newspapers as possible.

I was pleasantly surprised by the seriousness with which the Europeans had studied and catalogued their political cartoons. When I got back to Montreal, I was loudly complaining at the Montreal Press Club one night about the lack of any extensive history of Canadian editorial cartooning. Within two days, my office phone rang. (By this time, I had moved over to the *Montreal Gazette*, where I have been a fixture ever since.) It was Ian McLaren, a hotshot producer at the National Film Board (NFB). He had overheard my rant and suggested I stop complaining and do something. "How about helping me put together a documentary on Canadian political cartooning?" he asked.

Before I could agree, I had to talk to Duncan. I wanted his reaction to the potential project and, if possible, to secure his commitment to participate in some form. He was the country's pre-eminent cartoonist, so there was no going forward with the film – or the subsequent book – without his cooperation.

To my relief, Macpherson was quite taken with the whole idea; I believe he expected his work would be the principal focus of the film. I began travelling regularly to Toronto to meet with him. We would discuss the content and approach for the film – then we would socialize.

By 1975, McLaren and the team had produced a delightful film called *The Hecklers*, which received excellent reviews when it aired on the television arm of the Canadian Broadcasting Corporation (CBC).

McLaren got the NFB's renowned animation studio to bring to life a number of the cartoons included in the movie. In addition, Macpherson allowed us to film him – through a glass plate and from below – as he created an original cartoon of Pierre Trudeau.

Macpherson and his work did feature prominently in the movie, but we also got good interviews with John Diefenbaker, Robert Stanfield, Pierre Berton, and caricaturists Len Norris and Robert LaPalme, among others. Although the sitting prime minister, Pierre Trudeau, declined to

LEFT | The National Film Board's shooting stage, 1973. Ian McLaren watches Duncan Macpherson sketch.

RIGHT | John Diefenbaker being interviewed in his Parliament Hill office by Terry Mosher and Ian McLaren for the film *The Hecklers*.

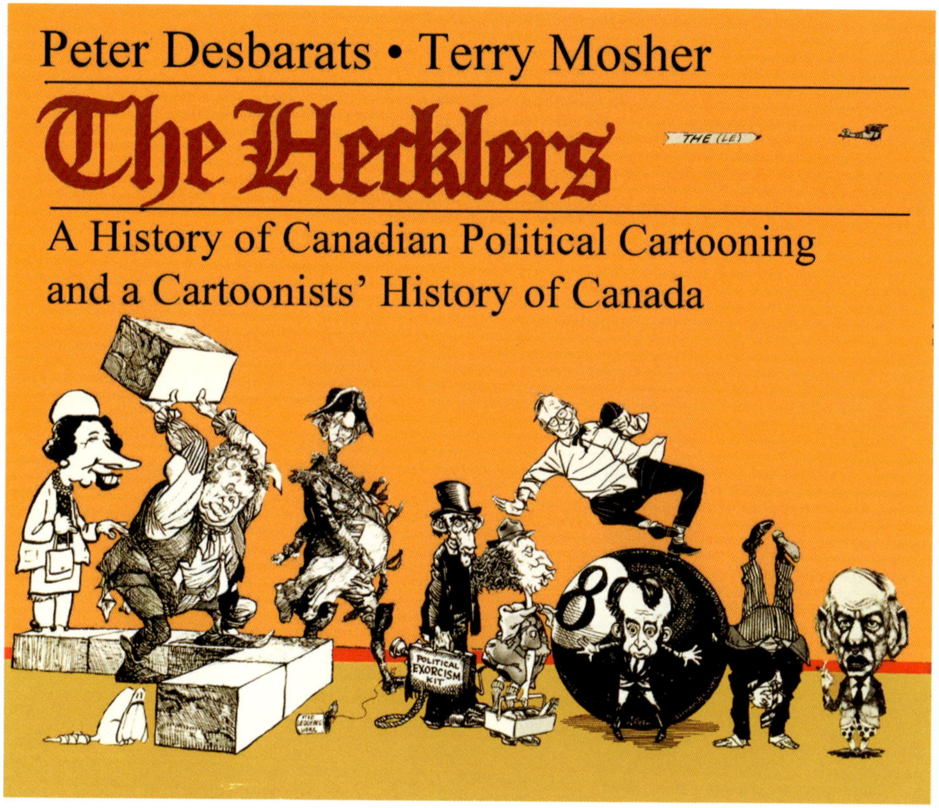

"There is no way in which you can deal with a heckling cartoonist. If he's good, you know he's good, and you just have to take it." Robert Stanfield (1975), from the film *The Hecklers*.

be interviewed, many other politicians agreed to participate. Even the delightful Joey Smallwood spoke to us on camera.

Because we had a generous budget – those were the days! – we were able to compile a lot of valuable historical material. Obviously, much of it couldn't be covered in an hour-long film, so my basement filing cabinets were crammed full of unused research. On a visit to Toronto, I talked to Anna Porter, then at McClelland and Stewart, about the possibility of producing a book. She agreed, and signed author Peter Desbarats to work with me. Desbarats and I pored over the material for several years, choosing the best and most representative pieces. *The Hecklers* was published in 1979, and although it is due for an update – so many talented cartoonists having come on the scene since then – it remains the book of record on the subject of political cartooning in Canada.

Sometime afterwards, I asked Macpherson if he had actually read the book, and if so, what he had thought. "Yes. Excellent!" he said. "Very good, very good. But then, I only read the bits about myself."

ADVICE

As we got to know each other better through working on the film, Macpherson became my mentor. It wasn't that he influenced my drawing style so much as that he gave me great advice on managing my professional progress. In 1975 Macpherson finally told me I should have enough confidence in my own abilities to quit the *Montreal Gazette* as an employee. He recommended that I negotiate a new agreement with the newspaper, this time as an independent contractor. He showed me the contractual arrangements he had hammered out with the *Toronto Star* so I could use them as a template.

Thankfully, the *Gazette* had a great publisher at that time by the name of Mark Farrell. He agreed to almost everything. Popular *Vancouver Sun* cartoonist Roy Peterson learned what I had negotiated, so I sent him a copy of my final agreement with the *Gazette*. He in turn took this contract to his editors. The editor-in-chief was quite shocked and, to quote Roy, "talks ended in a Mexican standoff." Although he didn't get everything he hoped for, Peterson's terms of employment eventually did improve, especially when he won multiple National Newspaper Awards (NNAS) in the 1980s. Thus it was that Macpherson paved the way for a number of Canadian cartoonists to better their working conditions.

I can't pretend that it was always a pleasure to be with Duncan. When he was drinking, he could be heavy-handed, arrogant, and a troublemaker. He freely acknowledged these faults, but insisted I was worse. I'm in no position to judge.

One Friday night, the two of us managed to get barred for life from the Toronto Press Club. We were standing at the bar with Des English, art director at the *Toronto Star*, when Macpherson wandered off to speak to someone. A few minutes later, I heard a great crash. Macpherson was flat on his back, a giant towering over him. I am 5'8". What I lacked in height, I made up for in foolhardiness. I charged down the bar, made a leap at the guy, and simply bounced off him. A general bar fight ensued. Macpherson grabbed me by my bloody shirt and dragged me out of the place, going up and down several sets of stairs. We then re-entered the Press Club by a secret back door, which led to another part of the bar. Macpherson demanded more drinks for us both. No one would oblige.

Only later did I discover that the giant towering over Macpherson was a former Canadian Football League player who was then a sports columnist for the *Toronto Sun*. Apparently

Duncan's devilish self-portrait.

Duncan had only stumbled, and the other fellow was just about to help him up. I sent an apology to the Press Club. Duncan was reinstated. Among the multitude of Macpherson stories, I know this one at least to be true.

Times were different then. You could generally get away with that sort of behaviour, although we were considered by our colleagues to be belligerent characters. There's no getting around the fact that, back in the 1970s, Duncan and I were both functioning alcoholics, as were many others in journalism.

Whenever I went to Toronto, I'd give Macpherson a call about 4:00 in the afternoon,

The look.

knowing that he would be wrapping up his cartoon for the following day's newspaper. "Press Club for a few drinks?" I'd ask. This invitation would usually entice him out of his lair at the *Star*. By 5 p.m., we'd be at it, with no idea what the night might bring.

By the mid-1980s, I'd had enough. It was time for me to give up alcohol and a few other bad habits I had picked up along the way. With time, I was successful. Since then, I've managed to stay sober 99.9 per cent of the time. As for 0.1 per cent, well, nobody's perfect.

While Duncan may have regretted his conduct on occasion, he never expressed a desire to quit drinking. He felt, as many do, that not drinking might somehow kill his creativity. In any case, he kept at it. The drinking, along with being a smoker all his adult life, undoubtedly contributed to his early death. Nevertheless, Duncan squeezed a lot into his too short life.

For two years in the early 1990s, I tried working for both the *Toronto Star* and the *Montreal Gazette*, travelling back and forth between the two cities on a weekly basis. It was exhausting. At the same time, I was preoccupied with some personal matters that would eventually lead to the dissolution of my marriage. It was becoming clear that neither newspaper was getting my best effort. What pushed me to take action was that Haroon Siddiqui, the editorial-page editor of the *Star*, killed seven of my cartoons over those twenty-four months. During the same period, my *Gazette* editor, Joan Fraser, spiked only one. I decided I should go home to Montreal for good.

I was finishing up at the *Toronto Star* that spring of 1993 when, on 3 May, *Star* publisher John Honderich walked into my studio to tell me that Duncan Macpherson had just died. It was an awful shock, as Macpherson was only sixty-eight. I was very shaken, and while I drew an *in memoriam* cartoon for the *Star*'s editorial page, I was never happy with it.

In 2012 the Association of Canadian Editorial Cartoonists (ACEC) held a convention in Montreal, in collaboration with the McCord Museum. Wes Tyrell was elected the association's new president, a position he still holds today. Shortly after the convention, Wes was contacted by someone in the United States who informed him that a small museum in New York State had eight hundred Duncan Macpherson originals in its possession. No one was quite sure how they had ended up there, but the museum was apparently willing to let them go for the right price. Both the *Toronto Star* and the Webster Foundation in Montreal generously contributed to a fund that allowed us to bring the cartoons back to Canada. They are now housed at the McCord Museum.

While this deal was being worked out, I met several times with Dorothy and Ian Macpherson. During one of these meetings, Ian told me that his father had written a personal journal running to about three hundred and fifty pages. As far as he knew, no one outside the family had ever read it. He wondered whether I might be interested. Naturally, I jumped at the chance.

The journal was an eye-opener. Macpherson was not shy about his opinions or sharing his particular version of events. He sometimes chose odd stories to pick apart. As an example, he devoted many pages to his theories about the assassination of President John F. Kennedy but made absolutely no mention of his six National Newspaper Awards. Despite its oddities and meanderings, it was clear that the journal would be the perfect inspiration for this book, a project I had been imagining for years.

It wasn't always easy to read Macpherson's mood. He had a big, gap-toothed grin that could be interpreted in many ways. People close to him knew that it paid to be wary. As Ian said: "Sometimes Dad would get a look on his face that meant you were better off getting out of the room."

Although we had got along well from the beginning, I wasn't certain how Duncan actually felt about me in the early days of our friendship. So, in 1976, when I asked if he would write an introduction to a collection of my cartoons titled "Okay, Everybody Take a Valium!" I did so with some trepidation.

"Sure," he said, "you'll have it in a week." The envelope duly arrived. I opened it cautiously and read his handwritten introduction. I sheepishly felt a little like Sally Field at the Academy Awards: "He likes me! He really, really likes me!"

In 1971 S.A. Longstaff and Sarah Henry wrote an excellent profile of Duncan Macpherson for the left-wing, Winnipeg-based magazine *Canadian Dimension*. The article covered Duncan's early years as the cartoonist for the *Toronto Star*. The thoughtful essay asserts that "Macpherson matters to us because of his success in doing something that is very difficult and rare in graphic satire – evoking reality through the eyes of its casualties and victims. Indeed, in Macpherson's vision, to be Canadian is to be a victim, an underdog of sorts, at the prey of national and international forces that leave us bewildered, seemingly powerless, frozen in inaction. His success in representing this part

The cover of an issue of *Canadian Dimension* featuring Macpherson's work.

A prized possession: an original drawing of Charles de Gaulle that Duncan Macpherson gave to the author.

INTRODUCTION

Terry Mosher is an irritating man and a genius. His collection of cartoons and reportage has the amazing pen name Aislin on the cover. Inside the book you find genius—a complete example of the cartoonist himself.

In two hundred years of satire through cartooning, there are less than a dozen artists who have advanced the intellectual and artistic skills of the medium. Mosher is well on his way to joining this group.

Man has been on earth for three million years, and it is only in the last few thousand that he has extended his tool-using ability to scratch pictograms on a cave wall. Since then, many art forms have developed—and the latest of these forms is the satirical drawing that reflects the inanities of human society. It is in this that Mosher excels—particularly in the use of caricature rather than the "situation" cartoon.

Inspired satire in visual art requires two qualities: one is acquired; one must be there at birth. The acquired discipline is the cartoonist's pen, the love of drawing, an absolute must to translate the moving vision and the intellectual intent into one cohesive and telling graphic design. Mosher has it.

The "born" quality is difficult to describe, for it deals with insight and sense of proportion. It is an instinctive "lens" that sees—regardless of environment and education—particles and pieces of the truth. Mosher has it.

I know there is a stratum of Canadian society that will recoil from Mosher's observations—rather too indelicate for the drawing rooms of the non-thinking genteel whose ideas of history and culture are collecting butter churns, old pop bottles, and a few chocolate-box Krieghoffs. This same stratum—whether they be politicians, establishment, management, or labour—is the very subject matter that angers and motivates Terry Mosher. And without the ridiculous, there is no satire.

Duncan Macpherson

Duncan Macpherson's introduction to one of the author's books, beside a Mosher cartoon of Macpherson.

of our experience makes him one of our few authentic voices, and it is time we became more self-consciously aware of his importance to us."

I wholeheartedly agree.

In a journal entry made less than ten years before he died, Duncan Macpherson left a note for a potential future biographer: "A word of advice. If a biography in print is ever contemplated, the publisher must be American; no goddamn pennywhistle Canadian bankrupts or English incompetents."

I have not fully respected his wishes, but I think he would forgive me. After all, Macpherson was a great Canadian – Canadians should be telling his story. I also believe he would have been pleased with this tale about a cartoonist, by a cartoonist. I hope you enjoy it and come away with an appreciation for this remarkable man, and for his creative genius.

Terry Mosher

PLAINS OF ABRAHAM
MAITRE CHEZ NOUS
Macpherson TORONTO STAR

Canada

Ken McGoogan's 2010 book *How the Scots Invented Canada* was enormously successful, eagerly bought by multitudes of Scots-descended Canadians, of which there may be as many as five million. Mass emigration from Scotland to North America in the eighteenth and nineteenth centuries was partly the result of evictions from the land (the Highland Clearances) as well as Scotland's poor economic conditions. Young people were often forced to move abroad, as either soldiers or traders, or, in the case of well-educated young Scots, for professional or managerial jobs.

This displacement continued into the twentieth century as countless Scots crossed the Atlantic to the United States and Canada. Duncan Macpherson's parents were among them.

When they met, Alexander Macpherson and Margaret Matheson had already left their small Scottish towns behind. They got to know each other when Margaret was working as a nurse aboard a transatlantic ship and Aleck was making one of many crossings to establish his new trading business. In 1921, like many before them, they chose to leave their home country officially and settle in Canada. Although their son Duncan was born at the Toronto General Hospital on 20 September 1924, it took some time for the Macphersons to put down roots in their new environment. Aleck, a fledgling importer of goods to his adopted country, found it necessary to travel back to Scotland for extended periods so as to have easier access to merchandise on the Continent. He often took his wife and young son back to the Isle of Skye (Inner Hebrides) with him.

> *My mother said that I drew on everything – nickel drawing books, the backs of shirt stiffeners for posters – even on the porcelain kitchen table top.*
>
> DUNCAN MACPHERSON

2

FROM TORONTO TO SCOTLAND AND BACK

ABOVE | An image of a Highlander by *Globe and Mail* cartoonist Brian Gable.

RIGHT | Like Macpherson, contemporary Halifax cartoonist Bruce Mackinnon is of Scottish descent. This is his impression of a Scot with a typical attitude.

As a result, Duncan Macpherson's earliest memories were not of Toronto but of the small coastal town of Lower Breakish on the Isle of Skye. His family would stay with aunts and uncles who were crofters and cattle drovers. His sister, Fiona, was born there in 1926, and it was there that Duncan first attended school. Although he was quite young at the time, he retained very strong memories in later years of having stone pencils and a piece of slate on which to write and draw. At the end of the lesson, a child would take his or her personal wood-framed slab of slate and, using a damp cloth (the girls) or spit and an elbow (the boys), they would literally "wipe the slate clean."

While serving with the Royal Canadian Air Force (RCAF) during the Second World War, Duncan returned to the Hebrides and became reacquainted with his extended family. In his 1984 journals – which he wrote as background for a possible autobiography – he recorded his conflicting impressions of the Macpherson side of the family. On the one hand, he considered them unusually well educated despite their rather rural and isolated upbringing. He was told, for example, that his Aunt Catherine had held a senior position in the Department of Health for Scotland. On the other hand, Duncan found the Macphersons as a group to be distant, secretive and suspicious, and a touch greedy. Furthermore, he thought them overly prone to superstition and obstinately disinclined to countenance anything "new."

The Macphersons of Skye were indeed a tough lot. The family crest features the motto *Touch not the cat bot a glove* ("bot" meaning without), a metaphorical warning to other clans that they should think twice before interfering in Macpherson business.

In a 1973 article in *Toronto Life* magazine, John Gault, another Canadian-born Scot, observed: "Duncan Macpherson is a hold-over from the warring clans, a Highlander hurtling down the hill, screaming, tartans billowing, swinging a mighty claymore round and round over his head. Macpherson doesn't attack with clever repartee but with bellowed curses."

A *shieling* cottage near Lower Breakish on the Isle of Skye. Painting by Mary Hughson.

While visiting Skye as a child, Duncan had been taken on a number of family trips to the Outer Hebrides, specifically to the communities of Upper and Lower Shader on the Isle of Lewis. His mother Margaret's family, the Mathesons, lived there. One family member had moved to Edinburgh to study nursing, but the family Duncan knew remained happily on Lewis, in a world where Gaelic and English met. He retained pleasant memories of riding bareback on a family horse and hiking on the moors with

ABOVE | The region of Scotland where Macpherson's family came from.

BELOW | A painting by Duncan Macpherson of King Harald, a ninth-century Norseman who is said to have conquered the Orkneys, the Hebrides, and the east coast of Ireland.

the occasional overnight stay in a "shieling." Someone who grew up almost next door to the Mathesons, and now lives in Toronto, explains that a shieling was a rough Highland shelter for use when bringing the cows up to summer pastures. The drover could spend the night in this stone cabin, sleeping on a makeshift heather bed, and then, in the morning, milk the cows and return to the croft with the vitally important milk. Duncan seems to have enjoyed this simple life, even helping out with family chores like cutting and collecting peat.

As an adult, Macpherson generally seemed fonder of the Mathesons than of his father's relations, and certainly felt closer to his mother and his sister than to Aleck, who, he felt, "in spirit never left Scotland." His father always seemed to have pressing business interests elsewhere and was seldom around. Macpherson's journal notes that Margaret, "with sagacity and graciousness, did cut her Scot ties, seeing Canada as a new land of Opportunity." Macpherson continued: "Well, so much for Scotland. It does haunt me from time to time, but, like mother, I much prefer Canada."

He may have felt he had put Scotland behind him, but those early childhood experiences must have left their mark.

In the 1980s, in semi-retirement in the small Ontario town of Beaverton, Duncan Macpherson revisited his origins, carefully researching and painting six historical Scottish figures. The colourful series, titled "Celtic Hexagon," now hangs in the Beaverton Public Library, where he spent many happy hours. For the interested visitor, the library is a bit of a Macpherson shrine.

The Macpherson family moved back to the very different world of Toronto in 1930. Duncan's 1984 unpublished personal journals record his memory of the return to Canada. "When I was around five years of age, we returned from Scotland. I remember we docked in Quebec City. There are then fractured memories of being aboard a train: I was in bed, looking down on lights and a river in the night, and there was a commotion of some sort involving my mother, Margaret. I brought the memory up to her years later. She laughed and said my father Aleck was smuggling a case of whiskey from the ship to Toronto. All of the contraband was under my mattress. Aleck had thought that the customs inspector would not disturb a five-year-old boy asleep in his bunk."

The Macphersons and the Great Depression arrived in Toronto at just about the same time. Toronto was being hurt by the economic crash

LEFT | Attending John Fisher Public School, *circa* 1935, Duncan Macpherson is in the second row from the top, wearing a white jacket.

BELOW | Toronto's Yonge Street Mission in the 1930s, close to where the Macphersons had settled.

A twelve-year-old Duncan Macpherson, second from the left, top row, at John Fisher Public School. His baseball team didn't lose a game all season.

as much as any other North American city. The unemployment rate climbed to 30 per cent, and for those fortunate enough to have jobs, salaries plunged by almost two-thirds.

Establishing themselves in Toronto in the middle of the economic crash was challenging for the newly arrived Macpherson family. Yet, in his journals, Macpherson recalls his childhood in downtown Toronto as being a relatively happy and active one. "I was neither depressed nor sad. The Depression itself caused most people to live an austere life. But, as a young child, what was one to compare it with?"

The first Macpherson home was in the Oakwood area, but the family moved frequently over the next few years as a result of the changing fortunes of Aleck Macpherson's import business and his near constant travel. Indeed, there were years when he barely seemed to live in Toronto.

Since Margaret was a proud woman and never talked to her children about these things, it is not clear how the marriage or the family's economic well-being fared during this period. Mrs Mac worked for a while as a nurse but later gave classes on wool spinning in her home and even opened a British woollens shop. She also tended a plot at the corner of Broadway and Bayview where "she grew all our vegetables: potatoes, turnips, lettuce and so on."

The frequent moves meant that Duncan and Fiona changed schools many times during their young years. Macpherson did not remember his time at public school with fondness: "I certainly didn't learn a damn thing and school was just something to put up with. Other than art, my studies were by rote – something to be endured and, in my case, forgotten."

While classroom learning faded quickly for Macpherson, his memories of climbing trees in summer and skating on ice in winter were vivid. "The City of Toronto, in an enlightened moment, set up summer playgrounds in all the schoolyards and public parks. They were supervised, with all sorts of sports equipment supplied by the city for basketball, floor hockey and so on."

Duncan took full advantage of these facilities. Fiona was a good athlete too. An excellent runner, she won most of the competitions she entered. Fiona would jokingly insist that she had to be fast to keep ahead of her older brother.

Macpherson wasn't cut out for the classroom, but he found an outlet in sports. By his second year of high school (he had failed his first), he had grown to six feet. At a track-and-field event

NEVER LOST A GAME CHAMPIONS' RECORD

Star Cup Won by John Fisher School Juniors—Girl Sets New Record

With a record of 10 wins and one tie out of 11 games played, the junior baseball team of John Fisher public school won The Daily Star's championship cup this season. The school paraded yesterday when Trustee Donald M. Fleming, Ward 9, handed the trophy to Walter Peppiatt, captain of the team.

The pins accompanying the trophy were presented to the players by William D. Dodd, on behalf of The Star. Principal W. R. Kingston introduced the speakers, and Coach L. M. Hart was also [illegible]

Olive Busby, pupil of the school, was handed her certificate as breaker of the record for the 75 yards race for girls seven years of age. Olive made a new record of 11 seconds at the Toronto schools sports meet recently. "The first time in Toronto a girl seven years of age ever ran that distance in that time," said Mr. Fleming, handing over the parchment, neatly framed.

Ross Sinclair, Stanley Lynch and Bruce McGee, also received certificates for w[illegible] in the city schools athletic meet.

The baseball champions were: Clare Duhig, Cliff MacFayden, Roy Pallister, Irving Moxford, Len Cullen, Andy McMillen, Dunc McPherson, Jack D'Arcy, Jack Anderson, Frank Powell, Walter Peppiatt (captain), Al. Stephens and George Ovens.

NEWS OF WEEK IN CITY SCHOOLS

Items of Interest About Pupils and Pedagogues

DAILY STAR TROPHY FOR BALL CHAMPIONS

Record of 10 games won, one tied and none lost, is the season's story of the junior baseball team of John Fisher school. ABOVE The Star's camera man shows the team in the background, while IN FRONT, from LEFT to RIGHT, are: L. M. Hart, teacher and coach; Trustee D. M. Fleming, who presented the trophy to the winners; Walter Peppiatt, team captain, and Principal W. R. Kingston.

Memories of childhood antics during the Depression in Toronto.

in Montreal several years later, he managed to clear 5'9" over the high jump. As he later wrote: "Sport was the most enjoyable part of my young life: running, jumping, baseball and soccer in public school, with hockey, track and field, and baseball in the playground."

Drawing was just as important to the young Macpherson as sports. "Was I encouraged to draw as a child? No, I wasn't. But I wasn't discouraged either. My mother said that I drew on everything – nickel drawing books, the backs of shirt stiffeners for posters – even on the porcelain kitchen table top." Margaret once got a deal on some cheap, white indoor paint and asked her son to paint his room. He did that, but then promptly covered the walls with dozens of very funny hand-drawn cartoons. Word got around the neighbourhood; people began knocking on the Macphersons' door wanting to see the boy's sketches. It was the first public exhibition of Macpherson originals.

Of economic necessity, Duncan was industrious. As soon as he was old enough, he took any part-time work he could find to provide himself and the family with a bit of cash. He paid for his own clothing, schoolbooks, and even a bicycle. He worked for a while making deliveries for Cowan's butcher shop. While waiting for orders to be prepared, he started drawing funny faces on the eggs in the exposed cartons. That got him fired. But because the shop didn't have its own bicycle, he was rehired at once.

Macpherson's first connection to the *Toronto Star* was having a *Star Weekly* delivery route. During the summer, he would set up a card table and sell lemonade on Eglinton Avenue in aid of the Star Fresh Air Fund. He also worked as a camp counsellor at the Star camp near Bolton, Ontario.

The young Duncan would draw on anything – with any tool at hand, like this girl's clipped pigtail.

As a boy, Duncan Macpherson drew all sorts of things but never thought much about it. "I was always a scribbler by nature. But I didn't – nor did anyone else – take it seriously." Until, that is, he was picked for special instruction. Every year, two or three children from each public school were invited to Saturday morning drawing classes at the Art Gallery of Toronto, now the Art Gallery of Ontario (AGO). James Houston, the Toronto

Toronto's storied Central Technical School, which artists such as Lawren Harris, Bruno Bobak, and Aba Bayefsky attended. The school was used as a locale for the film *Good Will Hunting*.

artist who went north to discover the wonders of Inuit art, was one of those lucky young students. It changed his life and, through his work at the Cape Dorset Co-op, the lives of many others. As for Duncan Macpherson, he was thrilled to be one of the children chosen from his school. "I began to realize the social importance and respect that drawing had in a community. That class was the cornerstone of my career as an artist. And what did I learn at that time? Concentration."

Duncan was taught by his mother to be "respectful and polite." When people laughed at his cartoons, however, he learned something important. "I discovered an avenue of expressing insolence, of being impudent, even boldly disrespectful. This period may have incubated my satirical attitude towards society." This sums up the personality of many humorists: perfectly good-natured people who become savage with a pen in their hand.

The Macpherson stubbornness was in evidence early on. Margaret said that, when he was only six, Duncan refused to continue going to Sunday school. When she asked if he didn't want to learn more about the saints and heaven, he said no, he didn't. "I'll meet them when I get there."

Two of Macpherson's experiences as a teenage student helped shape his artistic career. While he was attending North Toronto Collegiate Institute (NTCI), he took exchange courses at the adjoining Northern Vocational School. There, he studied technical drafting and found he loved the discipline of it.

Equally important was a short-lived transfer to Central Technical School. Macpherson wanted to take regular art courses in his third year of high school but knew his father would disapprove. "My father was an intellectual snob and believed in a 'classical' education. In his view, one was not educated without Greek and Latin." So Macpherson enrolled in secret.

Duncan's teacher at Central Tech, Charles Goldhamer, was very impressed with the young man's drawing ability and placed him in the third year of a four-year course. "Goldhamer taught design and poster work, and a man named Bob

Ross taught me life drawing, a strong influence on me. A master of the scalpel line, his final drawings had all the volume and movement of the model. It is the most difficult method of drawing – but it turned out to be my best discipline over the years."

Macpherson was eventually found out, all because his father was a voracious reader. "He didn't just read the newspaper, he scrutinized every line of type – including the want ads. He discovered my name in the paper in a football line-up – playing for Central Tech! After a domestic explosion, I was hustled back to North Toronto. The school welcomed me back, not because of my scholarship, but to play football."

Duncan was back at NTCI and in his third year, absolutely convinced he wouldn't pass. He wasn't sure what to do. Then he remembered that there was a war on in Europe – he could join up!

He looked into his options and discovered that the Royal Canadian Air Force was doing pre-recruitment for those not yet of age. However, to join an aircrew – the guys who actually flew – he needed to have completed his third year. He went to see the principal of NTCI and explained his predicament. Colonel Frank Wood was a First World War vet and very sympathetic. While acknowledging Macpherson's academic shortcomings, he nevertheless granted the young man his third year – on the condition that he never return to North Toronto Collegiate.

"Mother, who had lost two brothers in World War I, was against me joining up. Anticipating that, I was on strength before I told her. Father? I don't recall telling him – or even seeing him before I left. At the time, I couldn't have cared less, but, as with a lot of judgments, it was unfair."

Duncan Macpherson joined the RCAF on 22 September 1942. He was discharged on 1 April 1946 – "fittingly," he said, "on April Fool's Day."

Macpherson was a championship high jumper, eventually clearing six feet while serving in the Royal Canadian Air Force.

Duncan Macpherson creating work for the Knights of Columbus. London, 1943.

When Duncan Macpherson decided to enlist with the RCAF, he couldn't have known that a childhood game would ruin his chances of becoming a pilot.

As children, Duncan, Fiona, and their friends sometimes played the aptly named hide-the-ball-bearing. On one occasion, Duncan put the bearing – the remnant of a discarded roller skate – into his ear, where it promptly disappeared. Although Duncan was generally a healthy and active child, he later contracted scarlet fever and was confined to the Riverdale Isolation Hospital for several months. No visitors were allowed. His sister remembered travelling to the hospital with their mother and waving sadly to Duncan who was standing at an upper window. The one benefit of that confinement was that the missing ball bearing was discovered and surgically removed. However, the procedure resulted in Macpherson having some permanent hearing loss and inner-ear problems. Fiona (Macpherson) Williams believed this is what disqualified her brother from being trained as a pilot, but he never spoke of it.

Macpherson's thoughts about basic training in Canada were somewhat cynical: "Haircut, kit issue, lower bunk and hundreds, if not thousands, of recruits; mustard gas exposure to acquaint one with a gas mask." The recruits were told that, as gas is heavier than air, all they had to do was head for the nearest tree and climb it. It was not a sophisticated protocol.

Macpherson's final training before being shipped overseas was in navigation, simulated flying, instrumentation, and aircraft recognition. On his own initiative, Duncan drew up a cartoon

Although I was no longer a schoolboy, I certainly hadn't matured. (I doubt that I ever will.) What I had turned into was something that the military abhors – a son of a bitch that takes great delight in bucking the system.

DUNCAN MACPHERSON

3

DUNCAN'S WAR

Macpherson (on the left), like so many others, started to smoke and drink during the Second World War.

manual of German aircraft as an addendum to the recognition training materials. It was used for years after he left.

The sorting out of positions – pilot, navigator, or gunner – was the next step before the crews were shipped out. Duncan's hearing problems ruled out him as a pilot and he was too tall to be a gunner. So if he hoped to be a daring fly boy, with all the attendant glamour, he had to aim for the role of navigator. Macpherson passed his mid-term examination on airplane recognition – of course – but then failed the navigation course. The commanding officer (CO) explained that he might eventually be able retake the test, but he never did.

"So far, it had been a great war for me. But then conditions deteriorated. I was so goddam mad, I was nearly speechless. And I stayed mad at the authorities for the rest of the war."

His hopes dashed, Macpherson shipped out to Britain aboard the troop ship the SS *Louis Pasteur* with other young recruits. In those days, the voyage across the Atlantic was fraught with danger. Every convoy out of North America from Halifax or St John's had to run the gauntlet of German U-boats. Sinking of the Allied ships and the Canadian corvettes that escorted them were all too common and took a heavy toll on Allied forces. The losses were so heavy that at war's end, when Winston Churchill was asked what he feared the most, he simply replied, "The U-boats."

Having reached England safely, and established himself at his new station, Duncan gave his rebellious side full rein. He was not shy about making his resentment of authority clear. Throughout the war, Duncan kept pocket-sized sketchbooks handy so he could make sardonic observations on the situations he encountered.

Officially, Macpherson's principal duty now was packing bombs. Unofficially, he waged a characteristic, long-running war against military discipline. He had been placed in a classification called General Duties. "There wasn't a lower rank, so they couldn't use the threat of busting me. I spent a lot of time in the Mess Hall washing dishes – and doing any other rotten manual job that was called for."

The first time Macpherson was confined for running afoul of authorities, it was for damaging cutlery during a typical outburst of temper. He later told Toronto publisher Doug Gibson that he had only been complaining about the lousy

A dramatic Macpherson woodcut of British prime minister Winston Churchill.

ABOVE | Relations between the enlisted men of the RCAF and their RAF allies weren't always cordial.

OPPOSITE, ABOVE | Loading bombs to a tight schedule.

OPPOSITE, MIDDLE | The front lines of the mess hall.

OPPOSITE, BELOW | On leave from the base, and crossing the River Ouse in Yorkshire.

food. In the mess line, he picked up the stack of forks, bent them into spiky circles, and threw them at the cooks. He was charged with "willful destruction of His Majesty's property." It wasn't the only time he landed in the guard house. In his journals, Macpherson seems quite pleased, even gleeful, about all this.

Once, returning from a group activity, Macpherson saw that some brushes and cans of white paint had been left outside. In the dead of night, he returned and painted a massive 8' x 10' caricature of his CO on the parade ground. It was still there the next day during a full parade. "It gave the whole station a lift," he said. His CO's reaction is not recorded.

Over the next couple of years, Macpherson carried out general duties and engaged in "short-lived mischief" on a number of bases in the south of England. A posting to Royal Air Force (RAF) base Linton-on-Ouse, thirty-two kilometres east of the city of York, however, brought the reality of war closer. The station was home to mostly Canadian personnel and two bomber squadrons. Macpherson was assigned to the bomb dump, "a job requiring a strong back and no brains." Personnel worked round-the-clock shifts servicing inward and outward-bound Lancaster and Halifax bombers. Between sorties, the ground crew passed the time with various amusements. One day they were playing baseball against a neighbouring station. Macpherson was on second base when a Lancaster "wobbled in and pancaked, followed by a spiraling Halifax that had caught fire. They had been shot to hell by ack-ack [anti-aircraft gunfire] and other fighter planes. All the crew was killed except for one tail-gunner who was thrown clear. It was a strange image, players and spectators frozen on the playing field like wax dummies, watching this decimated squadron returning. There I was, standing on second base, watching the war."

With King George VI and Queen Elizabeth about to visit the Canadian bomber group at Linton-on-Ouse, the station was in a tizzy. There was no Blanco to clean and whiten parade webbing, gloves, belts, and other equipment. It would not do to have a sloppy-looking honour guard to greet the royal couple. "I suggested that we get wash-tubs and builder's lime and just dunk the webbing and gloves in them to dry. What I didn't know was that the lime was unslaked! [Unslaked lime is akin to acid.] Within minutes, the white-gloved guards had bleeding hands. It was back to the Guard House for me. My cell was a corner room smack alongside the entrance gate. I waved through the bars at the royal limo, which was only feet away, and – it's true – George VI waved back at the person behind the barred window: me!"

Ever the freelancer, Macpherson would paint cartoons on the noses of bombers for "a quid a plane." He also drew caricatures of his comrades' daily lives. In one, a few fellows have managed to get some drinks on the sly. Duncan himself developed a fondness for drinking in the local pub with his pals.

At this point, Duncan was signing his cartoons with a simple MAC, but when he discovered that another cartoonist was using the same pen name, he then went to the full MACPHERSON signature for the rest of his career.

Duncan was in the habit of reading the educational officer's daily bulletin board. He noticed an invitation to all servicemen to enter a War Bond poster contest. Scrounging some paint and a card, he drew a stack of bombs coming out of a bomb bay. He entered this in the competition (the piece has unfortunately been lost) and won third prize, as well as some very welcome cash. It is telling that, when Macpherson eventually saw the first- and second-place entries, he was thoroughly disgusted with the quality of the work, even

A Lancaster lands very close to the bomb dump.

though they were by actual commissioned war artists. Macpherson was not a humble artist. Throughout his career, whenever he felt his work was better than others' (which was most of the time), he wasn't shy about letting everyone know.

Winning a prize in the poster contest gave Macpherson a chance to change his situation once again. At Linton-on-Ouse, he had drawn as much as possible in his spare time. His pocket-sized notebooks came to the attention of the company adjutant who asked if Duncan would draw a memento for the station's archives. Macpherson agreed, but asked if in exchange he could travel to London to collect his poster prize, and perhaps talk to the editor of the RCAF magazine *Wings Abroad* about doing some cartoon work. He was already demonstrating a talent for negotiating a good deal.

A secondment to London was arranged. Arriving in the capital with high hopes, Macpherson headed to RCAF headquarters in Holborn with his transfer papers to *Wings Abroad* in his pocket. Disappointment awaited. "No one had a clue about my posting, and I was again set adrift. My first job was to shovel coal from one bunker to another below the sidewalks around the building that housed HQ." Other lowly, make-work chores and humble, pointless postings followed.

Then, a bit of serendipity. On a London street one day, Duncan happened to run into Charles Goldhamer, his former teacher at Central Tech in Toronto. The chance meeting with this Canadian war artist changed the course of Macpherson's remaining wartime experience.

It had been the brainchild of New Brunswick's Max Aitken (later Lord Beaverbrook) to sponsor a group of Canadian artists to paint events at home and abroad during wartime. The War Memorials Fund for the First World War drew in many of Canada's finest artists, including David Milne, whom Duncan Macpherson came to know much later back in Canada. During the Second World War, the Canadian War Artist movement was revived. Regrettably, Duncan Macpherson came along too late to be part of the program, but Charles Goldhamer was an important member.

Goldhamer was a war artist for the RCAF. He painted a number of dramatic combat scenarios, but his most striking work was done in Sussex in 1941. A group of severely burned airmen undergoing plastic surgery formed what they called the Guinea Pig Club. Goldhamer made a number of drawings of these men at the Queen Victoria Hospital in East Grinstead, where the most advanced reconstructive surgery of the day was being carried out. Several of these drawings are now housed in the Canadian War Museum.

Goldhamer made sure that Macpherson received the prize money for his War Bonds poster and then introduced him to several other war artists with studios in Holborn.

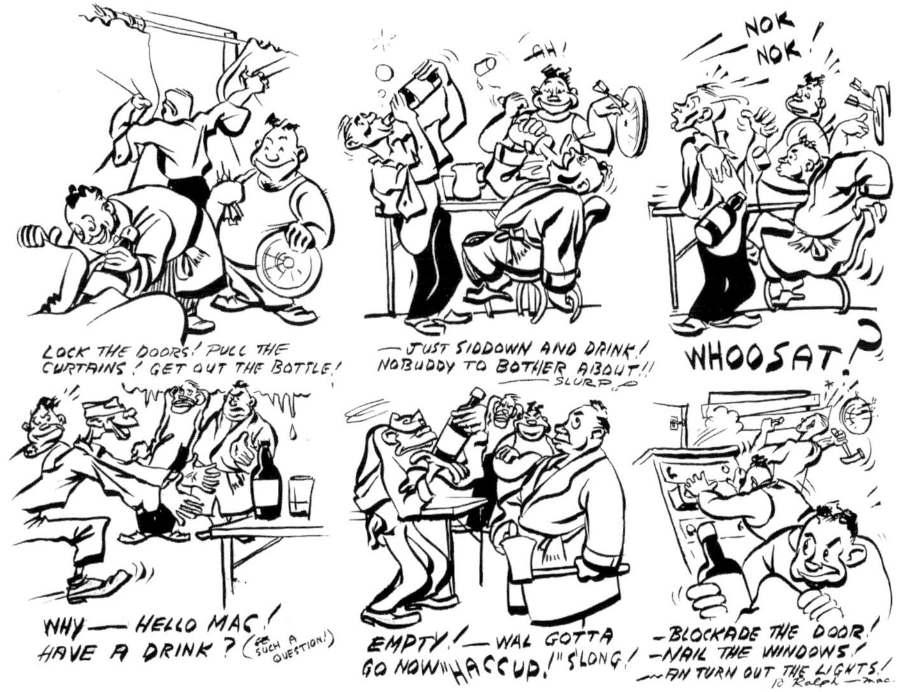

A gag cartoon by Duncan for his pals.

Soon, perhaps thanks to Goldhamer, Macpherson found himself steered in the direction of the Knights of Columbus, even though he wasn't Catholic. Through their contacts, he did odd jobs painting numbers and letters on aircraft. More to his taste, he also did quick caricature studies of the brass for their amusement. He coached and played basketball and found time to play hockey for the RCAF HQ. This was much more to his liking than whitewashing walls.

During his time in London, Macpherson experienced several terrifying "buzz bomb" air raids. When a bomb once landed close to him, he was lifted off his feet and thrown almost thirty metres. He was miraculously unhurt.

One of his friends in those days was Queenie Curnoe, who was stationed at RCAF headquarters. She remembers the buzz bombs (V-1 flying bombs) very well: "The locals called them doodle-bugs. As they came in, they sounded exactly like a Ford motorcar. When they went silent, you knew they were about to land. All we could do was wait."

Although Queenie and Duncan kept in touch after the war, she says, "There was no girlfriend-boyfriend thing; we were all too busy. We were just a bunch of pals who enjoyed Duncan's company. We would have dances for whoever was around. Duncan drew up hilarious, hand-painted posters that everyone thoroughly enjoyed."

Despite the threats from overhead, Macpherson loved wandering the city, often visiting the offices of the official war artists. He was very taken with Carl Schaefer's large watercolours of airfields in Bomber Command and also admired Charles Comfort's portrayals of Canada's war effort abroad.

British war artists like Charles Ginner and Henry Moore impressed Macpherson with their reflections of wartime London. Duncan said, "Moore's subway drawings were superb. With his stylized renderings, Moore caught the nightmare of his time. Great art. Timeless."

Henry Moore was too old at forty-one to enlist for the Second World War, but he and his wife stayed in London during the early months of the Blitz, and Moore was recruited as an official

LEFT | Duncan was unimpressed by other poster designs submitted to the competition.

RIGHT | Footloose on the streets of London.

war artist. As he travelled on the Underground, Moore observed Londoners camped out on the platforms to avoid becoming air-raid casualties. He made discreet sketches in small notebooks and would then work these up into larger, dramatic compositions back in his studio.

Initially, no cartoonist influenced Macpherson's work more than David Low. Born in New Zealand, Low was a self-taught cartoonist and the best-known caricaturist at work during the war. He was so effective that his name was added to Adolf Hitler's "hit list." His body of work leading up to, during, and after the Second World War may be the best artistic record of those dramatic times. Low worked for Lord Beaverbrook's newspaper out of the Daily Express Building on Fleet Street, where his cartoons were on public display. Macpherson spent hours studying them.

Many years later, Lord Beaverbrook, owner of the *Daily Express* and the *Evening Standard*, was on the hunt for a cartoonist to rival the talent of David Low. Already familiar with Macpherson's work, Beaverbrook invited him to be the guest cartoonist at the *Daily Express* during Macpherson's visit to Britain in 1964. Beaverbrook hoped to convince him to come on board as the *Evening Standard*'s new cartoonist. As a sweetener, he wined and dined Duncan, who enjoyed the attention but turned down the job anyway, because, he said, the money wasn't good enough.

During the last months of the war, Macpherson found he had time to enrol as an art student at the Holborn Polytechnic Institute,

Goldhamer's studies of burned airmen being prepared for plastic surgery, now housed at the Canadian War Museum.

Charles Comfort's painting of the landing at Dieppe, now held by the Canadian War Museum.

where he had his first, startling introduction to nude models. He quickly got over the novelty. "My drawing improved somewhat, but the real benefit of those classes was the development of my intense interest." Macpherson knew that, one way or another, art was what he wanted to do.

With the cessation of hostilities, the war was over and Macpherson had to go home. This time, his voyage across the Atlantic was free of U-boats, and he made it back to Canada safely.

Macpherson's conviction that war was stupid and meaningless was inspired to some degree by the powerful work he saw in London by Henry Moore and David Low, but he had already had experiences of war that disgusted him. On one occasion, he had been ordered to collect a dead man's clothing and belongings and sort them according to what belonged to the crown, what was personal, and what was to be returned to the man's family. "It hit me quite hard that war is a completely insane exercise. I decided that, from then on, I would only go through the motions. To rebel was stupid, but I did decide then and there to coast through the rest of my time in uniform as a spectator – not a participant." Later in his career, many of Duncan Macpherson's most forceful cartoons for the *Toronto Star* reflected his complete loathing of war.

Tube Shelter Perspective, 1941, by Henry Moore. The shelter in question was at the Liverpool Street station.

Macpherson's cutline for this Vietnam War cartoon: *PS. Nobody likes the war, but it is good for business.*

Macpherson's cutline for an anniversary of D-Day: *When politics are left to the generals.*

Four Horsemen of the Apocalypse over a battlefield in the Middle East.

U.S. President Lyndon B. Johnson.

Ever the joker, Duncan pretends to carry a heavy block of ice while helping his uncle Bill in Boston with deliveries. This photograph dates from 1946.

Drawing was as natural to me as breathing. I could move through half a dozen studies while the rest of the class was labouring over one.

DUNCAN MACPHERSON
IN REFERENCE TO HIS LAST YEAR AT THE ONTARIO COLLEGE OF ART (OCA)

4

LEARNING HIS CRAFT

Lots of people who are called "artists" don't actually draw all that well. Those rare ones who do always started with some innate talent and, through training and discipline, developed their skills. From my own experience, I know that after years of practice, you reach a point where you are able to draw almost anything. Your eye captures the image and transmits it to your brain. The signal travels from your brain, down your arm, and through your fingertips to a pen, a pencil, a crayon, or a brush. Then – scribble, scribble, scribble – there it is!

Sometime in his late teens, Duncan Macpherson realized he had in-born talent, which he put to good use while posted in England during the Second World War. At war's end, Macpherson returned to Toronto, ready to take up serious studies in art and drawing.

Like other returning veterans, Macpherson was offered support from the federal government to help him reintegrate into civilian life. "I had four years of education and living-out allowances to use before being forced to find work." Applying to the Ontario College of Art, he was told there was a waiting period of a year for the courses he wanted. Since a veteran could apply to any institution anywhere if courses were not available in Canada, Duncan decided on the School of the Museum of Fine Arts in Boston, where he was able to board with his Aunt Bella. "Bella put me to work painting the house shutters, etc. – and I helped her husband Bill with his fuel and ice deliveries on Saturdays."

While soaking in the classic art education – art history, anatomy, sculpture, and

LEFT | Macpherson's etching of a clown, created when he attended the School of the Museum of Fine Arts in Boston, demonstrates his interest in pursuing a variety of graphic techniques and styles.

RIGHT | Titled *Death*, this early lithograph that Macpherson produced at the School of the Museum of Fine Arts shows the influence of the European expressionist Käthe Kollwitz.

printmaking– offered by the school's excellent instructors, Duncan was also able to pick up some part-time illustration and cartoon work. "The Open Road for Boys, an American magazine with an enormous circulation, used my drawings, and eventually allowed me to do a two-page spread. The magazine did a biographical piece on me, forecasting that I would become a famous artist."

In 1947, when Duncan was two years into his studies in Boston, Margaret Macpherson phoned from Toronto to say that Aleck was on his deathbed. Duncan immediately left for home but didn't reach Toronto before his father died.

Aleck had worked as a manufacturer's agent during the war and had done very well, once telling his son that, no matter what his financial circumstances had been during the Depression and later, he had always sent Margaret money. "I said nothing," Duncan remembered, "but I certainly didn't believe him because of the penurious life we lived during that time." Decades after Aleck's death, Duncan learned that his father had been telling the truth after all. "Throughout Aleck's lifetime, I regarded him as a pompous lead-swinger [someone who shirks their duty], without any sense of family responsibility. I was dead wrong – but he was long dead before I could have apologized."

With his father now gone, Duncan's mother "assumed that I was now going to drop all this frivolous art nonsense and carry on father's business." That was never in the cards. After devoting considerable time to tying up loose ends, and figuring out how best to look after his mother, Duncan resumed his student life, enrolling at the Ontario College of Art for third-year studies.

Duncan considered one of his instructors, Russian-born painter Eric Freifeld, to be a "brilliant artist and teacher." The admiration was mutual. In an interview years later, Freifeld talked enthusiastically about Macpherson's skill as a draftsman and the impact that particular talent had on his work and ideas. "All art is excellent only when the ends are worthwhile and qualitative – and when the means are so good as to become inseparable from the ends."

As a student, Duncan Macpherson was such a star that his graduation from OCA in 1951 was announced in *Maclean's* magazine. It was a highly unusual thing for the magazine to do, but his work had already been featured in the publication and elsewhere. In fact, several of Macpherson's teachers had become aware of their student's success as an illustrator and had asked him to use his influence to get their own work published.

While Macpherson was still in Boston, it was the art director at the *Montreal Standard*, Dick Hersey, who first got him published in Canada. The *Standard* was one of the best weekly publications in Canada at the time. Shortly after the war, Hersey had seen an exhibit of "servicemen's art" in Ottawa, including some of Macpherson's work.

Young Man Going Up

EDITORS have headaches, all right, but there are compensations, too. One is "discovering" real talent. We think we have a young man with just that. Forecasting is always risky, but we'll stick our necks out:—watch Duncan MacPherson, "doodler," cartoonist, *artist*. The lad has a true artistic flair.

Dunc, 22, hails from Toronto. Four war years in the R.C.A.F. included tireless sketching, painting. Then came a famous Boston art school. Presently we got a peek at his portfolio—and began to write checks for the canny Scot.

This page and the next two indicate why. Unless art school strait-jackets his natural ability, this young Canadian is going places!

Macpherson

AUGUST, 1947 7

LEFT | Duncan Macpherson's cartoons were first printed in Boston, in the magazine *The Open Road.*

RIGHT | Students at the Ontario College of Art in Toronto, *circa* 1950.

The Last Pay Parade

A 1951 drawing for the Ontario College of Art magazine *Sketch*, showing professors moaning over their paycheques.

(The artist himself had no idea how it had ended up there.) In 1948, during Macpherson's second year at art school in Boston, Hersey had contacted him and asked for artwork to illustrate articles by a prominent Toronto author, Greg Clark.

Greg Clark (1892–1977) was one of the most popular writers of his day. He had served in the First World War as a soldier, receiving the Military Cross in 1917 for his heroism at Vimy Ridge, and after serving as a war correspondent in the Second World War, he had been awarded an OBE. His columns originally appeared in the *Star Weekly*, but thirty years into his association with the paper, a bitter disagreement with management caused Clark to take his talent and his weekly column to the *Montreal Standard*. (He once told me that, after that disagreeable parting, he never read the *Star Weekly* or the *Toronto Star* again.)

Clark's stories for the *Standard* – often of failed fishing or hunting adventures – were illustrated by Jimmy Frise, a cartoonist who had gained fame in English Canada through his *Star Weekly* comic strip titled "Birdseye Centre." Frise was a household name in those days and a popular portrayer of small-town Canadian life.

When the Clark-Frise partnership ended in 1948 with Frise's death, the hunt was on for someone to replace him. Half a dozen well-known illustrators were approached. All copied Jimmy Frise's style – all except Duncan Macpherson, who came up with his own look. Hersey had in fact been looking for a new approach, and so he selected Macpherson to illustrate the stories. Duncan characterized this as "the beginning of my career."

As was the case with Jimmy Frise, Clark and Macpherson became pals, even if Clark was in the habit of calling his friend "Drunken" Macpherson to his face. Duncan, like many young men who had served in the Second World War, brought his boisterous, social-drinking habit home with him from the war.

"After a visit to Greg's home at High Park, he waved goodbye from his verandah and shouted a remark I'll never forget: 'Beware of little guys!' I gagged with laughter because Clark himself was knee-high to a grasshopper." It was only later that Macpherson realized Clark was probably referring to small-minded people.

LEFT | One of a series of humorous best-selling books by Clark and Frise.

RIGHT | Greg Clark (centre) and Jimmy Frise (right), in conversation with an unknown individual.

Montreal painter John Little (the author's godfather) became one of the more popular *Maclean's* cover artists in the late 1950s. John tells a story about first trying to get established as an illustrator in the late 1940s. Living in the Montreal suburb of the Town of Mount Royal, he borrowed his father's car one day to drive downtown to see Dick Hersey at the *Montreal Standard*. After a quick look at John's portfolio, Hersey asked John to drive him and Mavis Gallant, then a feature writer at the *Standard*, to a bar in the west end where the three of them drank away the afternoon.

That wasn't unusual behaviour for those times – or for Hersey. The *Montreal Standard* was located at 321 St James Street West, in the heart of the old financial district and in the same building as the *Montreal Star*. In the basement was a tavern called the Ticker Tape, where Hersey would often gather with as many as a dozen illustrators. They would pull together a few tables, drink some beer, and look over roughs, discussing layouts and considering future projects. According to Macpherson, Hersey achieved wonderful results with this approach. "To try something new was dear to Dick's personality, and his illustrators excelled."

Macpherson liked to reminisce about those times: "There were extraordinary artists I competed with – many becoming friends – in the hectic era between the end of the war and 1959, a magic

Everyday life with Clark and Frise: the two men on deadline in their shared office.

period for magazine illustrations." In his journals, he mentions people like Jimmy Hill, Jack Bush, Bruce Johnson, Jack Reppen, Franklin Arbuckle, Rex Woods, Al Fleming, and Harold Town.

Hersey had other illustrators at his beck and call, like the multitalented Oscar Cahén (a member of Painters Eleven), Ed McNally (who became the editorial-page cartoonist for the *Montreal Star* in the 1960s), the very funny and sly gag cartoonist Peter Whalley, and Doug Wright, whose best-known work – then a weekly comic strip titled "Nipper" – began appearing in the *Standard* in 1949. In later publications such as *Weekend Magazine* and *Canadian Magazine*, the popular strip carried on and was called "Doug Wright's Family."

Years later, Whalley, a superb Montreal cartoonist, remembered something else that made Hersey very popular. "Most of the time, we artists were broke, so Dick would hand out cash advances. As a result, he always got great work from all of us."

Although Hersey and Macpherson were great pals, there were disagreements from time to time, as this story from Bruce Johnston, another fine illustrator from Montreal, demonstrates. Bruce was part of Dick Hersey's retinue. He recalls being with Hersey in Toronto at the Lord Simcoe Hotel sometime in the late 1950s.

> Dick's room was on the 19th floor, and he threw a riotous party for a group of his Toronto illustrators. He was in town to discuss some Macpherson illustrations – a series of flowers representing all the Canadian provinces. Dick told Duncan that one of his drawings was a piece of shit! "Okay," Macpherson says, and he walks across the room and, one by one, starts throwing the sketches out the window. We all watched them flutter down onto King Street. Hersey got up and said: "Here, let me help you with that," and threw a few out himself. All the while, both of them were standing there exchanging insults. It was really something to behold. Nevertheless, everyone sobered up. The drawings were recovered somehow, and used exactly as they were in *Weekend Magazine*.

Apart from his work for the *Standard* and *Maclean's*, Macpherson did freelance illustrations throughout the 1950s for corporate magazines and advertising agencies. His work appeared in newspapers and on billboards across Canada.

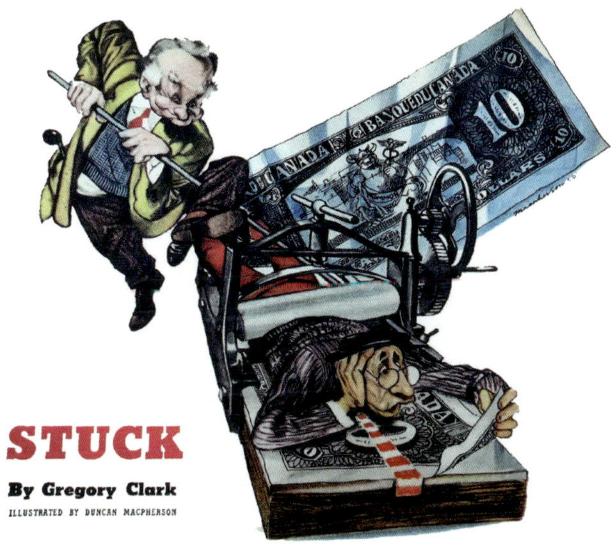

Macpherson illustrated Greg Clark's adventures for the *Standard* in a striking new style. Here, Greg and friends on money, driving lessons, the farm, and moving day.

The cop fixed me with his eye. "Can you explain?" he inquired stonily, "what he is doing driving a stolen truck?"

At this time, the most popular illustrator in North America was Norman Rockwell, who produced many covers for the *Saturday Evening Post*. Macpherson showed some influence of Rockwell in his Greg Clark illustrations.

The commissions involved doing hundreds of drawings, but, as Macpherson said, "I was fast and unstoppable in those days."

It started to dawn on Duncan that he wasn't making a nickel from the ongoing commercial popularity of his work for these corporate clients. Until then, he hadn't thought about the importance of retaining copyright. Thereafter, he became a pioneer in selling only "first rights" of his work whenever possible.

Despite the good pay, Macpherson was generally not enamoured of the world of advertising. "I'm a prickly person, and lightening quick on perceiving bullshit. Advertising is 100 per cent that, and my tolerance for the jobs exploded when it became too bloody crass."

All his life, Duncan Macpherson was fascinated with the Arctic and made several trips north. On one visit he had a chance meeting with the great explorer Vilhjalmur Stefansson. Born at Arnes, Manitoba, in 1879 to Icelandic settlers, Stefansson went on to become a legendary – and very controversial – Arctic explorer, up until his death in 1962. Stefansson told exciting stories of drifting dangerously among ice floes and discovering large Arctic islands, but his academic theories were disputed and people lost their lives on one of his ill-planned expeditions. Controversial he may have been, but in meeting him, Macpherson was encountering a major Arctic figure. His own experiences in the Arctic inspired Duncan to create a comic strip involving two characters named Ig and Loo. "The subject matter was to be a blend of the historical, the contemporary and Eskimo mythology – and Stefansson was enthusiastic about the idea."

Macpherson drew up a series of panels, in black and white and in colour, and sent them off to a cartoon syndicate in Chicago. After some time, the panels were returned to him. The syndicate complimented him on the concept and the quality of the artwork but judged the content to be "too highbrow" for their readers' tastes. Macpherson was only temporarily disappointed. "Thinking back, I thank my lucky stars that I abandoned the strip. It would have been sheer hell on earth to go through life drawing Ig and Loo for a living. At the same time, this was the beginning of my incorporating satire in my work – and a precursor of the editorial cartoons that I eventually undertook."

Although they didn't become Macpherson's life's work, Ig and Loo would often appear in later *Toronto Star* cartoons in sympathetic portrayals of the plight of the Inuit.

LEFT | Doug Wright's family.

BELOW | A John Little cover for *Maclean's* shows neighbours watching a Montreal Royals baseball game at Delorimier Downs from afar.

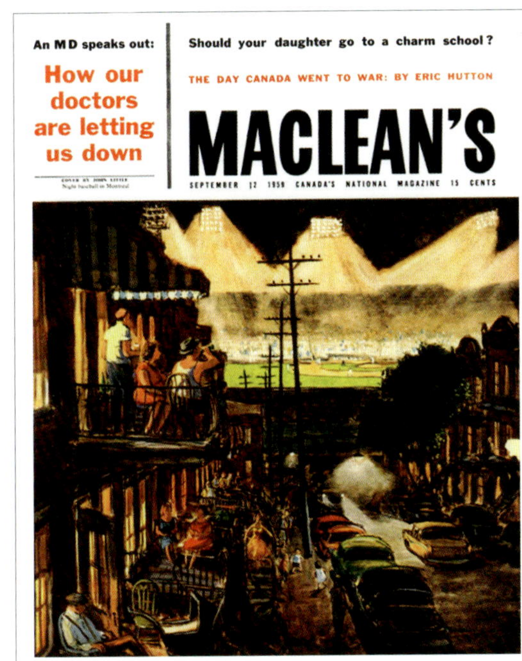

Macpherson's illustration of a trillium – Ontario's official flower – was painted for *Weekend Magazine* in 1957. It is famously said to have survived being tossed out a nineteenth-storey hotel window.

The ongoing adventures of Ig and Loo.

"… WHERE'S THE CAN OPENER?… WHERE'S THE CAN OPENER?… OVER AND OUT."

In 1978 television had just arrived in the Northwest Territories. Macpherson drew a group of Inuit, gathered around their new TV, laughing uproariously at "the white man's news."

Inuit reaction to Quebec's French-only language bill. This is an excellent example of Macpherson's ability to render clothing.

A Christmas card of Duncan, Dorothy, and Ian playing hockey in Uxbridge, Ontario.

When he came home to Toronto from Boston following his father's death, Duncan's interest was sparked by a "dark-haired and vivacious" young lady named Dorothy Blackhall, an old school friend of Fiona's. She and Duncan got to know each other better by going out to lunch on a regular basis. His attraction to her became more intense, and he made a number of visits to Beaverton on Lake Simcoe, where Dorothy's family had a summer cottage. He proposed to her there on a late summer evening, just before he entered his final year at the Ontario College of Art. "I still remember her expression – a long and silent side-long look. What she was thinking of, God knows, but, after a period of quiet contemplation, she agreed."

The young couple married in 1949 and moved into a small apartment on Bathurst Street. They had many good years together, and while there were also periods of separation, Dorothy was with Duncan when he died forty-four years later.

Duncan Macpherson had always liked the idea of living in a small community. "Duncan is engaged by smaller places where there is light and space – and everyone knows each other," according to his friend Jack Brehl. Macpherson did in fact spend the last dozen years of his life in Beaverton, but there was an even earlier experiment in small-town life.

Around 1950, Duncan and Dorothy settled in the sleepy little town of Uxbridge (an hour's drive northeast of Toronto), where they stayed for four years. The locale had been suggested to them by a mutual friend, Dr Don Davis. The Macphersons' son, Ian, was born during their

Duncan is engaged by smaller places where there is light and space – and everyone knows each other.

JACK BREHL

5

UXBRIDGE

LEFT | Dorothy Blackhall and Duncan Macpherson.

time in Uxbridge, and the couple seemed quite happy for a while. At first, money was very tight: the long-standing *Montreal Standard* contract to illustrate Greg Clark's stories had come to an end. Initially, the Macphersons rented several rooms in an old house, but as things improved, they bought a small place on 1st Avenue in the heart of the village.

Duncan also found himself a very interesting art studio, with an amazing backstory.

"I noticed a large upper-story window – north-facing – above a street-level drugstore. The druggist owned the building called the Willis Block, and, much to my surprise, said that it was being used as an artist's studio – and that the artist was moving out that very day. Climbing two flights of stairs, I pushed open the studio door. There, sitting on a packing crate, was a gnomish man puffing on a pipe. He introduced himself. It was a thrill that I still remember: the gnome was David Milne."

Unbeknownst to Macpherson, the former war artist in the First World War had settled in Uxbridge in 1941 with his second wife and their son. The American art critic Clement Greenberg described David Milne as one of the three greatest North American artists of his generation. Even though Milne was overshadowed by the Group of Seven early in his career, he is now recognized as one of Canada's foremost artists, and his works are shown in every major gallery. However, in Uxbridge at least, Milne's

Hotel and Garage, painted by David Milne in 1942.

talent was not highly rated. A neighbour often minded the Milnes' son after school, so Mrs Milne offered the woman one of her husband's paintings by way of thanks. It was handed back to her with the comment, "I wouldn't hang *that* in my house!" A local dentist also turned down an offer to trade paintings for dental work. He presumably regretted this decision later on.

As in most small towns across Ontario, times have changed since the Milne painting reproduced here was completed: the garage is now a Coffee Time and a Circle K; there are no more gas pumps; and while the hotel structure remains unchanged, it now contains a fish-and-chips restaurant and a NEXUS gaming store. Directly across the street, the building that once housed the pharmacy above which the Milne/Macpherson studio was located is now a Vape Shop. The big studio window on the second floor has been replaced with two smaller windows to match the others. Some of Milne's charming watercolours of Brock Street in downtown Uxbridge were painted directly from that upstairs studio.

Interestingly, Milne did hundreds of paintings featuring Uxbridge but never identified the

ABOVE | *Visiting the Bootlegger in Uxbridge*, an etching by Duncan Macpherson.

BELOW | Macpherson started to dabble in free-form watercolours, probably under the influence of David Milne.

location. He was apparently trying to prevent his first wife – who he claimed was a bit of a "stalker" – from figuring out where he was living, should she happen to see his paintings on exhibit.

Macpherson was told that David Milne had been paying $8 a month for the studio. He offered $10 and moved his equipment into the space. "I bought and carried my own coal for the small stove in winter – and I was delighted with my new studio."

Before Milne died in 1953, Duncan had a chance to get to know and respect him. He would often meet Milne on the Toronto-bound train. "Reaming his pipe, he would point out compositions in the landscape that interested him. Colour and form were Milne's strength, and landscapes were his religion." Macpherson even helped to organize an exhibition of Milne's best unsold work at the Uxbridge Town Hall.

Years later, in an online discussion about Macpherson, one of his former neighbours, the artist Gary LeDrew, told a funny story about his father taking the train to Toronto with Duncan Macpherson and David Milne. "David pointed out the window and remarked what a beautiful green a haystack was. Duncan said that he was crazy – that the haystack was red. Dad – also an artist – didn't say anything, but that haystack sure looked yellow to him."

Gary LeDrew has led an interesting life as a bosun, band manager, scriptwriter, and, most importantly, artist. He is currently based in Cape Breton. Although he was very young when his family lived near the Macphersons, he says he was aware of Duncan having a well-deserved reputation as a bit of a wild man, and had heard that Macpherson was banned several times from the Uxbridge Legion for bad behaviour. One winter, Duncan got the flu and sent Dorothy over to the LeDrews' house to borrow a bottle of rum (there was no liquor store within thirty kilometres). Says Gary, "My mother was aghast when Dorothy returned the rum the next week. Unpretentious Dorothy carried the new bottle in her hand – no bag – marched down to the drugstore where mother worked, and just handed it to her." One wonders what Mrs LeDrew's boss thought.

Macpherson portrayed Uxbridge in a more humorous way than had David Milne. In the etching included here, some gleeful locals visit a bootlegger while elderly ladies look on disapprovingly. This image is very evocative of the time. LeDrew says the town's Ontario Provincial Police officer during that period, "Slim" Wilton, estimated that there were thirty-three active bootleggers in Uxbridge. "There was Morley's, Pearl's, Thelma's, and Gravel Gertie's. Some featured appetizers of smelts or morels depending on the season. Others were good for cards or

LEFT | Duncan seemed able to laugh at his incompetence as a hunter.

RIGHT | This oil painting of Dorothy and Ian was an early experiment in portraiture. It demonstrates Macpherson's ability to capture hands.

Thankfully for everyone, Duncan eventually graduated from shooting at nature to studying it.

darts – and all were great for gossip and companionship. Great memories!"

Macpherson devoted at least half a dozen pages in his journal to his duck-hunting exploits while the family lived in Uxbridge. That's surprising, because while he was enthusiastic, he was very bad at it. According to Ian, "Dad was the world's worst duck hunter. It was terrifying whenever he picked up a gun."

Accompanied by a yellow lab named Buff and several neighbours, Duncan would haul his homemade hunting contraptions to a large swampy area about eight kilometres northeast of the town. Over the course of his hunting "career," he devised a number of Rube-Goldberg-like vessels, "one a bit smaller than a bathtub." All he asked was that they support his two hundred pounds while transporting him across the bog for better shooting. None of these ersatz boats ever floated for more than thirty seconds. There were also inventive pieces of clothing, including special wading boots. Nothing ever worked, but, according to Duncan, they did provide his companions – "the local vet, the plumber, the druggist and others" – with a great deal of amusement. In fact, the town plumber's tale about one of Macpherson's inventions, called "Big Mac's Jesus Boots," quickly became part of Uxbridge folklore.

"Big Mac" eventually gave up on duck hunting. His friend Bruce Palmer, whose hobby was stargazing, had inspired Macpherson to leave off shooting at the region's animal life.

By the mid-1950s, Macpherson had sold the house in Uxbridge, since he and Dorothy were going through a rocky period. Dorothy and Ian returned to her family's home in Toronto, while Duncan moved back in with his mother on Duplex Avenue. It was one of several times the couple parted. Duncan doesn't say much in his personal journals about these separations, and Dorothy would only ever remark, "Duncan certainly had

Macpherson put together a rough spread of a proposed illustrated article for *Weekend Magazine.*

his demons." Having witnessed Duncan's obstreperous behaviour first-hand, I offer this thought: while Duncan was known not to suffer fools gladly, the same could be said of Dorothy.

Reconciliation would inevitably follow a separation. They moved from one rented apartment to another, from house to house, until the couple finally bought an old Victorian home on Blythwood Road in north Toronto. Ian settled into school. Macpherson said, "The body of our lives together took place on Blythwood Road."

Macpherson's days of illustrating the Greg Clark stories were over, but the *Montreal Standard* – later *Weekend Magazine* – still

Winter ice fishing on Lake Simcoe. Always the observer, Macpherson didn't fish much himself.

occasionally asked him for work. These contracts would often be for two-page illustrations, usually rural in theme, for which he could have free rein to come up with his own ideas. Macpherson did a number of illustrations for *Weekend Magazine* on the subject of Canadian outdoor activities. The 1958 spread on fishing included here is typical.

By this time, Macpherson was fully settled in Toronto and starting to do steady work for *Maclean's*. Since both his professional circumstances and his living arrangements had changed, it was time to think about a new studio space. He looked at a number of locations, even trying out his mother's sun porch.

In the end, he managed to rent one of the six studios in the Studio Building. (All had the northern exposure – sometimes called reflected light – that artists prefer.) After the move, Macpherson's status went up considerably. Now a National Historic Site of Canada, the

A philosophical type claims that God never made a more calm, quiet, or innocent recreation than angling.

A travelling salesman never leaves his tackle at home, stopping at every likely looking bridge to try his luck.

red-brick building is located at 25 Severn Street, on the edge of the Rosedale Ravine, right beside the subway. Constructed in 1914, in its earliest years the building was used by Lawren Harris, Tom Thomson, A.Y. Jackson, Arthur Lismer, and other members of the Group of Seven. At one point, Emily Carr was a fascinated visitor to Lawren Harris's studio.

Macpherson produced many of his best illustrations while working at this location. The Studio Building, which now sits beside Lawren Harris Park, was home to several other prominent artists of the day, such as portrait painter Gerry Scott and illustrator Don Anderson; it continued to attract artists like Harold Town through the years.

Macpherson wrote that this move "was a big boost to my morale. I moved in an easel and a printing press for etching. I planned to segment my time so I could pursue painting and drawing in a serious sense. But making a living got in the way."

Toronto's famous Studio Building, nestled among skyscrapers, with subway cars passing by.

One of hundreds of small illustrations Macpherson did for *Maclean's* in the 1950s.

By the mid-1950s, Duncan Macpherson had started doing a lot of work for *Maclean's*, illustrating fiction pieces and painting the occasional cover, as he did for the 1957 Christmas issue. The magazine had wanted to feature a star-filled view of Montreal from the vantage point of the cross atop Mount Royal, with the glowing city lying below in the background.

In a world before Google, illustrators had to do a lot of actual legwork to research their subjects. Macpherson rarely worked from photographs, preferring to prepare rough sketches on site for use as source material back in the studio. For this *Maclean's* job, Macpherson took the train from Toronto to Montreal. He then walked up Mount Royal with the idea that this would give him the best bird's-eye view of the city. Spotting the CBC/Radio-Canada transmission tower, Montreal's highest structure, he thought he might as well climb it. He had got a very little distance in his climb before acknowledging it was a dangerous idea, so he abandoned the attempt. Macpherson then walked back down Mount Royal to reconnoitre, and soon decided that the top of the new Montreal General Hospital would suit. He was fortunate to find an access point to the roof and a convenient spot among the vents to sketch a series of cityscapes. During the overnight train ride back to Toronto, he assembled those sketches into a rough layout, and the next morning he returned to his studio to paint the final illustration. When he arrived at *Maclean's* with the canvas, the paint was still wet.

As always, Macpherson had delivered: on brief and on time.

What the hell, kid, what you've got to understand is that cartooning is a living.

DUNCAN MACPHERSON, BEING INTERVIEWED BY CHRISTINA MCCALL

6

MACLEAN'S MAGAZINE YEARS

Montreal by night: one of my favourite Macpherson Christmas covers for *Maclean's*.

In his journal, he explained that "the *Montreal Standard* had paid very well in comparison to *Maclean's*. However, *Maclean's* was coming on like gangbusters with a first rate lineup of authors: Robert Thomas Allen, W.O. Mitchell, McKenzie Porter, Blair Fraser, Sid Katz, June Callwood, and others. Another early and regular feature was 'Jasper,' a panel cartoon by Simpkins. If ever there was an all-Canadian panel cartoon, that was it."

Macpherson had actually preferred working for the *Standard*, because he had more freedom there and the atmosphere felt a lot less buttoned-up than in Toronto. Still, working for *Maclean's* suited him very well. Located at the corner of Dundas Street and University Avenue, it was close to home – not a train ride away in Montreal – and the magazine had two fine art directors in Gene Aliman and his assistant, Des English.

Christina McCall was a great Canadian journalist who, with her husband, Stephen Clarkson, wrote a much-lauded biography of Pierre Trudeau (*Trudeau and Our Times*). In an introduction to Macpherson's 1978 collection of cartoons, she recalled an enlightening conversation with Duncan when she was a twenty-two-year-old researcher at *Maclean's*. "I was just out of university – earnest, ambitious, and in awe of managing editor Pierre Berton."

She said that "Berton wanted to write a feature on cartooning, and asked me to do some background research for the piece. I spent hours in the library, analyzing the great caricaturists of the past, and then persuaded Duncan Macpherson, a contributor to *Maclean's* at the time, to talk to me about his work. I spun out torturous theories about the social import of Daumier and Hogarth, David Low and Herblock. Seriously uncomfortable with all this, Duncan would answer my ponderous questions with a 'yep,' a 'nope' or a 'maybe.' Then he looked into my serious, eager young face and said: 'What the hell, kid, what you've got to understand is that cartooning is a living.'"

"We both started to laugh uproariously."

Maclean's superb editor in those days was former war correspondent Ralph Allen, originally from Oxbow, Saskatchewan. One of his most successful initiatives was a new feature at the magazine: writer Robert Thomas Allen's funny short stories about life with his wife and two daughters.

Although he is almost forgotten now, Robert Thomas Allen (1911–90) was as popular a humorist in the 1950s, 1960s, and 1970s as Stephen Leacock had been in his day. Allen played an important role in the evolution of Duncan Macpherson's career.

Allen was born and raised "on the Danforth" in Toronto, so close to the Don River that he and his pals spent the hot summer days swimming there. Later, Duncan Macpherson was to produce a magical vision of those boys – not a swimsuit among them – horsing about in the water, choking on illicit cigarettes, or leaping off an overhanging willow branch into the river. It became the popular cover for Allen's 1977 book, *My Childhood and Yours: Happy Memories of Growing Up*.

After finishing school, young Bob Allen was glad to get work in the consumer- catalogue business, where Duncan Macpherson also put in some time. These mail-order catalogues were essential reading in Canadian homes across the country and, later, in the nation's paper-starved outhouses. With no further education – because money was always tight – Bob Allen tried his hand at writing and began to submit humorous articles

"Boy! Do I need a shave this morning!"

ABOVE | Jasper, drawn by Jim Simpkins, was Canada's most popular cartoon strip after the Second World War.

BELOW | Robert Thomas Allen as Don Quixote.

A book cover: Duncan Macpherson and Robert Thomas Allen, working in tandem.

about everyday life to various magazines and newspapers. They were published and actually brought in money. His popularity made him a sought-after contributor to major popular magazines like *Reader's Digest*, *Imperial Oil Review*, *The Canadian* – and, of course, *Maclean's*.

Bob Allen was a short, shyly smiling man who was always dressed in a suit and tie, with glasses perched on his nose – a strikingly old-fashioned figure. Yet his way of working would resonate with today's millennials, sitting and peering intensely at their laptops in a Starbucks. Allen would spend his days wandering around downtown, pausing to do his day's work in a cheap café, scribbling on a napkin or a scrap of paper. When asked why he worked this way, Allen just mumbled something about liking to be around ordinary people. The result, however, was far from ordinary. It won him the affection of millions of readers and the Stephen Leacock Award for Humour in 1956 (*The Grass Is Never Greener*) and again in 1970 (*Children, Wives, and Other Wildlife*).

Maclean's editor Ralph Allen hired Duncan Macpherson to be Bob Allen's illustrator. It was a match made in heaven. Duncan was delighted to illustrate these articles, since he considered Allen to be one of the best humour writers in North America.

Allen's stories most often centred on life at home with his wife and two daughters. Macpherson enjoyed the tales and provided affectionate cartoons of the four family members. However, the caricature of Allen morphed over time into a separate new character, a rumpled,

LEFT | Lewis Parker by Duncan Macpherson – and Duncan Macpherson by Lewis Parker.

RIGHT | A Robert Thomas Allen family gathering.

ABOVE AND OPPOSITE | Macpherson's caricatures of Robert Thomas Allen, produced for *Maclean's*, evolved into his "Everyman," a mainstay of his *Toronto Star* cartoons.

bespectacled "John Q. Public," who was later regularly featured in Macpherson's work for the *Toronto Star*. American writer and critic Edmund Wilson, writing in the *New Yorker*, expressed his appreciation for Macpherson's undersized common man, someone he said was "gopher-nosed and chinless – surrounded by predatory monsters who bewildered him, bullied him and left him in tatters."

Allen wasn't thrilled about being identified with these "little guy" portrayals, particularly when he and Duncan both ended up at the *Toronto Star*. Despite these minor frictions, Macpherson was always grateful for the association: "Thinking back, illustrating Robert Thomas Allen's stories was the highlight of my association with *Maclean's*."

Macpherson also enjoyed his role in another of Ralph Allen's projects for *Maclean's*, which was to reacquaint Canadians with their history. Allen started by commissioning articles covering different eras. Macpherson recalls: "The period I

covered mostly was early Montreal and Quebec. I found that I enjoyed the process of meticulously researching the time period before beginning the drawings."

Maclean's was starting to devote more space to news events, so Ralph Allen created a new feature called *Up Front*: two yellow pages at the front of the magazine to highlight breaking news. These were the last pages printed, so the work had to be done quickly. Within a couple of hours, Macpherson would spot-illustrate the section with thumbnail sketches. "The section grew, and two other illustrators came on board: Lew Parker and Bert Grassick. The three of us specialized in fast art, all being brush men."

Duncan Macpherson was an excellent illustrator, of course, but there were many who were better known. It was his cartooning – not his illustrations or paintings – that was about to put him into the "genius" category.

The charmed period for artists like Macpherson was about to end. Hand-rendered

ABOVE | In 1849 rioters burned the Parliament Building in Montreal. This carefully researched drawing by Macpherson records the only thing saved from the fire: a portrait of Queen Victoria.

BELOW | For an article in *Maclean's* by Bruce Hutchison, Macpherson illustrated the historical importance of Halifax Harbour as a naval base.

illustration was becoming passé. According to Duncan, "quite simply, photography was faster, cheaper and not as much of a headache in terms of color separation."

During the Second World War, *Maclean's* covers generally alternated between photographs of war scenes and photos of pretty girls. After the war, the magazine turned to illustrators (many of them mentioned previously) to provide cover art. Much as the *Saturday Evening Post* was showcasing American art and artists, *Maclean's* featured paintings of interesting Canadian scenes. Taken as a collection, these images provide an invaluable reflection of Canada during the 1940s and 1950s. In those days, photographs were rarely used as cover art. *Maclean's* first issue of 1961 was a turning point: from that edition on, the magazine's covers were almost exclusively photographs and montages. During the next dozen years, cartoons were featured only twice. In 1963 Duncan Macpherson drew a futuristic cover and foldout relating to the upcoming World's Fair in Montreal (later called Expo '67). Almost a decade later, during the Canada-Russia hockey series, *Maclean's* put my cartoon of Phil Esposito on the front cover.

The 1950s really were a magic age for magazine illustrators. Maybe the sun always seems brightest just before it sets.

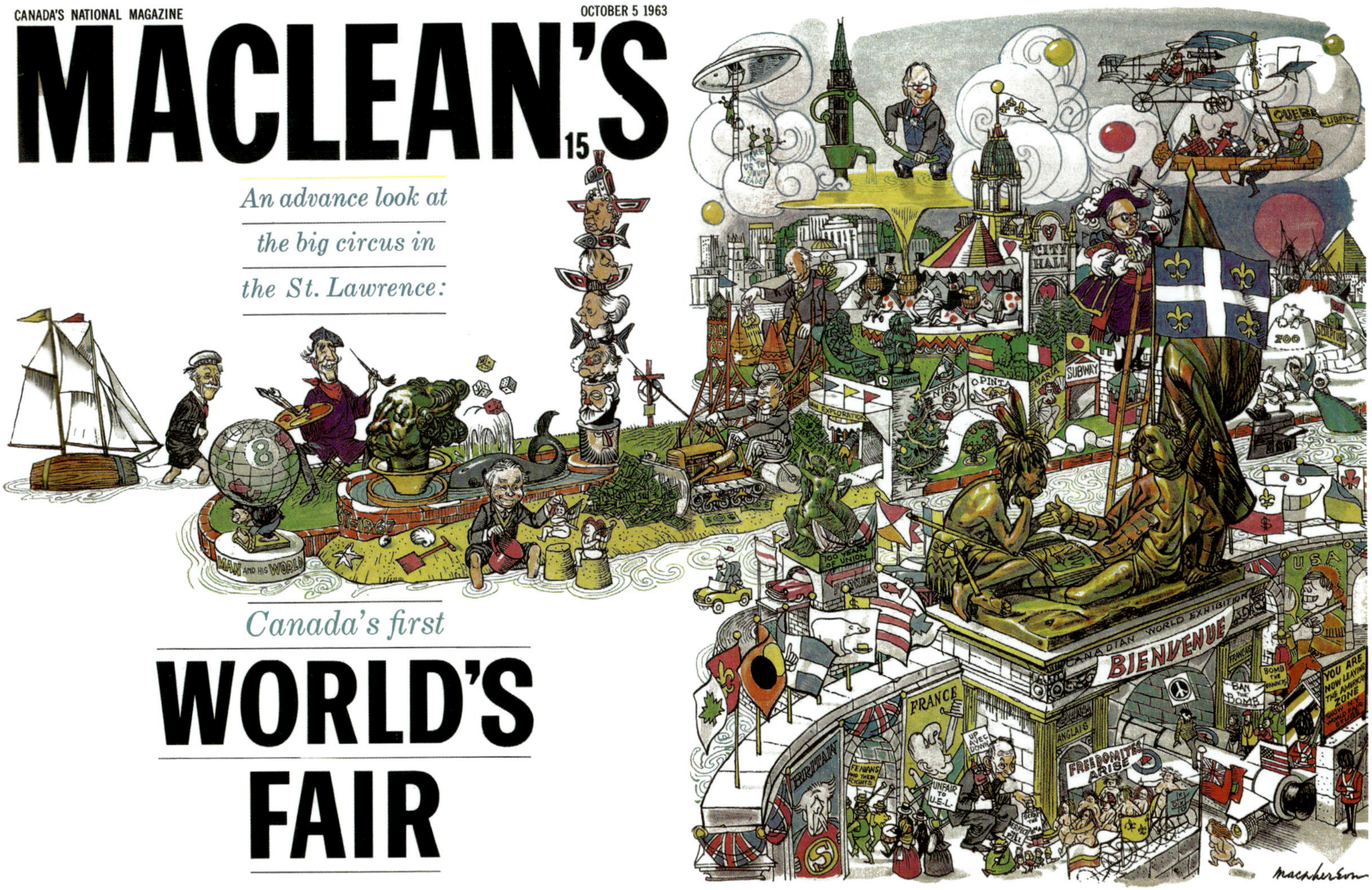

Macpherson's vision of what was to become Expo '67, published as a *Maclean's* cover foldout nearly four years before the actual event.

Duncan Macpherson's 1962 caricature of Pierre Berton as an adventurer and roving reporter for *Maclean's*.

It is impossible to talk about Duncan Macpherson's career as a political cartoonist without crediting the person who first recognized his potential to shine as a caricaturist: Pierre Berton.

Berton was a bit of a Renaissance man. Raised in the Yukon, he went to the University of British Columbia in Vancouver before enlisting for the Second World War. He later became a prolific journalist, editor, newspaper columnist and travel writer, children's book author, and television personality. A commanding figure who filled every room he entered, Berton won numerous awards over the course of his long career and was named a Companion of the Order of Canada. He is probably best remembered for his many best-selling books on Canadian history, including *The Last Spike*. These massive successes sold hundreds of thousands of copies and may have kept his beleaguered publisher, Jack McClelland, in business.

Berton was part of the liberal intelligentsia who helped establish Canada's identity as a tolerant and inclusive country in the second half of the twentieth century. A progressive to the end, Berton appeared on the CBC's *Rick Mercer Report* just a month before he died in November 2004 and discussed his forty years of recreational use of marijuana, giving tips on how to roll a joint.

While majoring in history at the University of British Columbia, Berton took a few art classes on the side since he thought he might like to be a cartoonist. Sketches from the time showed him to be proficient, but his innate cleverness just didn't shine through. He eventually abandoned the idea

I taught myself how to see.

DUNCAN MACPHERSON

7

PIERRE BERTON AND THE *TORONTO STAR*

of drawing for a living and, as Toronto illustrator Tom McNeely used to joke, "Pierre then moved on to lesser things."

Paul Berton, Pierre's son, is the current editor-in-chief of the *Hamilton Spectator*. He notes, "My father's interest in drawing never waned, although he recognized that it was never going to be more than a diversion. He always carried a pencil in his ear and was an irrepressible doodler on dinner napkins, manuscripts and newspaper margins. As a kid I always admired those sketches."

Fortunately, Berton had a good eye for other people's talent. He had moved to Toronto shortly after the end of the Second World War and had risen to become managing editor of *Maclean's* in 1953. In that position (and later as associate editor of the *Toronto Star*), he hired a number of brilliant cartoonists, all of whom contributed to elevating the state of visual humour in Canada. Duncan Macpherson was not the only person whose career benefited from Pierre Berton's benign interest.

For instance, the work of English-born *Maclean's* illustrator Len Norris caught Berton's eye. He suggested to his contacts at the *Vancouver Sun* that they hire Norris as a cartoonist. Norris's intricate, sardonic drawings exploring the foibles of British Columbia's politics and social pretensions very quickly made him a household name in the province. His cartoons, originally inspired by the work of Giles in England, rapidly took on an eccentric look of their own. The *Sun* published an annual collection of Norris cartoons for twenty-seven straight years. To this day, they

RIGHT | Pierre Berton's own sketches from his book *Cats I Have Known and Loved.*

A typical cover for one of Len Norris's many *Vancouver Sun* cartoon collections.

remain the best-selling compilations of their kind in Canada. Walt Kelly, the author of comic strip Pogo, admired Norris's work from afar, calling him "the best in the business."

When Macpherson started out as a political cartoonist, he experimented with a number of styles. Several of his early cartoons were clearly influenced by the work of Norris, who was by then a successful cartoonist at the *Vancouver Sun*. Very rapidly, though, Duncan began working in his own unique way. For his part, Norris was one of Duncan's first professional admirers: "Duncan Macpherson is the best political cartoonist that Canada has produced, and he ranks among the best in the world, head and shoulders above anybody else in North America."

Berton was also responsible for introducing the brilliant gag cartoonist George Feyer to the

Canadian public in the 1950s. Feyer, then a recent immigrant from Hungary, later did live television work, particularly during nationwide hockey broadcasts. His best work on religion, sex, and politics was too outrageous for the time and remains largely unpublished to this day. Always ambitious, Feyer moved to Los Angeles in the mid-1960s to work in television production. Sadly, he committed suicide in 1967.

During the 1950s, Duncan Macpherson was freelancing for *Maclean's* and other Canadian publications. While there were better-known artists in Toronto, Pierre Berton's attention was caught by Macpherson's illustrations of Robert Thomas Allen's humorous columns for *Maclean's*. This led to Berton asking Macpherson to illustrate the American version of his best-selling book *The Golden Trail: The Story of the Klondike Rush*. Painstakingly, Duncan came up with dozens of rough sketches for the book, which was eventually renamed *Stampede for Gold*.

Pierre Berton thought Macpherson was a great illustrator. But he also believed that Duncan would make an excellent political cartoonist. Macpherson himself had doubts. "He was very unsure of himself," Berton recalled. "He was a disciple of Gillray and Rowlandson [eighteenth-century British caricaturists] and had a real respect for the profession. He just didn't think he was good enough. For years at *Maclean's*, I was terrified that some newspaper would find him and steal him. After I joined the *Star*, I went back to him with a proposal."

LEFT | In this early cartoon about a royal visit to Toronto, Macpherson shows the influence of Len Norris's style.

RIGHT | An unpublished George Feyer cartoon on the Last Supper.

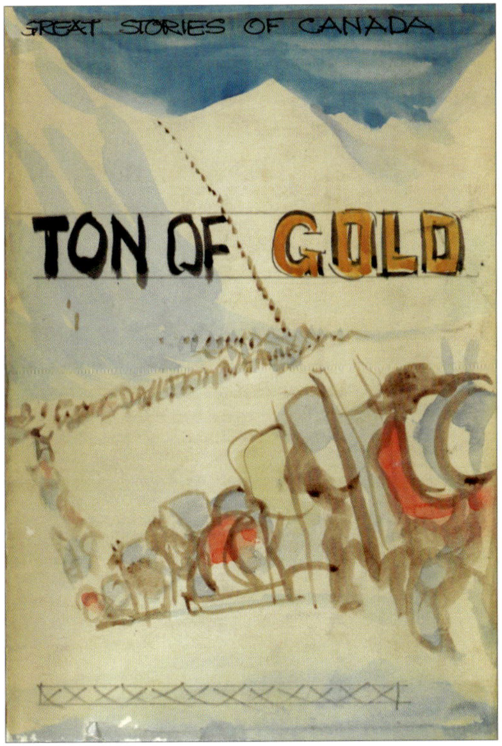

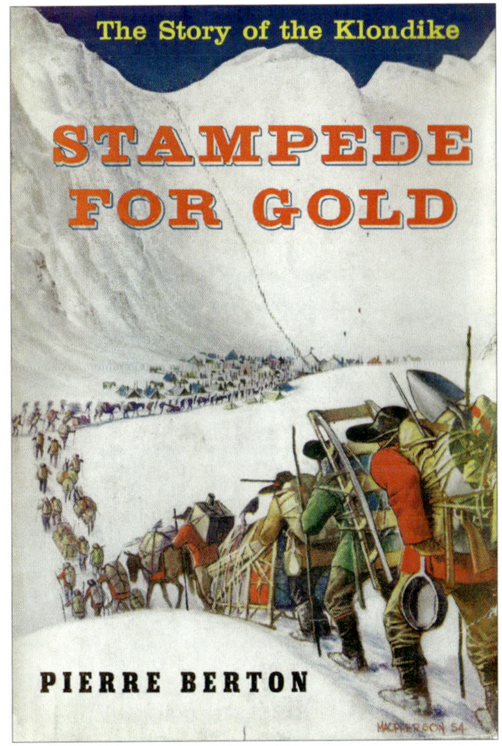

Rough sketches and final drawings for a Pierre Berton book on the Klondike.

Toronto Star publisher Beland Honderich in his office, with Macpherson originals on the wall.

Pierre Berton had moved to the *Star* in 1958 as a daily columnist and the associate editor of the *Star Weekly*. He quickly became the most popular columnist in town. The late 1950s were exciting times at the newspaper. The *Star* was abandoning the sensationalist and crime-beat reporting that had been the paper's bread and butter under former publisher Harry Hindmarsh, and bringing on board a new crew of intelligent and talented journalists like Nathan Cohen, Robert Fulford, and Ron Haggart. There were other defections to the *Star* too: Robert Thomas Allen himself came from *Maclean's* in the 1960s, and Peter C. Newman became a *Star* contributor at about the same time.

The driving force behind the changes was Beland Honderich. Born in 1918 in Kitchener, Ontario, "Bee" Honderich came from a farming family that had been particularly hard hit by the Great Depression. He dropped out of high school to find work and in 1935 landed a job as a cub reporter at the *Kitchener-Waterloo Record*. Just eight years later, Honderich was hired by the *Toronto Star* to fill in for reporters who were serving overseas during the Second World War. He himself had tried to enlist with the RCAF but was rejected because of his poor eyesight.

After rising through the newspaper's ranks, Honderich was appointed editor-in-chief in 1955 and tasked with improving the *Star*'s circulation relative to its perennial rival, the conservative *Toronto Telegram*. He was a strong proponent of the principles first adopted by the newspaper in the early 1900s under managing editor Joseph E. Atkinson. Atkinson had a vision for his newspaper's role in society, which was to promote a strong, united, and independent Canada; social justice; individual and civil liberties; community and civic engagement; and the rights of working people. He also wanted his staff to live by this business mantra, which was printed on employee recognition awards: "Get the news first; sew it up so the opposition cannot get it; leave not a crumb or a morsel or a tidbit uncollected; play it big."

Like Atkinson, Honderich focused on creating a bond with readers, giving voice to their needs and interests over those of big business. This was a credo that lined up very well with Duncan

A Christmas Eve sketch at the Salvation Army in Toronto.

ABOVE | Pierre Salinger with Duncan Macpherson and Pierre Berton at a press event in Toronto.

SHALL WE DANCE?

Macpherson's own philosophy. After researching thousands of Macpherson cartoons for this book, I didn't find one drawing in which he wasn't clearly sympathetic to those down on their luck.

Pierre Berton recommended to Honderich that Macpherson be offered a contract as the paper's editorial-page cartoonist. Honderich had come to rely on Berton's advice about which journalists and illustrators would be an asset to the paper, so it wasn't long before Berton approached Macpherson about moving to the *Star*. The cartoonist was non-committal about the opportunity but went to an interview with Honderich anyway, just to see how much the newspaper would be willing to pay. He refused the first number Honderich threw out and asked for an amount a third higher. "I figured that that was the end of the matter – and I returned to my pleasant routine of the studio and freelance commissions. However, a week later, the *Star* accepted my offer, and set up a meeting with the paper's brass. I should have asked for more!" The timing couldn't have been better, both for Macpherson and for the newspaper.

Berton and Macpherson became close chums in those early days at the *Toronto Star*. They are shown in the photograph on page 86 at a press function, along with President Jack Kennedy's press attaché, Pierre Salinger. Salinger arrived with a request: his boss would like the Macpherson original of Kennedy asking a demure John Diefenbaker to dance. Duncan obliged.

Macpherson's starting salary in 1958 was $11,500, an enormous sum in those days. He instantly became the highest-paid cartoonist in Canada, and possibly in North America. (The cartoonist known as Herblock at the *Washington Post* may have been making more in total, but he took much of his pay in stock options. Herblock died with $35 million in the bank.)

Although he was pleased about the salary, Duncan was definitely not impressed by the antiquated set-up in the *Star*'s newsroom: "It was out of the set of a pre-sound movie. The art department was a barricaded corner of wooden fencing and chicken-wire walls. Inside this compound was a group of men in shirts, ties and vests, peering silently at me like a collection of trapped orangutans. None of them had even heard about me coming to the newspaper."

The old *Toronto Star* newsroom in the 1950s.

Duncan had reluctantly parted with his Rosedale studio, accepting that he would have to set up shop at the *Star*, "but not with a group of caged artists." The building manager found him three rooms on the top floor – a corner suite – where he could set up his drawing board and art supplies. This was perfect for him, since it was well away from the newsroom.

Macpherson had a verbal agreement with Honderich to try out the job for one year. His

ABOVE | Bruce Palmer and Duncan Macpherson.

RIGHT | A wartime drawing by *Toronto Star* cartoonist Les Callan, whom Macpherson replaced.

cartoons were getting immediate, positive results for the newspaper, but in many ways, it was a difficult twelve months for Macpherson. He found himself working eight to ten hours a day, five days a week, on cartoons that didn't always satisfy him.

Toward the end of that first year, Macpherson strolled into Honderich's office and handed him a box of Cuban cigars. When the publisher asked what the occasion was, Macpherson said he was celebrating his departure from the *Star* for a new job back at *Maclean's*.

Pierre Berton recalled: "I was away on my first holiday and I came back and there was no Macpherson cartoon in the paper. So I called Honderich and said, 'What's happened to Macpherson – is he sick?' And he said, 'No, he quit.' I said, 'What do you mean he quit? He is the hottest thing you've got at this point.'" Macpherson had apparently asked the *Star* to allow him to cut back from five cartoons a week to three, and to let him travel, specifically to Cuba, where he wanted to sketch for the newspaper. Berton remembered Honderich explaining he had told Duncan that "he couldn't have everything." Berton continued: "And I said – why not? If he does three cartoons a week, it's still better than no cartoons a week."

Editorial executives at the *Star* suddenly began pestering Macpherson about negotiating a new deal. The newspaper's circulation was increasing rapidly, and it had become clear that his cartoons were instrumental. So Duncan asked his friend, lawyer Bruce Palmer, to be the one to present the contract demands to the paper. The meeting between Palmer and *Star* executives took place at the Lord Simcoe Hotel. To impart a little cachet to the affair, Macpherson rented a suite, complete with bar and deli. "The word got out about my renegotiation, and by four in the afternoon, much of the newsroom was in my suite having a picnic!"

CHARGE! Macpherson returned to the *Star*, doing what he did best.

" . . . don't turn that box around that way, Ricky . . . you know your father can't stand all that French in the morning . . . "

A typical suburban Sid Barron cartoon for the *Star*.

Macpherson said that at about 6:00 in the evening, Palmer burst through the negotiating room doors, yelling that his client would never work for the *Star* again! His brash negotiating style seems to have been effective. "In a day or two, Honderich contacted me, and said that we could come to an agreement if we could leave Palmer completely out of it."

Bruce Palmer had cleared the way for his friend. The agreement Duncan eventually reached with the publisher contained very favourable conditions, including a considerably higher salary. (Macpherson said that, in an unguarded moment, editor-in-chief Bob Neilsen complained that he was getting paid less than the cartoonist.) Macpherson was required to produce only four cartoons a week, and he would be paid even for cartoons that were rejected. He retained ownership over both the original drawings and the copyright, with the *Star* buying only first rights. Further, he would have six weeks of holiday, and the *Star* would cover all expenses related to research and business-related travel. There was more: "I would receive 50 per cent of money earned from syndication of my cartoons, an unheard of rate at that time. Also, I would never have to attend editorial meetings." Duncan really hated editorial meetings.

So the *Star* met Macpherson's demands, and the cartoonist returned to the newspaper to continue doing what he did best. This episode illustrates just how influential Duncan was, even at the outset of his career. He had used his popularity to bargain for a greater degree of independence than had ever been achieved by a Canadian newspaper cartoonist. Despite some initial misgivings about the new business arrangement, the *Star* was well aware of his value to the paper.

Macpherson's desire to redefine his business relationship with the newspaper was partly driven by his fear of being sidelined at some point in the future. He had been struck by how poorly the *Star* had treated Les Callan, the cartoonist already on staff when Macpherson first joined the paper. "They just pretended that he didn't exist any longer, after twenty-five years," he said. "That's why I've never joined the staff of the paper. It's a pretty cold-blooded business."

Les Callan had been hired by the *Star* before the Second World War. His cartoons were at best mildly amusing. Callan's most important contri bution to cartooning may have been during the war. He joined up in 1942 and began sketching for the Canadian Army's newspaper, the *Maple Leaf*. He followed Canadian forces through France, Belgium, and Holland, recording what he saw and writing down funny things that happened to him. After the war, the sketches were gathered in a best-selling book titled *Normandy and On … From D-Day to Victory*.

Editorial cartoonists started to take notice of the possibilities opened up by Duncan Macpherson's approach. Until his unprecedented contract, most cartoonists were part of an editorial-page team. They attended meetings of the editorial board and frequently illustrated ideas that had been proposed by other people. Macpherson's successful campaign to become more independent meant he could be recognized not just as an illustrator of the newspaper's editorials but also as a contributor to the editorial page in his own right.

Editorial writers don't sign their work, whereas columnists have always done so and have therefore been at liberty to express their own views. Duncan believed that political cartoonists should have that same freedom. This was a new attitude at the time, but one that most Canadian cartoonists have since adopted.

With the newspaper now allowing Macpherson more free time, Pierre Berton arranged for the talented Sid Barron to fill in whenever Macpherson wasn't around. (Barron and Berton had studied art together in Victoria in 1937.) Barron had already established a solid reputation as a cartoonist at the

This cartoon of Ottawa mayor Charlotte Whitton demonstrates Macpherson's extraordinary ability to draw drapery and clothing.

Victoria Times. Each panel of his cartoons was a pastiche of jokes on urban and suburban life. Robert Fulford admiringly called Barron "the poet of the mundane." Macpherson and Barron made a successful tag team – and they admired each other's work.

"Mac has a magnificent eye," said Barron. "The eye is not a reliable instrument until it's trained, and his eye is trained. He learned to draw how clothes hang on people; all the folds and the creases are done perfectly. I never learned that. I envy him."

In Macpherson's early days at the *Star*, some readers were taken aback by his style. "The first reaction to his cartoons was that they were cruel," "Bee" Honderich later recalled. Once the public got used to Macpherson's style, however, his work became extremely popular. No other Canadian cartoonist before or since has achieved the same prominence.

Duncan Macpherson's first workspace at the *Toronto Star* was on an upper floor of the old *Star* building at 80 King Street West. The twenty-two-storey Art Deco office tower was the headquarters of the *Star* from 1929 to 1970, when the newspaper's offices moved to a brand new building at One Yonge Street. Comic book artist Joe Shuster used the old building as inspiration for the *Daily Planet* offices in his "Superman" comic strip.

Toronto-born Michael Enright is a radio broadcaster and the veteran host of CBC Radio One's *Sunday Edition*, but one of his first jobs as a young man was at the *Toronto Star*'s offices. He remembers Duncan Macpherson very well.

"I was hired in the old *Star* building at 80 King Street West as a mail boy and messenger. My job was to deliver the bulldog [early] edition of the paper to employees around the building. I hated delivering to Macpherson; he scared me. He was a very intimidating man – tall, bulky, always with a cigarette dangling from his mouth. I do remember that he smiled a lot, showing a bottom row of fearsome teeth. He was always very pleasant to me, but I was in awe of him."

Enright notes that his very first published work came when he was thirteen or fourteen

80 King Street West.

TORONTO DAILY STAR

Established 1892—Joseph E. Atkinson, Publisher, 1899-1948
Published at 80 King St. W., Toronto 1, by Toronto Star Limited

JOSEPH S. ATKINSON, President and Publisher

Directors: WILLIAM J. CAMPBELL, Vice-President RUTH ATKINSON HINDMARSH
HARRY A. HINDMARSH, Secretary BELAND H. HONDERICH, Vice-President BURNETT M. THALL, Vice-President

The daily average paid circulation of The Daily Star for OCTOBER, 1963 was 352,345

Member of the Audit Bureau of Circulations

MONDAY, NOVEMBER 25, 1963

The rule of violence

The murder of Lee Harvey Oswald, the alleged murderer of President Kennedy, has provided a horrible sequel to the assassination of the president himself.

Although the authorities in Dallas claimed they had a complete case against Oswald, his guilt had not been legally proved. He was entitled by law to a fair trial, and to be presumed innocent until proved guilty. The man who shot him down disregarded these fundamental rights and constituted himself judge, jury and executioner without even hearing the evidence. This is the lynching spirit at its worst. Coming on top of the original assassination it cannot fail to strengthen the impression that the United States is a land of uncontrolled hatreds and lawless violence.

There is something peculiarly tragic in the fact that a would-be avenger of President Kennedy should thus trample on the principles by which he lived. At home and abroad, the president strove consistently to make reason and justice prevail. Today in Dallas violence is in the saddle and the rule of law is brushed aside.

Even if it is assumed that Oswald was guilty, his death is a disaster. It leaves the public in the dark as to the whole background of the president's assassination. What were the killer's motives? Was he sane or insane? Did he have accomplices? Did he contrive the crime himself, or was he incited to it by some other person or organization? We may never know the answer to any of these questions.

Some people may suspect, indeed, that Oswald was killed to prevent him from talking—or even that he was an innocent man used as a scapegoat to protect the real murderer. The extraordinary negligence of the Dallas police in protecting their prisoner will itself feed the darkest rumors.

It is easy to imagine the hell-broth of suspicion and fear that can rise from all this as extremists of the right and left accuse each other of responsibility for President Kennedy's death. This could poison the political life of the United States for years.

Fewer targets in Canada

The assassination of President Kennedy has called attention to one of the striking differences between Canada and the United States—the comparative absence of political violence in this country.

Four American presidents have fallen by assassins' bullets in the last 100 years, and attempts have been made on the lives of a number of others—and this despite one of the most elaborate security systems in the world. Yet during the same

The presidency of the United States is not only a great office; it is a terribly conspicuous one. The president is the head of the executive government, and he is also the head of the State. All official acts are done in his name, and he is nominally responsible for all appointments, from second lieutenants in the army up to cabinet ministers. At all national ceremonies he is in the centre of the picture. Inevitably he gets the blame, personally, when anything goes wrong

performed by the Queen and her representative the Governor-General. On ceremonial occasions, indeed, the prime minister is usually in the background. Technically he is the senior minister of the crown; in actual practice he is the chairman of a governing committee, the cabinet, which depends for support on the House of Commons.

Authority in this country is thus more diffuse and impersonal than it is in the United States. Canadians with

As Others See It

Raps Robarts' pension 'meddling'

Sir: Why does the Robarts government keep meddling and muddling in the pension plan when it is clearly a federal undertaking?

I, for one, was thrilled when the federal government announced they were working out the details for a Canada pension plan, but was astounded and dismayed when the provincial government straggled out with some cooked-up idea of a pension plan. I trust that Premier Robarts will see the light and forget his politicking and stop meddling with something so vital to every citizen of Canada.

Humans first

Sir: Alderman George Ben's suggestion for a decent zoo in Toronto (Voice, Nov. 9) is not a bad idea. But we also think that if Mr. Ben could spare some of his effort and energy in helping the people in his own Ward 5 to improve their living conditions, then we would have a decent residential area.

We have two factories right in the centre of our residential block which create fire hazards, air pollution, traffic and noise problems. We were talking about this problem with our

most of the benefits of what is currently considered a university education.

J. B. E. CRIPPS

Toronto 12

South Africa

Sir: Here is another shudder for Daniel Braithwaite (Voice, Nov. 13). I support Dr. Verwoerd for a multitude of reasons and would like to refute some of the statements made by Mr. Braithwaite.

The latest African "victims of persecution" were not executed for political reasons only, but

Right step

Sir: Uncle Sam is up on his hind legs beefing about the take-over of American interests by South American republics. But the expropriation of natural resources is in line with the policy of national development. As long as the use of natural resources is directed toward the benefit of the people instead of the personal aggrandizement of a privileged few it is a step in the right direction.

But American interests should be adequately compensated for the financial losses accruing

years old. He wrote a letter to the editor of the *Star* defending Macpherson's right to lampoon. The paper printed it, so he clipped the piece and carried it in various wallets for a very long time.

Macpherson's *Toronto Star* editors rarely took issue with cartoons that lampooned the cynicism and hypocrisy in Toronto's municipal politics. His biting commentary on international events, however, sometimes made them nervous.

Because of their satirical nature, cartoons tend to be rejected by editors more often than other newspaper features. In fact, some political cartoonists have their work cut multiple times a month. Macpherson estimated that no more than

The federal bandwagon.

twenty of his cartoons had been declined in his thirty-three years at the *Star*. That's a very low number. In truth, he often agreed with the editors after a period of reflection. He never identified specific cartoons that were killed, and none of his editors who did the rejecting are still with us. However, a former *Star* employee does recall one instance. In early November 1963 Duncan drew a bloodstained American flag in reaction to a brutal coup in Vietnam to which the Americans had turned a blind eye. Publisher Beland Honderich thought the drawing was too extreme and refused to print it. However, that cartoon soon became particularly apt, just in a new context.

Linda Sergiades (née Wright) worked as a secretary in the *Star*'s editorial suite during the early 1960s. She recalls the scene outside the office of the *Star*'s editorial-page editor, Bob Neilsen, on 22 November that year. "Bob walked out of his office and leaned up against the door jamb. His face was ashen, as he announced: 'Kennedy has been shot.'" In the wake of President Kennedy's death and the subsequent killing of assassin Lee Harvey Oswald, the *Star* decided to print that cartoon after all.

Sergiades found working in the editorial offices a great experience.

> Newspapers had a reputation of being uncomfortable places for young women to work, but at the *Star*, there were never any awkward moments. I worked with editors Bob Neilsen, Mark Harrison and many other talented individuals. All these gentlemen were very polite.
>
> Duncan was up on the twentieth floor, and it was often my job to get the printed proof of that day's cartoon to him for his files. He was particularly nice – even chatty – and I got to know him quite well. Still, I did hear stories about him. In the *Star*'s library one morning, there were whispered conversations about Duncan having destroyed the Thermofax machine [an early photocopier] the night before. He had been frustrated at not being able to get the thing to work!
>
> Sometimes I would watch Duncan draw. I marvelled at his renderings of stagecoaches and bandwagons as the centrepieces of his cartoons. He used no photos or other visual aids. When I asked about it, he simply shrugged and said: "I taught myself how to see."

Linda walked into Duncan's studio one day when he was puzzling over which cartoons to submit for the 1962 National Newspaper Awards. "I suggested he send in a brilliant drawing of Britain's Prime Minister Harold Macmillan trying to buy tickets from Charles de Gaulle for Commonwealth members to enter the Common Market. The cartoon had the cutline: 'Take it or leave it, no special rates for kiddies.'" The cartoon that Linda had suggested won Duncan Macpherson his third NNA.

Nathan Phillips was the eminently cartoonable mayor of Toronto (1955–62) when Macpherson began working for the *Toronto Star*. Duncan usually drew him eating. Here, Phillips crosses a picket line at the Royal York Hotel to get at a free dinner.

The first collection of Macpherson cartoons, published in 1962, was an instant best-seller and is today considered a valuable collector's item. Fully half the book is devoted to Macpherson's take on the goings-on at Toronto City Hall.

In the late 1950s, the city was going through a dramatic expansion. Naturally, there was drama, infighting, and behind-the-scenes finagling – perfect subjects for a cartoonist. The introduction to the book was titled "Comments from the Caricatured" and featured remarks by Frederick G. Gardiner, Allan Lamport, Mayor Nathan Phillips, and Premier Leslie Frost. Municipal Controller Jean Newman's note read: "Priceless … in detail, originality and perception. Macpherson must be the one Robbie Burns was hoping for when he said, 'to see ourselves as others see us.'"

Municipal politics claimed a good deal of Macpherson's attention in his first years at the *Star*. "You couldn't miss with Nate Phillips," he said. Phillips's election as the first Jewish mayor of Toronto was a sign of change as the city began to evolve from a Protestant, conservative, and staunchly British metropolis to a modern, multicultural city. Phillips took Macpherson's needling with good grace and got his hands on as many original Macpherson cartoons of him as he could find. He later donated them to the City of Toronto Archives.

Macpherson also enjoyed caricaturing "Big Daddy" Gardiner, the designer of the eponymous expressway that sweeps along the city's waterfront. One of his earliest and strongest cartoons

As a subject – and often a target – of Duncan Macpherson cartoons, I gladly pay tribute to his skill and art.

TORONTO MAYOR NATHAN PHILLIPS

8

TAKING TORONTO BY STORM

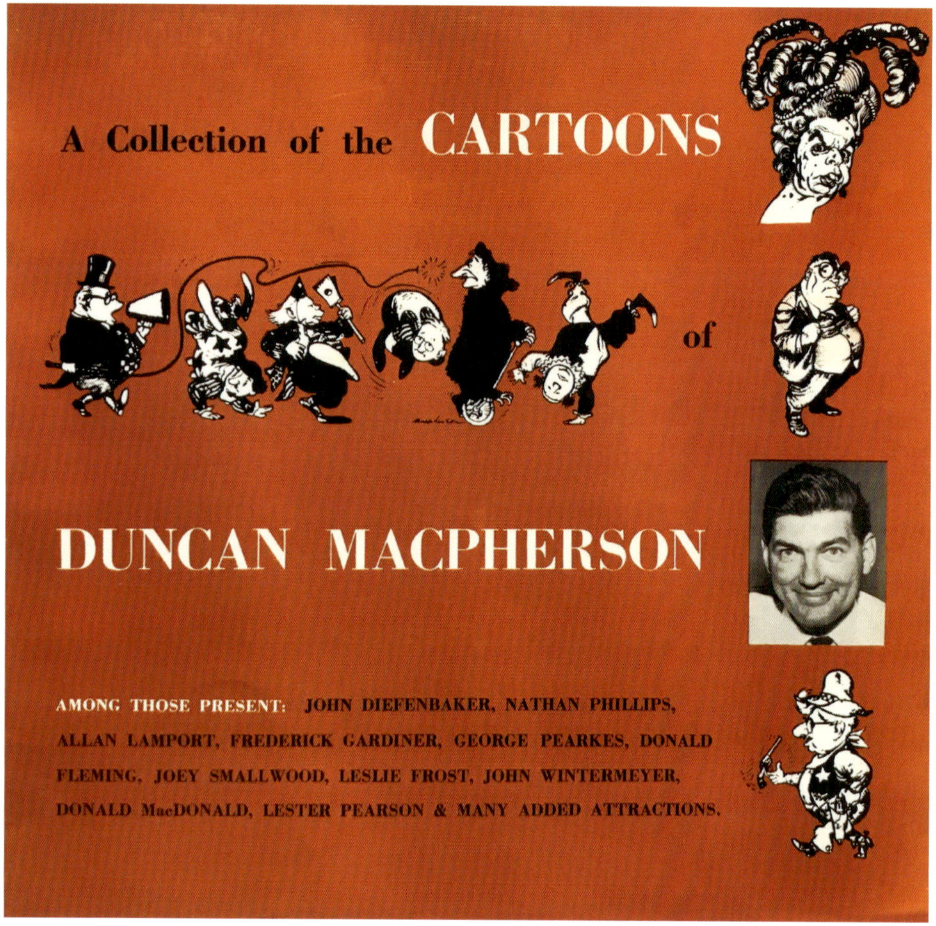

of Gardiner is reminiscent of the work of the great American caricaturist, Thomas Nast.

Gardiner was the first chairman (from 1953 to 1961) of the Metropolitan Toronto council. As Metro chairman, Gardiner was a staunch advocate of growth and expansion, and was responsible for many capital works projects, including the Don Valley Parkway.

Philip Givens served for many years on Toronto City Council, becoming mayor in late 1963 following the unexpected death of sitting mayor Donald Dean Summerville. In the municipal election the following year, Givens ran against Allan Lamport, a former Liberal MPP (1937–43), mayor of Toronto (1952–54), and city councillor, whose confrontational style practically guaranteed Givens's re-election. (Lamport once called Henry Ford a "black-hearted American Quisling" for his perceived lack of support for Canada's war effort.)

Allan Lamport's speeches were works of unintended genius: "If I get stabbed in the back," he once shouted, "I want to be there!" Macpherson's cartoons of "Lampy" got so much play that the candidate asked for permission to use some of them – even the nastier ones – in his election campaign. "Lampy says a knock is as good as a boost," Duncan said, laughing. Lamport lost the election, and Givens served as mayor until 1966.

In his cartoon to mark the opening of Toronto's brand-new City Hall, Macpherson depicts Philip Givens partying it up, a clever reference to the famous eighteenth-century Hogarth cartoon "Gin Lane," which portrayed the debauchery of London street life.

Givens campaigned tirelessly to have the city purchase Henry Moore's sculpture "The Archer" for installation in front of the new City Hall. City Council would not approve the funding, but Givens was eventually able to purchase

the piece with contributions from private donors. The sculpture was unveiled in 1966. He had achieved his dream, but the controversy led to his downfall.

William Dennison (mayor of Toronto from 1967 to 1972) grew up on a farm in Renfrew County. He left home at age fifteen to work in the lumber camps of northern Ontario, trekking west to Saskatchewan in the summers to earn money by helping with the harvest. His 1966 campaign for the mayoralty was based on providing "a strong voice for labour in city affairs" and opposing the pro-development policies of incumbent Phil Givens. He was elected, despite being opposed by all three daily newspapers. Although Dennison was a social democrat, Macpherson always portrayed him as having conservative tastes.

While the *Star*'s readers loved Duncan's lampooning of local public officials, there was also an appetite for artistic representation of important public occasions. Macpherson would go out and sketch these events on behalf of the newspaper. Here are several of his drawings from Queen Elizabeth's 1959 visit to the city of Toronto.

LEFT | Macpherson saluted Jean Newman as a real presence on City Council: "It's a bird, it's a plane, no … it's SuperNewman!"

RIGHT | Nathan Phillips changes his tastes to reflect the new demographics.

Phillips's 1967 autobiography featured a Macpherson cartoon.

Mayor Phillips had his office walls plastered with cartoons.

TAKE A JUMP IN THE LAKE!

For a time, Nathan Phillips was feuding with Toronto's three daily newspapers.

Metro Chairman Fred Gardiner (with the shovel) and Mayor Phillips were often at odds.

HE'S TRYING TO WRECK MY CASTLE!

Duncan Macpherson (ABOVE) settling in at the *Toronto Star*, sketching Metro Chairman Fred "Big Daddy" Gardiner (RIGHT).

Macpherson made Toronto politician Allan Lamport a frequent target.

BACK IN THE SPOTLIGHT!

Nathan Phillips Alley (after Hogarth's "Gin Lane").

THE ARCHER.

William Dennison contemplates Henry Moore's *The Archer*.

Helpful tips to solve Toronto's parking problem.

— waiting for the duke

All set
for the parade

"Shouldn't you pass behind it, father?"

"—and what does your husband do?"

Queen Elizabeth II's visit to Toronto.

THEN LET THEM EAT CAKE!

9

DIEFENBAKER AND PEARSON

I'm simply against the wrongness in public life.

DUNCAN MACPHERSON FROM THE 1975 FILM *THE HECKLERS*

John Diefenbaker, Canada's thirteenth prime minister, was the leader of the Progressive Conservative Party when it was elected with minority status in 1957, the year before Duncan Macpherson joined the *Toronto Star*. Macpherson was quite fascinated by him. He once said, "Diefenbaker has always given me the feeling of a Billy Sunday [an American evangelist], a circus barker, and a third-rate actor, all put together. I had more fun with Diefenbaker than anybody – absolutely no restraints at all. I had him going as a wild man in my imagination, and that's the way he turned out."

The *Toronto Star* had always been a Liberal paper. When the Progressive Conservatives under Diefenbaker were re-elected with a majority in 1958, *Star* journalists, editorialists, and cartoonists ramped up the pressure on the prime minister. Right at the front of the pack was Duncan Macpherson. In fact, it was just the third cartoon Macpherson did for the *Star* that turned out to be the most famous of his caricatures of Diefenbaker: his portrayal of the prime minister as an out-of-touch, cold-hearted Marie Antoinette. It was an instant classic and has probably been reproduced more often than any other Canadian cartoon.

The prime minister had recently announced the government's controversial decision to cancel development and production of the Avro Arrow, a Canadian military aircraft. This would jeopardize the jobs of thousands of highly skilled Canadian workers. Diefenbaker took a cavalier attitude toward those workers, prompting the Macpherson cartoon. (The core of the

TEAM DIEFENBAKER!

Avro team later went to NASA – and after that, Canada started buying U.S. military aircraft.) "Before then, Diefenbaker could do no wrong – worse, he believed he could do no wrong," Pierre Berton recalled. "This puncturing of the sacrosanct, saintly Diefenbaker image started a landslide of people poking fun at the prime minister. From then on, he became fair game. The cartoon was the beginning of the Diefenbaker slide."

Pierre Berton had been absolutely right about Macpherson's talent and his potential as

CAPTAIN AHAB.

THEN "KAPOW!" I'LL FLATTEN THE OPPOSITION.

a political cartoonist. Thanks to this caricature, Macpherson established himself almost overnight as the pre-eminent cartoonist in Canada. Given the fame of the cartoon in its day, Ottawa cartoonist and historian Guy Badeaux (Bado) has called the Marie Antoinette cartoon Canada's own Mona Lisa. As for Diefenbaker, he was caught on film in *The Hecklers* snorting that the cartoon was far too intellectual, and no one would ever understand it.

For years, every time Macpherson was introduced to someone, almost the first thing they mentioned was that Marie Antoinette cartoon. "It was beginning to haunt me," he would say ruefully. "I mean, I've done a lot of work since that time."

Although the Marie Antoinette cartoon became the enduring symbol of Macpherson's treatment of the prime minister, it was followed by increasingly outlandish caricatures of Diefenbaker. For a cartoon titled Election Swim, Macpherson drew the prime minister as a godlike figure walking on water, to the astonishment of a pair of boaters. The prime minister paraded across the editorial pages of the *Star* in a bewildering variety of preposterous disguises: as a variety of sporting figures, Captain Ahab, Batman, and even Quasimodo.

Macpherson continued to lampoon Diefenbaker at a steady pace. If the prime minister saw himself as the central figure in a sweeping national drama, Macpherson portrayed him as the manic ringleader of a political circus. Over the years, in cartoons, Diefenbaker's front teeth grew more prominent, the eyes wilder, and the antics more demented.

Diefenbaker was not initially a fan of Duncan Macpherson's humour. He particularly disliked the Marie Antoinette cartoon and was extremely unhappy to learn that parliamentary correspondents had hung a copy of it in the Press Gallery.

When he was first introduced to Macpherson at the annual Press Gallery dinner, "Dief the Chief" gave the cartoonist an icy greeting before striding quickly away, pointedly leaving a Macpherson cartoon of himself unautographed. He eventually mellowed, once even inviting Macpherson to accompany him on a fishing trip – or so it is rumoured. The former prime minister grudgingly praised Duncan as a great cartoonist, one with the ability to get to the heart of things: "I like a cartoon that is devastating without wounding. It's like Parliament. I like to be strong in argument without hurting."

Diefenbaker continued to appear in Macpherson's cartoons for years after the prime minister's defeat in 1963. Ultimately, he was depicted as a shawled pensioner, a needlepoint Union Jack in his lap, telling the new Progressive Conservative leader, Joe Clark, to "run along and play."

Macpherson was a brilliant caricaturist, but he didn't always immediately hit on the best way to capture his subject. On the eve of the 1963 federal election, he confessed he was afraid that if Opposition leader Lester Pearson got in, he'd be lost. "He doesn't have a good face," he said. "No excesses that a cartoonist can take apart. I'm not satisfied with my caricature of Pearson. It's recognizable, I know, but I haven't got what I want."

Cartoonists Ed McNally at the *Montreal Star*, Peter Kuch at the *Winnipeg Free Press*, and Normand Hudon at *Le Devoir* were already adept at capturing the bow-tied "Mike" Pearson. Macpherson worked hard to develop a Pearson caricature and finally came up with an image that pleased him: a rumpled, befuddled character the public could instantly identify as the leader they viewed with both affection and exasperation. A characteristic cartoon was one depicting the prime minister as a pianist in a bordello that was being raided. The caption read: "I always wondered what they did upstairs." It is interesting

As Diefenbaker became less popular, Macpherson drew him as Quasimodo, the protagonist of Victor Hugo's novel *The Hunchback of Notre-Dame*. Quasimodo was feared and loathed by the people of Paris.

In this celebrated cartoon, John Diefenbaker and Finance Minister Donald Fleming go cap in hand to Washington.

MY FRIEND AND I WOULD LIKE TO CONSOLIDATE OUR DEBTS.

P.C.
LEADERSHIP

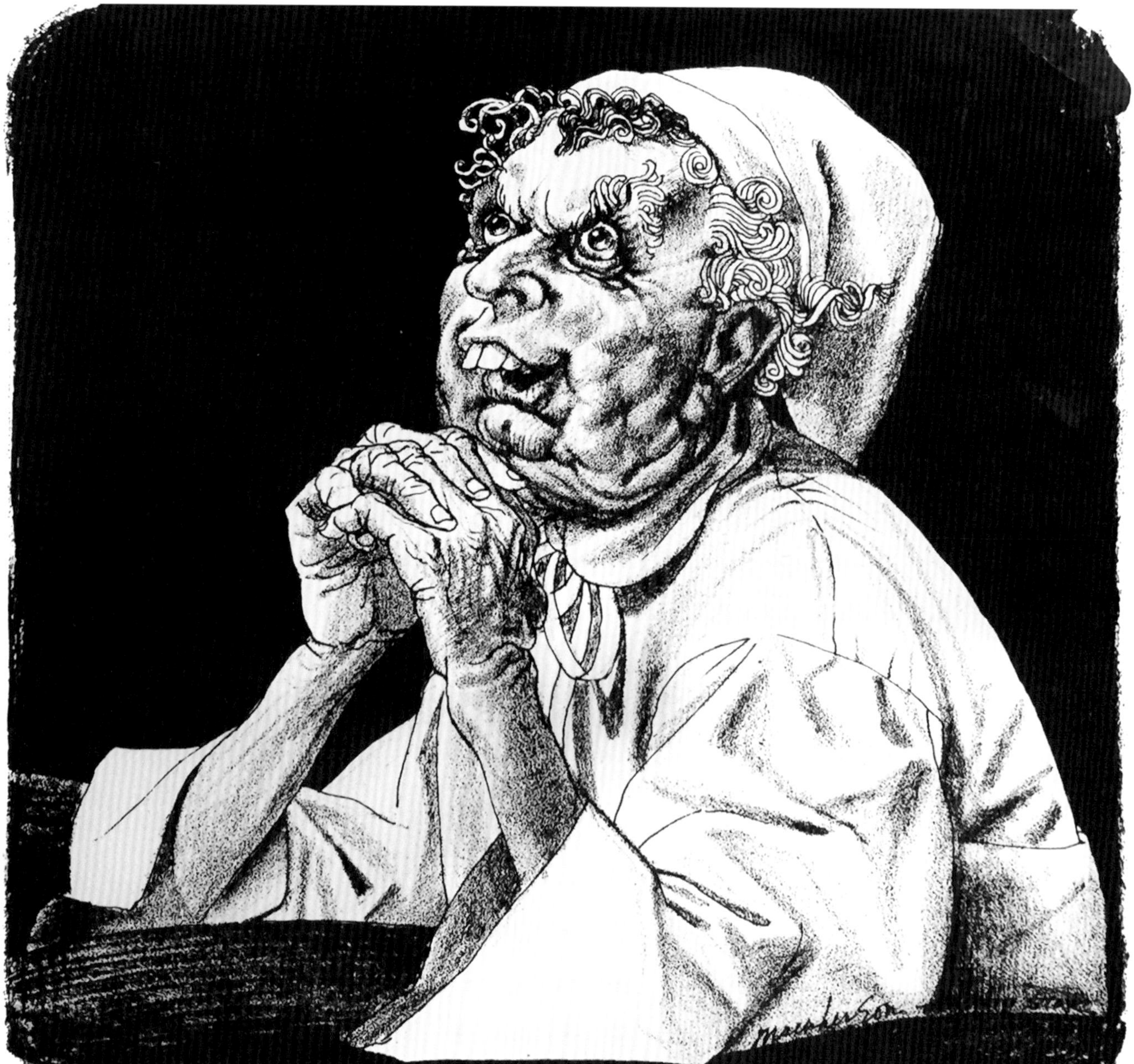

JOHN G. DIEFENBAKER SPEAKING.

SOLIDARITY
UNITY
CONCORD
HARMONY
PLAY BALL!
OF COURSE, OF COURSE,
RUN ALONG AND PLAY.
P.C. MANIFESTO

Lester Pearson was elected as the prime minister of Canada in the federal election of 1963.

that Duncan signed this cartoon "MacBrehl." This probably meant that the idea was suggested to him by his friend Jack Brehl.

In fact, Duncan was somewhat kinder to Pearson than were other caricaturists. They had met and genuinely liked each other. Furthermore, unlike Diefenbaker, Pearson had a fondness for self-deprecating humour. His office walls were hung with cartoons in which he figured prominently.

In 1997, on the centenary of Pearson's birth, the National Archives of Canada (previously known as the Public Archives of Canada, and renamed in 2004 Library and Archives Canada) was commissioned to produce an exhibition on his life, featuring photographs tracing his experiences as a young pilot, a diplomat, a politician, a Nobel Prize winner, and a prime minister. In order to give a genuine sense of the era, a number of cartoons were included in the mix, most of them by Duncan Macpherson.

According to Ottawa author Andrew Caddell: "Macpherson was not overly kind to Pearson as his government became prone to scandal. However, Pearson was always depicted as something of a naïf: a boy scout or a 'helpful fixer' in the political world, surrounded by people who were more ambitious or ruthless than him." Although history has all but forgotten the failings of the Pearson government, his leadership mandate was ultimately undermined by several less than edifying incidents. Influence peddling involving a drug smuggler brought down the prime minister's parliamentary secretary; charges of bribery related to licensing of a race track cost a cabinet minister his position; and a shady furniture-trading business involving two Quebec cabinet ministers shattered their careers.

Michael Pearson, the prime minister's grandson, told Caddell that his grandfather "liked

Macpherson and admired his skills as a cartoonist, his sense of humour and his general 'take' on the world of politics." The family has several of Macpherson's cartoons framed at their home and cottage near Ottawa, most of which are keepsakes from Lester Pearson's Parliament Hill office. Michael Pearson has said that their favourite is "a baseball-themed one titled 'the old smoothie,' depicting (in four panels) LBP as an outfielder chasing down the 'national unity' fly ball, juggling it, falling in a cloud of dust, and coming up with the ball in his mitt at the end."

As with Diefenbaker, Pearson is now often remembered exactly as Duncan Macpherson drew him. A permanent display in the Lester B. Pearson Building on Sussex Drive in Ottawa (home of the Department of Global Affairs) features many Macpherson cartoons.

Although he drew each of these prime ministers brilliantly, Macpherson seemed at his very best whenever he drew Diefenbaker and Pearson together.

As the authors of *The Hecklers* observed, Macpherson's cartoons demonstrate "an extraordinary ear for the comic properties of spoken and written English." He borrowed quotations from Jonathan Swift, Robert Burns, Lewis Carroll, W.S. Gilbert, Robert W. Service, and others – often distorting the original reference to suit his purposes. "Even more revealing," according to S.A. Longstaff and Sarah Henry,

> is the way he searches in offbeat literary and historical byways, always with an ear cocked for antique words and expressions. Books of magic, military manuals of yore, court proceedings, Canadian historian Edwin C. Guillet's books on travelling circuses – such are the curiosa he likes to ransack for verbal odds and ends.

Reflected glory. The United States created the Peace Corps in 1961, and Lester Pearson launched the Company of Young Canadians in 1966.

Is Premier John Robarts of Ontario, the richest province, really driving the car?

Quebec's Premier Daniel Johnson (Union Nationale) uses the threat of Quebec leaving Confederation to good effect against Pearson's Liberals.

$148 million to build a bridge to Prince Edward Island?

Pearson faces a non-stop barrage of questions from the Opposition over scandals within the Liberal Party.

No matter where Lester Pearson went, accusations of Liberal impropriety pursued him. The albatross became the symbol for the scandals in Macpherson's cartoons.

THE OLD SMOOTHIE.

> In this, he is a throwback. The great comic artists of the past – particularly Gillray and Nast – had to be literary men as well as artists. One is struck by the range of techniques Macpherson has under control. No contemporary comic artist attempts so much or has such an inexhaustible mental library at the service of his brush and pen.

Duncan Macpherson's drawings often evoked the cartoon styles of the nineteenth century: overtly theatrical, with their own plots and subplots, costumes, and historical references. He possessed the combined talents of two exceptional nineteenth- and early-twentieth-century Canadian cartoonists: Henri Julien (1852–1908) and John Wilson Bengough (1851–1923). Julien, Canada's first full-time editorial cartoonist, was a master draughtsman who built his reputation over twenty-two years at the *Montreal Daily Star*. Bengough had a flair for humorous creativity; it shone through in his political cartoons, which appeared in his own publication as well as in Canadian and international newspapers.

In approach, Macpherson is actually closer to Bengough than to his own contemporaries and immediate predecessors. Just as lampooning John A. Macdonald in the late nineteenth century helped to launch Bengough's satirical magazine *Grip*, caricaturing Diefenbaker gave Macpherson's career a flying start.

Macpherson would later recall how he "visited Mike Pearson in Ottawa the day the convention began that was to pick his successor as Liberal leader. I was tremendously impressed with the collection of Canadian art on the walls, the finest and most representative that I have ever seen. Mrs Pearson chose the work, the bulk of it shanghaied from the National Gallery, all to be returned when the Pearsons vacated 24 Sussex Drive. When Mrs Pearson wanted her way, she obviously got it." Maryon Pearson was known for her wit, once saying, "Behind every successful man, there stands a surprised woman."

It is telling that Duncan Macpherson was viewed with fondness and admiration even by his fiercest competitors, as is made clear in the many stories and tributes from his fellow cartoonists. One is Brian Gable, the award-winning political cartoonist for the *Globe and Mail*, who, with that newspaper's national reach, is the best-known cartoonist working in Canada today. "As a kid growing up in Saskatoon, I was only dimly aware of the newspaper business and journalism in general. Editorial cartoons were fun to look at even if the messages were sometimes difficult for a twelve-year-old to understand." The *Star-Phoenix* had its own editorial cartoonist, Ed Sebestyen, and occasionally Gable would see cartoons from other papers. That's when he became aware of the name "Duncan Macpherson."

Gable recalls that one of the earliest of Macpherson's cartoons to make an impression on him was a drawing of Lester Pearson, done in the early 1960s. "Pearson is rendered as an earnest boy scout. He is confidently guiding a hilariously drawn grim dowager, labelled 'BNA Act,' directly toward an open sewer, with a sign near the opening reading 'Provincial Premiers at work.'" What strikes Gable now is how well this cartoon works, even fifty years later. "It didn't matter how much a reader knew about the nuances of federal/provincial relations or Canada's ties to Great Britain. It was a wickedly funny image, which delivered its message effortlessly and succinctly. It remains a masterpiece of graphic design and exquisitely sophisticated drawing. Those two

John Diefenbaker loses the 1963 federal election to Lester Pearson.

PEARSONS
CELESTIAL
NAVIGATION
DIEFFENBAKERS
VISIONS
ON
HOROSCOPY
MACPHERSON TORONTO STAR

ORACLES ALL!

While the rest of the world dealt with major issues, Lester Pearson, John Diefenbaker, and Tommy Douglas were preoccupied with the debate over the Canadian flag. AUTHOR'S NOTE: Cartoonists may draw well – but they are notoriously bad spellers, as in Macpherson's treatment of MALAYSIA in the above cartoon.

Quoting Shakespeare's play *King John*, Macpherson has Diefenbaker ready to do battle over a proposed new design for the Canadian flag.

A typical J.W. Bengough caricature of Sir John A. Macdonald in *Grip* magazine.

Duncan Macpherson's take, many years later, on Canada's first prime minister.

phrases describe Duncan MacPherson's work perfectly. Looking back at those prairie years, I can see that the slow gravitational pull towards my own career in editorial cartooning was launched by early exposure to the brilliance of Duncan Macpherson's powerful art."

Master caricaturist Anthony Jenkins was also for many years a *Globe and Mail* cartoonist, working in tandem with Brian Gable. His childhood idols were Dick Duff, the former National Hockey League (NHL) player and head coach of the Toronto Maple Leafs – and Duncan Macpherson.

> Our family got the *Star*, or the *Toronto Daily Star* as it was known in those days. Stretched out on the floor as a boy, the first place I turned to was the editorial page, even before I knew what politics or satire were. I liked cartoons, and I liked the cartoons of the guy who signed his "Macpherson" best of all. Every Christmas I got a paperback Macpherson annual, along with shin pads, baseball mitts, and a lumber truck with real logs. Most of those boyhood treasures are gone. I still have the annuals.
>
> My childhood is remembered in black and white: TV shows, family photos, Macpherson cartoons. I began my Gladwell 10,000 hours of cartooning practice, drawing hands like Macpherson. I still can.
>
> I met Macpherson. Once. I was terrified. He was imposing. I think he wanted to be. "Draw bigger!" he advised me gruffly, flicking cigarette ash my way. Advice from master to beginner, for I was now a cartoonist!
>
> But not a peer. He had none. Then or now.

Generally, Macpherson was welcoming to up-and-coming cartoonists in those early years – but it always depended on the time of the day. In 1968 freelancer Ted Michener knocked on Duncan's office door at the *Star* hoping for a bit of advice. Ted was greeted with: "Come on in so that I can kill you for interrupting me!" Duncan must have been on deadline.

Graham Harrop had quite a different experience. Harrop's popular comic strip "Backbench" ran for years in the *Globe and Mail*, and these days he draws three editorial-page cartoons a week for the *Vancouver Sun*. When he was still an unknown, Harrop showed up unannounced at the old *Toronto Star* building on King Street, sometime around 1970. Under his arm, he had a number of comic strips featuring talking birds. He asked at reception whether he might see Macpherson. "My memory is of a very warm and gracious man who looked at and responded to each of my drawings. He had a hearty booming laugh – and such great humour in his eyes." Macpherson took Harrop's sketches down to editorial and secured a commitment to have them published for a two-week run. Although nothing more came of it, Harrop never forgot how Macpherson had extended a hand to a newcomer.

In the tribute sketch to Macpherson on page 135, Harrop, in effect, credits Duncan with creating an unforgettable image of John Diefenbaker looking far more like Diefenbaker than the man did himself (much as Bengough had done with his caricatures of Sir John A. Macdonald – and Thomas Nast had done in America, also in the 1800s, with Boss Tweed).

An 1877 Henri Julien cartoon on financial dealings between the United States (Brother Jonathan) and Canada (Johnny Canuck).

Following a 1964 meeting between the provincial premiers and Prime Minister Pearson to discuss the British North America Act, Macpherson drew Pearson as a boy scout attempting to lead the way. This remains Brian Gable's favourite Macpherson cartoon.

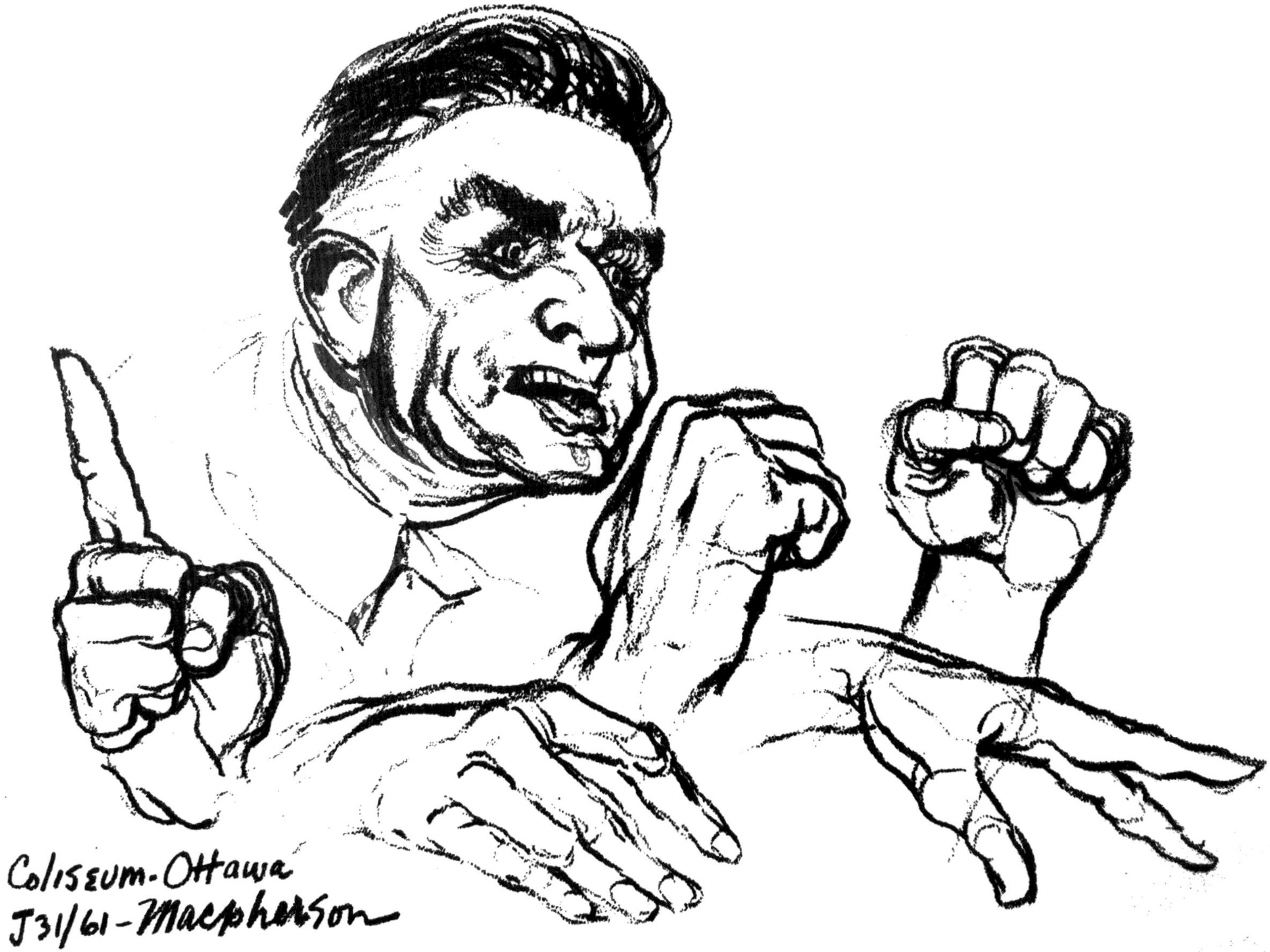

Macpherson sketches David Lewis's hands at the founding convention of the NDP in 1961.

A tribute sketch by Graham Harrop.

RESIGN!

SMALL COMFORT.

They were scared out of their boots of being Macphersonized!

PAUL HELLYER

10

CARTOON PORTFOLIO, 1959–67

Duncan Macpherson burst onto the editorial-cartooning scene in 1959 and quickly established himself as the most important cartoonist then working in Canada. In their 1971 article for *Canadian Dimension*, Longstaff and Henry underscored the serendipitous timing of Macpherson's employment at the *Star*. "The first clouds on the horizon of the Diefenbaker Vision were starting to gather. Had Macpherson arrived at the *Star* in, say, 1953 or 1954, it is doubtful whether then publisher Harry Hindmarsh would have been willing to fully unleash his talent against the Liberal government."

Although the general public may remember Macpherson principally for his caricatures of Prime Minister John Diefenbaker, he produced a great many exceptional cartoons on other subjects. As Mordecai Richler once said, "the true humorist must have 360 degree vision." Macpherson was always an equal-opportunity lampoonist, caricaturing prime ministers, cabinet ministers, the Loyal Opposition, provincial premiers, and mayors. Any public figure, Canadian or otherwise, was fair game.

John Fitzgerald Kennedy was elected president of the United States in 1960, at the height of the Cold War. During the short time before his assassination in November 1963, Kennedy's agenda was largely taken up with managing relations with the Soviet Union and supporting the growing civil-rights movement at home. He was not averse to flexing America's military muscle, authorizing a failed attempt to overthrow the

Defence Minister Paul Hellyer merged the branches of the Canadian Armed Forces in 1968, pushing a lot of military buttons in the process.

Cuban government of Fidel Castro and increasing the number of American military advisers in South Vietnam. Kennedy's successor, Lyndon Johnson, escalated the U.S. involvement in the war in Vietnam as American casualties soared and the peace process stalled.

In 1957 the Soviet Union grabbed the international spotlight – and first honours in the nascent space race – by launching Sputnik 1, the first artificial earth satellite. Nikita Khrushchev, the Soviet Union's premier from 1958 to 1964, emerged as a fierce spokesman for the Union of Soviet Socialist Republics (USSR) on the international stage, even as he backed several relatively liberal reforms at home. During Khrushchev's time in office, the Soviet Union's political relations with the world's other great Communist power – China – broke off as a result of doctrinal differences. And in the Middle East, Israeli-Arab tensions continued to ramp up, while people the world over fretted about the possibility of nuclear war.

Paul Hellyer – politician, engineer, and commentator – was first elected to the House of Commons in 1949. Today, at the age of ninety-six, Hellyer swims every day and is still pushing back against "the system." He is probably best remembered as Lester Pearson's minister of defence and the person responsible for the amalgamation of the Canadian Armed Forces in 1968. The decision was extremely unpopular among military personnel of all ranks.

Hellyer still seems proud of his knack for stirring up controversy. Pinned to his home-office wall is a yellowed clipping of a Duncan Macpherson cartoon from over fifty years ago. Hellyer had delivered a speech on the rather sensitive subject of atheism and religion at a church in Don Mills, Ontario. Macpherson imagined a mob of angry clergymen bearing Hellyer off to a "ducking pond," the old English method of punishing troublesome people.

In a 2019 interview, Hellyer recalled just how popular Duncan Macpherson was in the 1960s – and how nervous his fellow cabinet ministers were about how the cartoonist might choose to portray them. "They were scared out of their boots of being Macphersonized!" On the other hand, some politicians were mature and confident enough to appreciate having Macpherson poke fun at them. Walter Gordon, Lester Pearson's finance minister, always enjoyed a good laugh at his own expense.

For this, the first of the book's three portfolio chapters, I have selected my favourite of Duncan Macpherson's cartoons drawn between 1958 and 1967, and added a few stories and some background information.

TO THE DUCKING POND!

Walter Gordon, Pearson's finance minister, was the country's second most powerful politician. He was an economic nationalist, and his theories could be controversial, both at home and abroad.

WOT ABOUT THE DRAGON IN HERE?

Agnes Honderich, Walter Gordon, Beland Honderich, Duncan Macpherson, and Dorothy Macpherson celebrate the former finance minister's seventieth birthday in 1976.

During Canada's centennial year in 1967, Macpherson wondered who the perfect Canadian might be. What about a combination of Prime Minister Lester Pearson and Onondaga distance runner Tom Longboat? Or hockey player Eddie Shack blended with former governor general Vincent Massey?

Ellen Fairclough, Diefenbaker's immigration minister.

This 1959 cartoon shows Macpherson's Everyman bearing the weight of three levels of government, represented by Prime Minister John Diefenbaker, Ontario Premier Leslie Frost, and Metropolitan Toronto Chairman Fred Gardiner.

Donald Fleming, Diefenbaker's finance minister, shocked the country by devaluing the once-strong Canadian dollar to 92 cents American.

Paul Martin Sr was the secretary of state for external affairs under Lester Pearson. Although Canada remained officially neutral during the Vietnam War, the country reaped billions in profits from armament sales to the United States. Here Macpherson portrays Martin as an "angel with an angle."

After notorious Quebec criminal Lucien Rivard escaped from prison in 1965, there were allegations that the escape was facilitated through bribes paid by the office of Lester Pearson's attorney general, Guy Favreau. Nothing was proved, but Favreau was forced to resign.

NDP leader Tommy Douglas had for many years been premier of Saskatchewan, the first province in Canada to introduce Medicare. In 1962 a doctors' strike took place in Saskatchewan. This cartoon showed Douglas's prompt reaction to the doctors' labour action. It worked brilliantly because it told the whole story without the need for words.

The Tories' Big Blue Machine reigned supreme in Ontario. No one wanted to go up against them.

NOPE – I'M NOT INTERESTED IN THE LEADERSHIP OF THE PROVINCIAL LIBERAL PARTY.

Duncan Macpherson's body of work is peppered with cartoons on Canadian-American relations.

Patrons wait to withdraw their money from a bank following a nuclear attack.

Some of Macpherson's most powerful drawings were inspired by international themes. Here, U.S. President John F. Kennedy navigates the shoals of civil rights in America.

U.S. President Lyndon Johnson.

WHY CAN'T Y'ALL GET ALONG PEACEABLE LIKE?

Public school in the United States.

Russian Premier Nikita Khrushchev was one of Duncan Macpherson's favourite subjects.

The hammer and sickle, wielded by Mao and Khrushchev.

Millions of Chinese people starved to death in the first decades of Communist rule.

Macpherson's tribute to the work of the United Nations.

In 1961 the Russians successfully launched cosmonaut Yuri Gagarin into space, beating the Americans at their own game.

No matter how bad the news of the day, baseball remains popular.

MICKEY MANTLE STEPS UP TO THE PLATE ...

A crowd gathers for a military parade in Moscow's Red Square.

11

ACCLAIM

You must do a lot of looking
to see so much.

ANONYMOUS WOMAN, COMMENTING TO DUNCAN MACPHERSON AT AN EXHIBITION OF HIS WORK

Wherever cartoonists gather, the talk inevitably turns to style and technique. Most agree that one of the most difficult things to pull off is an instantly recognizable caricature of someone – from behind. Duncan Macpherson was a master at it.

In the 1960s, Nikita Khrushchev was one of the most recognized people in the world. The West knew him as the leader who pushed the USSR to take the lead in the space race, which it did by putting the Sputnik 1 into orbit. He was the first Soviet premier to visit the United States. At once mercurial, frightening, jovial, and crude, he was a figure whose humanity was on display for all to see.

Khrushchev was suddenly ousted in October 1964, with no official explanation. To mark that occasion, Duncan Macpherson drew a highly detailed cartoon of a military parade passing through Red Square, with ordinary citizens looking on. Then one notices, from behind, just another unemployed member of the proletariat: Nikita Khrushchev. There is no mistaking the man's identity.

The Khrushchev drawing was one of a handful of Macpherson's personal favourites and was featured in a February 1965 exhibition of forty of his cartoons at a one-man show at the Toronto Art Gallery (to be renamed the Art Gallery of Ontario the following year). A mere twelve months earlier, the great American critic Edmund Wilson, writing in the *New Yorker*, had speculated that Macpherson cartoon originals would someday be hanging in art galleries.

The Art Gallery of Toronto, with its staggering collection of Canadian, Inuit, and international works of art, was even then considered one of the most innovative and most important art museums in North America. To have his works exhibited there was a compliment to Macpherson's talent, all the more impressive in that he had been working seriously as a cartoonist for only five years. He became very popular, very quickly.

Macpherson's appearance at the exhibit opening was described by the *Toronto Star*'s Alan Edmonds: "Looking like an immaculately dressed stevedore who wandered in to a ballet dancers' tea party, Macpherson stood there and accepted the compliments. He seemed pleased that the gallery had decided to do this." Edmonds also commented on Macpherson's drawings: "His pen is dipped daily in a mix of humaneness – and horror at humanity's howlers, of compassion and pins to prick the pompous, of wit and wisdom – and a whopping sense of fun."

Other reputable institutions started to mount exhibits of Macpherson's work. A 1972 show at the McMichael Gallery in Kleinburg was launched by Ontario Premier William Davis, one of Macpherson's favourite targets at the time. Davis praised the cartoonist for "keeping politicians humble." Macpherson found that assessment debatable.

Although everyone attending the opening was complimentary, Duncan was most pleased with comments from the Group of Seven painter A.J. Casson, who spoke of the "marvellous control of line that makes his work so great. When I was young, artists were required to develop that level of penmanship. Now there are only a few men like Macpherson that excel at it."

Requests for Duncan Macpherson originals came from some very highly placed targets. Peter C. Newman recalls being a columnist in Ottawa

LEFT | In 1965 Duncan was on his best behaviour at the opening of his exhibition at the Art Gallery of Toronto (now Art Gallery of Ontario). With him are the three most influential women in his life: from left to right, his sister, Fiona, his mother, Margaret, and his wife, Dorothy. (The young girl in front is Fiona's daughter, Kathy.)

RIGHT | Ontario Premier Bill Davis takes in the Macpherson exhibition at the McMichael Gallery in Kleinburg.

for the *Toronto Star* in 1969: "Cabinet ministers who were victims of Macpherson's cartoons would fume and snub the paper … in public. In private they would get their executive assistant to call me at home and ask if I could arrange for the minister to get a copy of the cartoon."

Macpherson's work even attracted ongoing royal interest. The Toronto Press Club had to temporarily lift one of its several "lifetime" bans on Macpherson so he could present Prince Philip with a cartoon the latter wanted: Macpherson's "everyman" is holding a poster saying "Monarchy to the Wall" while he gives Philip a bomb.

In July 1967 Macpherson travelled to Ottawa with *Star* columnist Ron Haggart to attend a dinner at Rideau Hall for fifty-four of Canada's brightest young people. The glittering event was hosted by Queen Elizabeth, Prince Philip, and Prime Minister Lester Pearson. By then, Prince Philip had asked for – and received – his second Macpherson original: Charles de Gaulle and Quebec Premier Daniel Johnson welcoming the royal couple to Canada for Expo '67.

In 1971 the Canada Council presented Duncan Macpherson with its Molson Prize. It is given to those who have enriched the cultural or intellectual heritage of the nation. Macpherson's role as a social critic was described as being "a stylist in chastisement." This was just one of many honours to be bestowed on Macpherson during his life. He received the Royal Academy Medal for distinguished work in the visual arts, and in 1987 was named a member of the Order of Canada by Governor General Jeanne Sauvé.

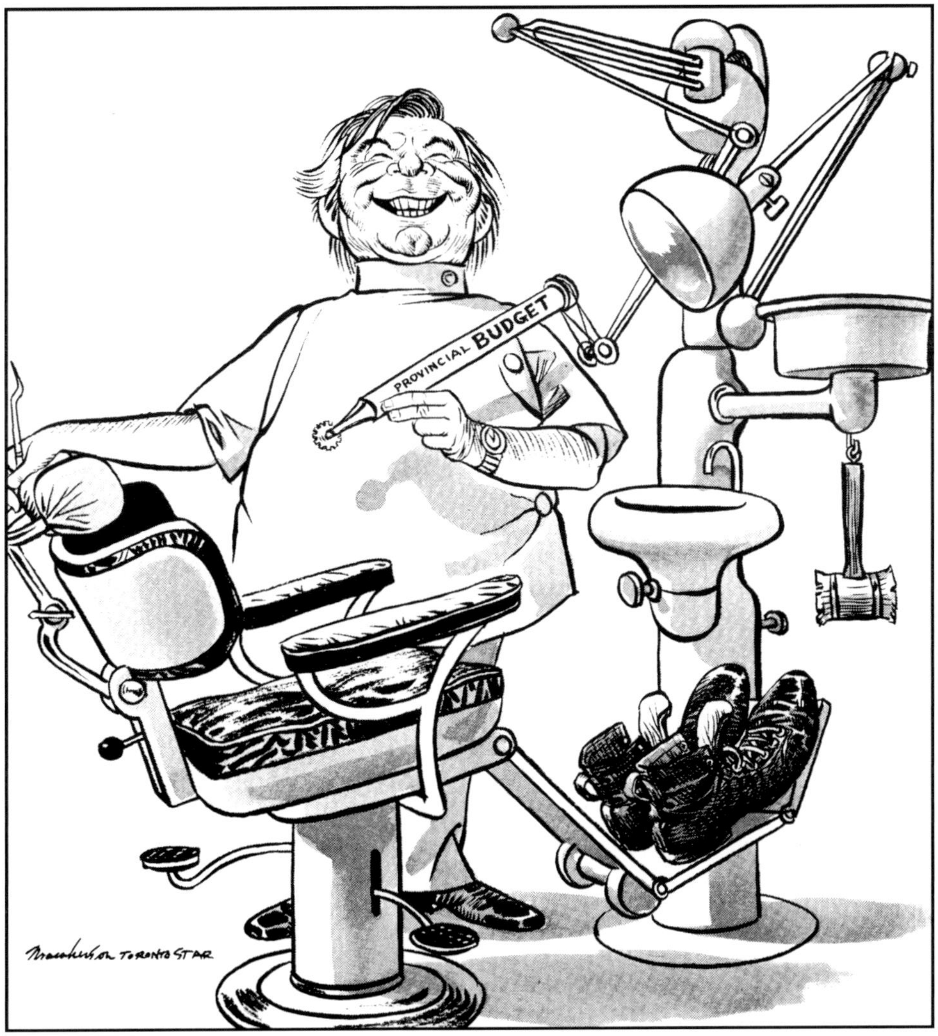

HIT A NERVE?

Macpherson was also named to the Canadian News Hall of Fame in 1976 after having won an unprecedented six National Newspaper Awards, more than anyone else in any category at that

Bill Davis was the Progressive Conservative premier of Ontario, Canada's richest province, from 1971 to 1985 without facing any sustained opposition – with the possible exception of Duncan Macpherson's cartoons …

point. After the sixth win, Ben Wicks, the most popular comic-strip artist in Canada in his day, said, "They should just give it to Duncan every year as a matter of course."

The cartoons chosen as NNA winners demonstrate Macpherson's broad array of styles and areas of interest, from local to international arenas.

Longstaff and Henry describe the late 1960s as vintage years for comic and satiric art. In Britain, cartoonists Gerald Scarfe and Ralph Steadman were savaging politicians and public personalities with their wicked drawings. In the United States, David Levine's pointed and sophisticated caricatures were all the rage in the *New York Review of Books* and other literary publications. There were a number of other brilliant cartoonists working in the United States at that time, people like Edward Sorel, Saul Steinberg, and Ron Cobb. Cobb, whose work appeared in the *Los Angeles Free Press* and in underground media, offered up "mordant renderings of genocide, police violence and other unpleasant themes." In the 1960s, even the American daily press had developed teeth. New cartoonists like Paul Conrad of the *Los Angeles Times* and Patrick Oliphant of the *Denver Post* were unsparing in their criticism of "their side" during the war in Vietnam. Duncan Macpherson was as popular in Canada as these cartoonists were with the American public.

Critic Edmund Wilson, in his book *O Canada: An American's Notes on Canadian Culture*, wrote that Macpherson's cartoons were the only ones in English Canada to contain "a high level of political satire." Wilson asserted that Macpherson's

LEFT | Prince Philip receives a Macpherson original at the Toronto Press Club.

RIGHT | Prince Philip requested the original of this cartoon, showing French president Charles de Gaulle and Quebec premier Daniel Johnson welcoming the royal couple to Canada during the country's centennial year.

work, which he compared to that of James Gillray, had the power to be "fascinating quite independently of our interest in or knowledge of the happenings it commemorates."

In a 1964 *New Yorker* article, the basis for his book, Wilson credited Macpherson with creating "a phantasmagoria for which the mediocre subjects themselves sometimes seem hardly adequate. His cartoons go far beyond the editorial. They are the work of a vigorous imagination, which, taking its cues from political events, expands them into gratuitous fantasies. It is known that a first-rate talent can be found in Toronto that ranks with Levine and Scarfe."

Nonetheless, Macpherson was relatively unknown in the United States – except among American cartoonists. At a gathering of the Association of American Editorial Cartoonists in 1972, the chairperson interrupted proceedings to announce: "Ladies and gentlemen, Duncan Macpherson is in the room!" This was greeted with a standing ovation and much gawking.

Several American cartoonists so admired Macpherson's work that they stole directly from him. For instance, when Robert Graysmith was hired as the regular cartoonist for the *San Francisco Chronicle* in 1968, he turned to his collection of Macpherson cartoon albums. Instead of producing his own daily cartoons, he did crude copies of Macpherson's work. Perhaps he felt Toronto was far enough away for it not to matter. He then discovered the annual collections of Len Norris's work and plagiarized his *Vancouver Sun* cartoons for a time.

Duncan meets Queen Elizabeth II at a reception in Ottawa in 1967.

Macpherson observed, "After some time, Graysmith wasn't stealing anymore … and started turning out some pretty good cartoons." Eventually, Graysmith stopped cartooning altogether and became a true-crime writer. His book *Zodiac*, about a killer active in northern California in the 1960s and 1970s, was later turned into a Hollywood movie.

Graysmith wasn't the only borrower from Macpherson's oeuvre. Cartoonist Paul Szep was born in Hamilton, Ontario, in 1942 but couldn't find work in Canada. He moved to Boston in the 1960s, his Duncan Macpherson collections under his arm, and was eventually hired as the *Boston Globe*'s cartoonist. His style was obviously cribbed from Macpherson, but the drawings were not as well executed. Most startling was the way he lifted whole ideas from Macpherson's work, adapting them to American scenarios.

There is an interesting epilogue to the Szep story, involving a cartooning legend from Quebec. Montreal-born Robert LaPalme was a painter as well as Canada's pre-eminent caricaturist from 1940 to 1960. For most of that time, he was the editorial cartoonist for *Le Devoir*. LaPalme became especially well known for lampooning the all-powerful Quebec premier Maurice Duplessis at a time when nobody else dared to do so.

He was also instrumental in launching the International Salon of Caricature in 1963. In its heyday, the Salon was the largest exhibition of cartoons in the world, making Montreal a mecca for caricaturists. LaPalme, the first cartoonist to receive the Order of Canada, told me, "I see cartoons from all over the world. And, at this point in time, there is no better cartoonist anywhere than Duncan Macpherson." So when Paul Szep won the 1974 Pulitzer Prize for cartooning, Robert LaPalme sent a telegram of congratulation – to Duncan Macpherson.

Alan King was once a backup cartoonist for Duncan Macpherson at the *Toronto Star*. He then moved on to become the editorial-page cartoonist at the *Ottawa Citizen*. Alan recently observed: "I notice Paul Szep, who stole Duncan's style and got a Pulitzer for it, is still producing – so Macpherson's spirit lives on!"

30 March 1960: Macpherson wins his first National Newspaper Award for commentary on the 1959 federal budget. Prime Minister John Diefenbaker shows John Q. Public his vision of a new dawn through a looking glass, while Finance Minister Donald Fleming picks the taxpayer's pocket.

FOR A SLIGHT TAX.

14 March 1961: Macpherson wins his second NNA for a cartoon showing a meeting between Fidel Castro and Nikita Khrushchev on top of the Statue of Liberty when both leaders were attending a meeting at the United Nations.

30 March 1962: Macpherson's third NNA-winning cartoon shows Britain's prime minister, Harold Macmillan, trying to buy a ticket from Charles de Gaulle to enter the European Common Market. Macmillan has the Commonwealth progeny in tow.

TAKE IT OR LEAVE IT, NO SPECIAL RATES FOR KIDDIES.

7 April 1966: Macpherson wins his fourth NNA for a cartoon of Prime Minister Lester Pearson racing toward an election majority, only to be tripped up by an albatross labelled "scandals."

6 April 1971: A drawing of impoverished children wins Macpherson his fifth NNA.

18 April 1973: Macpherson wins his sixth NNA for a cartoon drawn the day after Prime Minister Trudeau was re-elected with a minority government. The NDP's David Lewis held the balance of power.

Broadcaster Charles Templeton runs for a provincial seat as an Ontario Liberal. Templeton had briefly been Macpherson's editorial-page editor at the *Star* before entering politics. He had also worked as a sports cartoonist for the *Globe and Mail* in the early 1930s.

A Robert Graysmith rip-off of Duncan's work, changing the face to that of a San Francisco politician.

"Inside most of us there is a Duncan Macpherson. We suppress it." – John Gault, *Toronto Life*.

In those watering holes favoured by journalists, it was Duncan Macpherson's bizarre behaviour, as much as his cartooning, that made the man a legend in his own time. Once I let it be known that I was writing a book about him, a number of journalists and cartoonists wrote or called me with story after story about Duncan. I had a hard time figuring out what was merely legend and what was true.

Toronto journalist Robert Fulford described the difficulty in a 1976 interview for the book *The Hecklers*. "The problem is that, when everybody's drunk, Macpherson will threaten something like: 'I should throw that ugly, uncomfortable chair out the window!' Of course, he doesn't, but three years later, the drunks claim it really happened." According to Duncan's friend Jack Brehl, everyone had a Macpherson tale: it might be scary or weird, but it was always funny. Said Brehl, "Some of the stories are even true. Duncan is enraging, hilarious, maddening, unpredictable, explosive, sudden, unusually charming, and always vital."

After a hard day's work, Macpherson would head out the front door of the original *Toronto Star* building on 80 King Street West, fully intending to turn toward the subway and home to Blythwood Road. However, all too often, Duncan turned right, toward the Press Club, known fondly as the Yellow Submarine. It was then located just a block west of the *Star*, in the low-ceilinged basement of the notorious Prince George Hotel. Stories about Macpherson's unruly behaviour seem to share a common prologue: a stop at the Club for a few drinks.

Duncan Macpherson's pen was mightier than his sword – but his left hook wasn't bad either.

TORONTO STAR OBITUARY, MAY 1993

12

"HE HAD HIS DEMONS"

Metro Toronto Chairman Paul Godfrey, Ontario Premier Bill Davis, and entertainer Aileen Ahern celebrate at an event during the Toronto Press Club's heyday in the 1970s.

Amid the stories both true and exaggerated, the fact is that, over the years, Macpherson was given *four* lifetime suspensions from the Toronto Press Club. He was also awarded an honorary lifetime membership.

According to Brehl: "Drink wasn't a creator of his traits, just a stretcher of them."

Toronto Star staffer Roy Shields, who travelled to Cuba with Macpherson in 1962, offered the following analysis: "Duncan is a difficult man. Ghosts visit him in the night and he often over-reacts to their presence." But Shields also claimed that he hadn't ever seen the cartoonist so drunk that he was incapable of thought. "He doesn't do the irrational things of a drunk. When he's drinking heavily, he'll steal a potted plant, or sit on somebody, but all the time he's doing this, in his black way, he's releasing terrible tensions. He's a very tormented man."

In his journal, Macpherson calls himself a down-and-dirty street fighter. "Hit 'em hard – and first." Duncan may have learned this in his early days at the *Star*. At that time, Duncan was acquainted with Eddie Roworth, a police reporter. Eddie was only five foot seven or so but was very strong from working out regularly at the gym. On one occasion, when Eddie and Mac disagreed vehemently on some (probably unimportant) topic, they moved the argument out into the alley behind the Press Club. Several witnesses went along. According to long-time *Star* staffer George Gamester: "Eddie unexpectedly took Dunc out with one punch." It was back to the pugilistic drawing board for Macpherson.

Pierre Berton's description of Macpherson being "one over the eight" could equally apply to the man's cartoons: "Wild, expansive, sometimes bitterly sarcastic, often wicked and totally unpredictable. There is a sober Macpherson and a drunk Macpherson. The sober Macpherson is a shy, retiring man of utter humility. The drunken Macpherson is a loud egoist filled with bravado ... a goddamn pain in the ass!"

The *Toronto Star* and its revered history were not out of bounds as far as Duncan Macpherson was concerned. In 1899 Joseph E. Atkinson became the publisher of the *Toronto Evening Star*. Around the *Star*, even today, he is referred to as "Holy Joe." His task was to save the failing Liberal newspaper, then competing with six other papers in a Conservative-leaning market. Atkinson wanted the paper to focus on the concerns of ordinary people, which was highly unusual thinking at that time. By 1913, the *Evening Star* had the largest circulation of any newspaper in Toronto. By the time of Atkinson's death in 1948, the *Star* was on its way to becoming the largest newspaper in Canada.

One evening, Pierre Berton, Duncan Macpherson, and others were gathered at the Toronto Press Club. Berton is said to have challenged Macpherson to go over to the *Star*'s offices and steal the portrait of "Holy Joe" that was hanging in the lobby. Some people say Macpherson did take the portrait but threw it into a snowbank. Others claim that he painted a moustache on the beardless Atkinson, while another story has it that Macpherson secretly visited the portrait every evening for weeks, gradually changing the expression on the face with a hidden set of paints.

That was the thing about Macpherson's reputation: all those stories were equally plausible. However, I believe the truth of the event to be somewhat different. Here's my version, pieced together from later conversations. Once Berton had issued his challenge, and Macpherson had headed off on his quest, someone at the Press Club phoned a warning to the *Star*. The call was taken by columnist Ron Haggart, who happened to be working in the library. Haggart then contacted city editor Taras "Scotty" Humeniuk, the only employee around who was bigger than Duncan. Humeniuk intercepted Macpherson and talked him into abandoning the enterprise. The portrait remained in place. "Scotty" and the Scottish cartoonist then went out and got drunk together.

A cartoon of Duncan at the Press Club bar by *Toronto Star* cartoonist Patrick Corrigan.

Al Dickie and Duncan were great pals in the late 1960s and through the 1970s. Dickie worked briefly at the *Star* and then moved on to become a chief reporter for Canadian Press at Queen's Park. Al remembers Duncan often having a limousine waiting outside wherever they happened to be drinking in case it was needed. Often the chauffeur-driven automobile's sole purpose was to get someone who was too drunk to stand safely home.

Al remembers that, when they were in a fancy restaurant, Duncan would often fill the linen

The *Toronto Star*'s Joseph E. Atkinson.

tablecloth with sketches. When they returned to one north-end Italian restaurant, there was a framed tablecloth proudly displayed on the wall that Duncan had drawn on their previous visit.

There's another oft-told Macpherson tale that we can now confirm. Although in the telling this event takes place in a variety of locations and under wildly different circumstances with different people, here are the facts according to Al Dickie. Duncan hit someone in the face somewhere, leading to a bloody nose and stained shirt. Feeling contrite, Duncan gave the poor fellow his own shirt. The crowd moved on to a fancy restaurant where a tie was required. Duncan went to the washroom and, with a felt-pen marker, drew a colourful necktie on his white t-shirt. He was then allowed into the establishment.

Doug Gibson, the editor of Peter C. Newman's bestseller *Here Be Dragons*, enriched the book with a Macpherson story of his own that he swears is true.

> A very cruel person had once shown Duncan how to whip a tablecloth off a fully set table. There were a number of associated disasters at the Mark Hotel in San Francisco, during the time that Duncan and the luckless Allan Edmonds were in town covering a Republican convention. Edmonds grew used to wearily taking out his wallet to calm outraged restaurant staff.
>
> Macpherson finally succeeded in pulling off the trick. Then one night, at Harry Barberian's restaurant in Toronto, Duncan had a drink or three before spotting his friend the Russian ambassador sitting at a well-laden table. The ambassador's two bodyguards reached for their weapons as this large, wild man stalked over. The ambassador calmed them. Macpherson told all three men just to relax while he showed them something amazing.
>
> With a less than elegant flourish, Macpherson grabbed the tablecloth and yanked. The bodyguards, steaks and glasses of wine now in their laps, reached for their weapons in earnest as the ambassador frantically restrained them. "This is just my friend Duncan," said the ambassador.

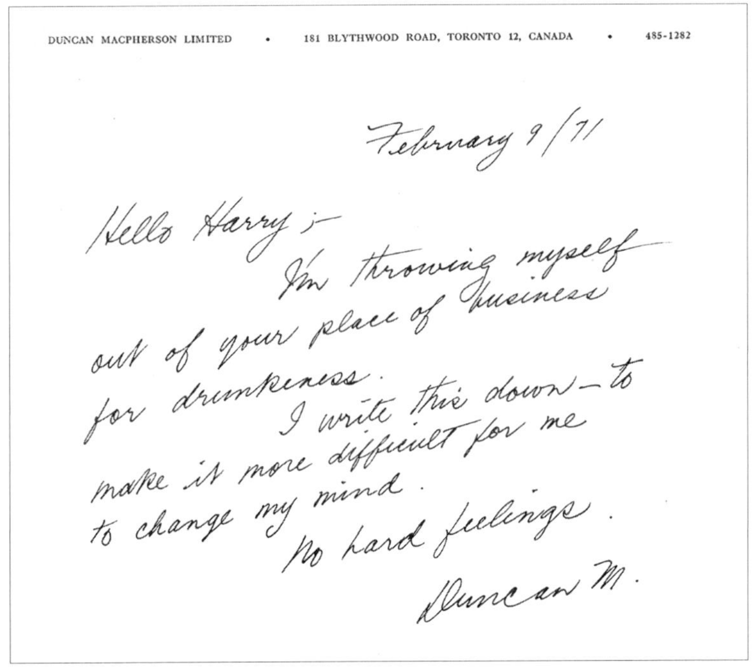

DUNCAN MACPHERSON LIMITED • 181 BLYTHWOOD ROAD, TORONTO 12, CANADA • 485-1282

February 9/71

Hello Harry –
I'm throwing myself out of your place of business for drunkeness.
I write this down – to make it more difficult for me to change my mind.
No hard feelings.

Duncan M.

At the time of Macpherson's 1965 exhibition at the Art Gallery of Toronto, *Canadian Art* magazine writer Joy Carroll observed, "Macpherson himself is larger than life, both physically and by temperament. He can be a docile and undemanding dinner guest: 'Just give me a grilled cheese sandwich.' Or he can be wild and unpredictable; in a single evening he has been known to break an antique bell jar, half choke a fellow guest, snap the host's braces until they disintegrated, and draw mammoth cartoons on the walls with a felt marking pen. After such an episode he is contrite, telephoning his apologies and sending along a decorator to repair the damage."

Star columnist Gary Lautens once described Macpherson as "a combination of Mary Poppins, Mark Twain, and Attila the Hun." Despite this bit of hyperbole, Lautens's view that at the drawing board Macpherson was actually rather orthodox is quite right: "All he employs is pen, paper and cackle." Lautens once asked Macpherson if drawing cartoons was a hard way to make a living. Duncan looked out his studio window. A steelworker was scrambling around on a thin girder, part of a skyscraper rising forty storeys into the air. "Not as hard as that," he replied.

Duncan loved a wager, particularly with the *Star*'s legendary sports writer, Milt Dunnell.

LEFT | Visiting Dutch cartoonist Fons Van Woerkom sketched Duncan attempting his tablecloth trick at Harry Barberian's restaurant.

RIGHT | An advance note from Macpherson to Harry Barberian, giving him permission to ban Duncan from the restaurant if he became too unruly.

ABOVE | Duncan's long-suffering friend, restaurateur Harry Barberian.

RIGHT | Life sometimes imitates art. Macpherson drew this cartoon of one politician (Bill Rompkey) pulling the tablecloth trick on another politician (Allan McEachern), a scenario with which Duncan was all too familiar.

Before one Super Bowl, the two decided to bet on the field conditions for game day. Macpherson, craftily checking weather conditions in the host city, bet on the field being muddy. On the Monday morning, Duncan sheepishly entered the newsroom wearing a paper bag on his head. The football game had been played in a domed stadium.

Another true story: One night in the early 1970s, artist Jimmy Hill hosted a game of craps at his house. Macpherson was soon cleaned out but wanted to keep playing; he offered up his new

$40 shoes, which he lost on the next throw. As Hill drove him home, Macpherson insisted that Hill take the shoes. Hill claimed to have no use for them. "Okay," said Macpherson, as he rolled down the car window and tossed the shoes out.

Even Duncan's sister, Fiona, to whom he was close all his life, was not entirely safe from her brother's particular sense of humour. She once hounded him to paint a nice portrait of her. An exasperated Duncan finally said that she could pose, but the process would take the better part of a week and she would have to sit still for several hours at a time. At the end of the week, a gleeful Duncan finally showed his sister the finished painting – of a giant gorilla. Fiona had forgotten that, whenever people asked for a drawing of themselves, Duncan invariably painted a picture of a monkey.

While Macpherson's rowdy behaviour is at the centre of most stories about him, he could also be thoughtful and generous. In the summer of 1975, cartoonist Ted Martin and his wife, Dawn, opened a storefront cartoon gallery on Avenue Road in Toronto. The popular establishment mounted a number of exhibits and became a gathering place for cartoonists from Toronto and elsewhere. A few days after the opening, Dawn rode her bicycle over to the *Toronto Star*. She was delivering a cheque to Duncan, since the gallery had sold one of his original drawings. As Dawn left the building, she saw a youth making off with her bike. She gave chase through a construction zone, but the young man disappeared. Dawn went back into the *Star* and was at the front desk when Duncan came by on his way to lunch with friends. He asked if she wanted to join them, but she said she had to report the theft to the police. A day later, Ted called Dawn to come to the gallery. She was reluctant, since it would involve a sweltering ride on a bus, but Ted was insistent. When she got there, there was a brand-new Raleigh 3-speed locked to the gallery porch, courtesy of Duncan.

When Sid Barron, Macpherson's reliable backup cartoonist at the *Toronto Star*, cut back on his production in the mid-1970s, Vic Roschkov was hired away from the *Windsor Star* to fill in. On Roschkov's first day, Macpherson asked him whether the *Star* had provided its new hire with a parking spot. It hadn't. Macpherson

Legendary *Toronto Star* sports writer Milt Dunnell loved playing poker and placing wagers – particularly at Duncan Macpherson's expense.

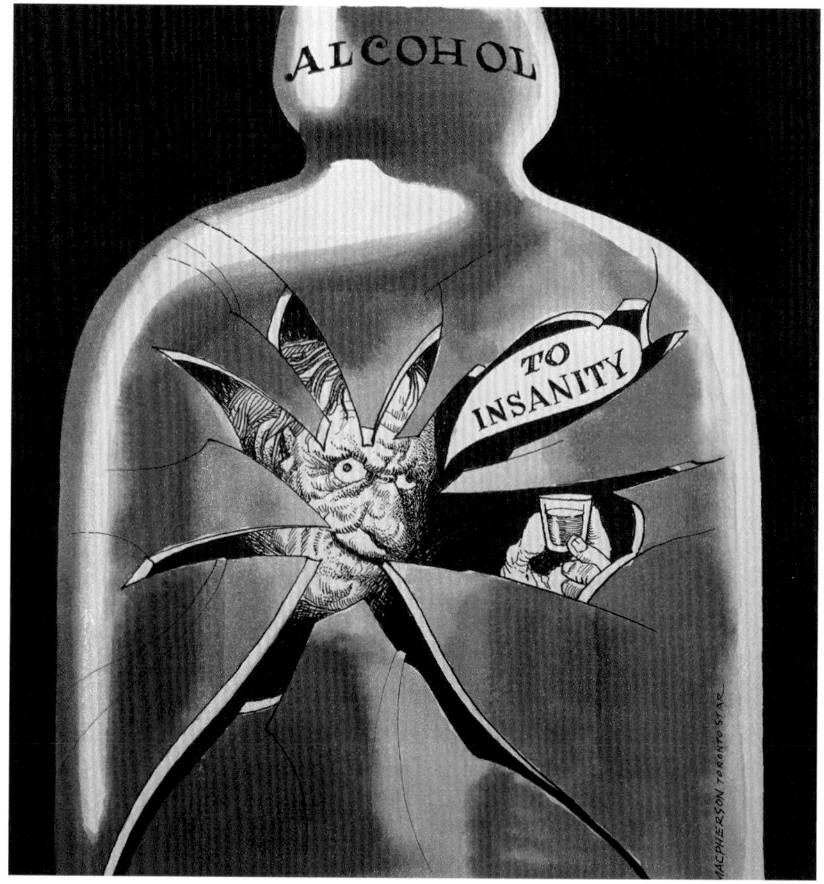

LEFT | Duncan and one of any number of friends.

RIGHT | An unusual cartoon for Macpherson, drawn in 1972 and pointing out the dangers of alcohol.

generously replied, "Well, take mine! I've just had my driver's licence suspended for six months." According to his son, Ian, Macpherson had been pulled over on a road near Beaverton, Ontario. As the police officer testified in court, Macpherson had been seen driving along with one leg dangling out the window. Once stopped, Macpherson stuck a $100 bill in the police officer's face and told the man to "fuck off." During the hearing, when Macpherson quietly wondered what his chances were of getting off, lawyer Bruce Palmer simply asked his client if he had brought a toothbrush. Luckily for Duncan, the suspension was the worst of it.

At the time, Roschkov, who didn't drink alcohol, was completely unaware of this incident. A friendship developed between the two men, and they often met, but just for coffee. This is

TO THE BARRICADES!

Roy Peterson's tribute cartoon after Macpherson's death.

perhaps why, even today, Roschkov thinks of his fellow cartoonist as a kind, outgoing man, with insightful advice on cartooning and the industry. Nevertheless, Roschkov had heard the stories and eventually witnessed Macpherson under the influence. "I played a lot of pool, and I was once at the billiard table at the Toronto Press Club on Richmond Street when Duncan marched over after he had been drinking. He immediately tried to lift the billiard table off the floor – and split his pants from stem to stern!"

Why did the *Toronto Star*'s management put up with Macpherson's erratic behaviour? The likely explanation is that publisher Beland Honderich recognized the value of having Duncan Macpherson in the fold. Honderich also knew that the *Star*'s competitor, the *Toronto Telegram*, had issued a standing offer to Macpherson; he could have crossed the street at any time and named his price.

Some people drink to excess to forget or mask pain in their lives. Others drink because it enables them to become the type of person they admire: creative, gregarious, and popular. I believe that Duncan Macpherson fell into the second category. Inevitably, there is a price to be paid.

Alcoholism is sometimes defined as an addiction to the consumption of alcoholic beverages. I don't know that that is correct in most cases. Very few problem drinkers are actually addicted to the substance so much as they crave the feelings that are produced by consumption. They like to get drunk. They discover early on that drinking changes them, and they like it – wanting to do it again and again. There is often much bluff involved, dismissing any embarrassing behaviour that took place. Either that, or they resolve never to get drunk again, but inevitably do so anyway.

A shy lad like Duncan Macpherson started to drink seriously (as many did) in the services during the Second World War. The experience turned him into a collegial, popular social drinker and smoker. He hated the war – but loved the pub culture and all that went with it. That comradely behaviour continued throughout his career with chosen friends and journalist cronies. Duncan continued to drink for the rest of his life, although he could clean up his act when called upon to do so, particularly by his wife. Dorothy, as we have seen, admitted that "Duncan had his demons." I personally think that Duncan was simply a bad drunk and often an unhappy person. This sometimes resulted in irascible behaviour on his part. When not drinking, he usually reverted to being a gentle, thoughtful, and even apologetic type.

Were there hidden reasons contributing to "Drunken Duncan"? Family? Genetics? Restlessness? Or simply a love of over-indulgence? Frankly, we don't know. He rarely writes of such matters in his personal journal.

The only known cure for problem drinking is to simply stop doing so. Macpherson, as far as is known, never took that route and never expressed any genuine interest in quitting. He even said on occasion that, if he were to do so, it might kill him. Now that is an odd thought. Was he perhaps thinking of his creativity? Undoubtedly, Macpherson's drinking led to eventual physical deterioration. A strong man, he never exercised much. He also had no awareness of good nutrition or its benefits. All this eventually had a catastrophic impact on his health, leading to his death of cancer at the far too young age of sixty-eight.

In spite of his reputation for trouble, Duncan Macpherson was recognized as a great contributor to Canada's artistic growth. A 1973 article in the *Vancouver Province* said it all: "The measure of the man's value in Canada, of course, does not rest with his escapades. It rests with his work, which promises to have a lastingly significant place in the country's cultural history."

Roy Peterson spent forty-seven years as the editorial-page cartoonist for the *Vancouver Sun*, in tandem with Len Norris. The influence of Peterson's style can still be seen today in the work of Malcolm Mayes at the *Edmonton Journal* and multi-award-winning Bruce MacKinnon at the *Halifax Chronicle Herald*. In MacKinnon's view, "Duncan Macpherson is the measuring stick by which all of Canada's best editorial cartoonists are gauged." When Macpherson died in 1993, Roy Peterson wrote a glowing tribute. "In the rich fabric of Canadian life, Duncan Macpherson is the pure platinum thread – the singular woven stitch somewhere between Oscar Peterson, Terry Fox, Sir John A. and Jack Shadbolt. No other cartoonist could, can or will be able to match his range, depth and breadth of talent. His mastery of technique is unsurpassed. His logic and analysis have distilled issues of the day to their quintessential nut and revealed their essence, however serious or ludicrous."

Judy LaMarsh's opinion of her fellow politicians was sometimes as jaundiced as Duncan Macpherson's.

Politicians often pretended to like the cartoons Duncan Macpherson drew of them so that no one could accuse them of taking themselves too seriously. A few even collected originals and hung them on their office walls, rather like battle trophies. It is also true, however, that politicians rarely invited Duncan Macpherson over for dinner.

Just occasionally, a politician would genuinely enjoy the laugh at their expense. Judy LaMarsh (1924–80) served a brief but eventful career in the minority government of Lester Pearson in the mid-1960s. As minister of national health and welfare, LaMarsh was an important figure who helped push through the legislation that created the Canada Pension Plan and the nation's Medicare system. However, LaMarsh was not an admirer of Pearson's successor, Pierre Trudeau, so she left politics in 1968. She then wrote three books, one of which was titled *Memoirs of a Bird in a Gilded Cage*, which featured Duncan's "portrait" of her on the cover and a great number of Macpherson cartoons. LaMarsh signed the cartoonist's own copy of the book: "To Duncan Macpherson – the only man who sees me as a raving beauty." In his personal journal, Duncan admitted to being fond of her, considering the former minister "a genuine outspoken character worthy of our respect." Library and Archives Canada has Judy LaMarsh's collection of cartoons of herself – some of which are quite harsh.

Macpherson also enjoyed producing illustrations for or about writers he respected. Many of those with whom he worked went on to win the Stephen Leacock Memorial Award for Humour. Publisher Doug Gibson, a fellow Scot, got to

I am not sure what an editorial page
editor is supposed to do in the way
of editing editorial cartoons.
I do know what I did: nothing.

GEORGE BAIN

13

WORKING WITH OTHERS

ABOVE | The cover of Judy LaMarsh's 1969 memoir was illustrated by Macpherson.

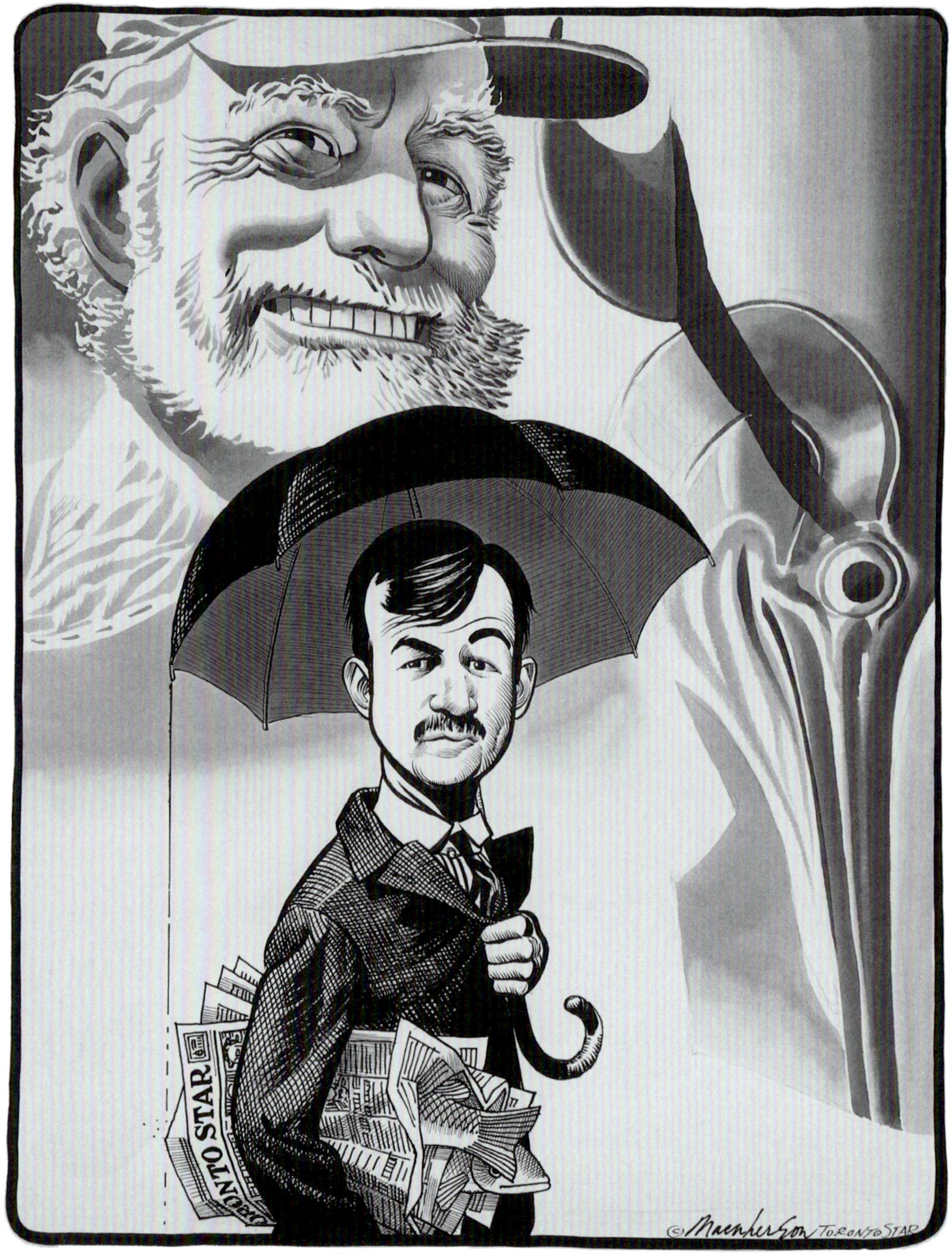

RIGHT | This is Duncan Macpherson's take on novelist Ernest Hemingway, who worked at the *Toronto Star* from 1920 to 1924.

know Macpherson the illustrator quite well. "Over the years, Duncan worked on a number of books for me. In some cases, he provided a cartoon for the book cover, as for a collection of funny columns by Richard Needham, a popular writer of humorous pieces in the *Globe*."

Gibson continues: "Indeed, I met Duncan through publishing books by Robert Thomas Allen. Duncan admired Bob Allen, and enjoyed working on his books so much that he came to my office and we chatted about the deal, bringing him in as the illustrator. When I was at Doubleday, I got Duncan to do the drawings for *Children, Wives and Other Wildlife* in 1971. It won the Stephen Leacock award that year. The illustrations had come from his previous work at *Maclean's*. Then there was *My Childhood and Yours*, which I brought out in 1977, after I had taken Bob and Duncan to Macmillan of Canada."

"We liked each other," said Gibson, "and things went very well. So I worked with him on a number of other books by Jonathan Manthorpe and George Bain – and I never had a moment's trouble. If Duncan liked you, things would go very smoothly."

Graham Fraser is the son of Blair Fraser, the highly respected Ottawa editor for *Maclean's* magazine in the 1950s. Before becoming Canada's commissioner of official languages (2006 to 2016), Graham had established his own bona fides working as a journalist for many of Canada's major media outlets. Starting out as a cub reporter for the *Toronto Star* in the early 1970s, Fraser remembers that when there was something that Beland Honderich, the *Star*'s chairman and publisher, didn't like, he would immediately let people know. "Honderich pored over every line of the first edition of the *Star* at the crack of dawn, and when there was something as minor as a one-column headline on page A16, he would phone an editor to get it

A GOOD MAN IS HARD TO FIND.

Secretary of State Judy LaMarsh, looking for a new leader for the CBC.

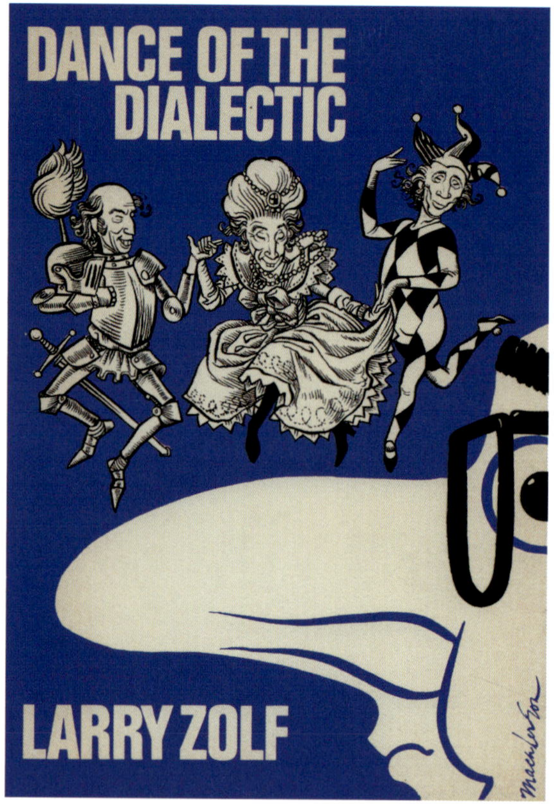

LEFT | Macpherson's cover for a book by his friend Larry Zolf, a well-known CBC gadfly.

RIGHT | A Duncan Macpherson cover drawing for a book by *Globe and Mail* humour columnist Richard Needham.

changed. I was once sitting talking to an assistant city editor – some four or five rungs down the ladder – when he got the call. "Yes, Bee … you're right, Bee, that's not a very good head; I'll get it changed for the next edition."

Yet Honderich rarely interfered with his lead cartoonist's work. Macpherson was once asked how many people knew him really well in his professional capacity. He came up with just two names. One was the *Star*'s Jack Brehl, a long-time journalist who had shared in many Macpherson revels and travels. The other was Beland Honderich.

Honderich may seem an odd member of that short list. He was feared by many of his staff and was not known for unbending with the people who worked for him. However, he and Macpherson developed a mutual respect and

Macpherson made it very clear from the beginning that he played no favourites and would thumb his nose at politicians of all stripes.

Duncan's Everyman, an object of sympathy for both the *Star*'s cartoonist and its publisher.

a good understanding of each other's values. It all started with a train ride. They were on their way to Ottawa together and started to exchange stories about growing up. Duncan recalled the conversation: "Beland described his days on the farm as a kid – poverty, hard times working on the railroad, and the bleak conditions of Depression days. I made it clear that I too had been through those days and understood.

"Honderich and I were both shaped by the Great Depression, but in different ways. Honderich, as chairman of a powerful free enterprise machine, emerged as a dreamer with strong beliefs about changing society. We both believed that ordinary people deserved a decent life. As an artist, however, I emerged as a realist and a doubter."

Macpherson's approach to cartooning political affairs was instinctual rather than intellectual, and aggressively critical. "You're a heckler, basically," he said. "It's the same as the old political meetings when you'd hire a couple of fellows to go into the hall and raise hell. And to be a good professional heckler, you've got to throw insults at all of them. I criticize my subjects the same way you'd criticize a hockey player for his play on the ice. You react to a situation, not because you're a moralist or anything like that. It's because you're a contrary sort of person, a cynic." Mac rejected the notion that he was ever needlessly savage. "I don't think that I ever intended a cartoon to be vicious in the sense of taking a vengeful attitude personally," he explained, "but if the only way to make a point is through a pretty tough delivery ... well, the point's going to be made."

Pierre Berton had his own view on Duncan's frame of reference. "I don't think Macpherson has any politics except the politics of the iconoclast. He reacts, and I think he reacts from the gut, and that's the best thing for a political cartoonist to do if he's not a political scientist, and Macpherson doesn't pretend to be." Some considered Macpherson's politics to be an amalgam of liberal and populist leanings. The cartoonist often said he liked to address his cartoons to the average drinker in a Toronto tavern. On the rare occasions that *Toronto Star* editors objected to a piece, Macpherson would poll the opinions of any copy boys, pressmen, or elevator operators he encountered in the building; he firmly believed that their views carried as much weight as those of his editors.

Duncan Macpherson was famously outspoken about political and commercial power players, but he wasn't shy about giving his opinions on personal matters either. After a few drinks, he would bluntly tell his newspaper friends all about their hidden traits. One pal began to greet him with: "Duncan, how am I?"

Macpherson didn't seem to mind being thought of as a difficult character, especially when it came to dealings with the newspaper's editors and publishers. During his over thirty years at the *Star*, Duncan worked with about ten editorial-page editors, all nominally responsible for approving his cartoons. Not all of them bothered, although a few understood and supported Macpherson's ferocious independence. Pierre Berton, for one, declared: "A political cartoonist, I believe, should work entirely on his own. He should be completely free of editorial control and not be required to illustrate the editorials as in the past. He should draw what he wants to draw."

When Duncan Macpherson's viewpoint was at odds with the *Star*'s editorial position, the paper was usually confident enough, both morally and financially, to tolerate the contradiction. Macpherson got a kick out of having the freedom to go his own way. "I must admit – and it wasn't deliberate – there have been days when the lead editorial would be in favour of something or other, and right next door in the cartoon, I'd be against it."

The 1950s and 1960s were times of relative prosperity for Canadian newspapers. Yet, even in that rosy environment, they did not welcome competition from other print media, which is why there was eventually some friction between Macpherson and *Star* management.

The Canadian edition of *Time* magazine, based in Montreal, hired Macpherson to draw several covers in the early 1960s. He was rather pleased, since *Time* paid him four times as much as he had been used to getting for similar work at *Maclean's*. But the American magazine's success

A few days before the 1962 federal election, this was Macpherson's cover for *Time*.

Both George Bain and Duncan Macpherson disagreed with Pierre Trudeau's decision to invoke the War Measures Act during the 1970 October Crisis.

in Canada made it unpopular with its Canadian competitors, particularly the *Toronto Star*. The paper eventually forbade the cartoonist from accepting more work from *Time*. Duncan was distinctly unhappy about the diktat: he hated having his pocketbook pinched.

Despite having worked with so many editors over the years, Duncan's personal journals make very little mention of them, with a couple of exceptions. He made it clear, for example, that he did not like dealing with George Radwanski, known throughout the industry as "the Rat." Indeed, Radwanski was a factor in Macpherson retiring from the *Star* in 1980. More on that in a later chapter.

Macpherson felt very differently about George Bain, the former RCAF bomber pilot. Bain was one of Canada's pre-eminent journalists in the 1950s and 1960s. He began his career as a copy boy with the *Toronto Star* and then worked as a reporter, columnist, and editor for several other newspapers, including the *Toronto Telegram* and the *Globe and Mail*. Geoffrey Stevens, a former managing editor of the *Globe*, remembers Bain as "one of the great journalists of the day."

In 1973 George Bain joined the *Toronto Star*, where he and Macpherson quickly developed a good rapport. It is telling that Bain was the only editorial-page editor Macpherson ever asked to write an introduction to one of his many cartoon collections. Their mutual respect may have originated in their common Second World War experiences and their shared distaste for Remembrance Day pageantry.

They also had similar views on current events, and both had made a career in humour. Bain was well known for his humorous writing, something that was generally unheard of among editorial-page editors. He won the Stephen Leacock Memorial Medal for Humour in 1966 for his book *Nursery Rhymes to Be Read Aloud by Young Parents to Old Children*. In 1978 he and Duncan joined forces on a book edited and published by Doug Gibson titled *Letters from Lilac*, a

George Bain approved publication of this dramatic caricature of Yasser Arafat.

collection of missives from a fictional character about life in a fictional town in Saskatchewan. Macpherson contributed a striking cover illustration of the launch of the local MP's campaign to become prime minister, as well as cartoons of sixteen of the community's most notable figures.

Bain described working as Macpherson's editorial-page editor this way: "By late morning, Macpherson would show me the rough sketch, as I had to approve the cartoon before it could be published in the following day's newspaper. He would come into the office, throw the rough in front of me, rest his meaty paws on the edge of the desk, look at me like a shark contemplating his lunch, and when I had a chance to study the cartoon – a time that might extend clear up to two or three seconds on days when he was in a benevolent mood – he'd say: 'Well?' I would reply, 'Yeah, Duncan, great,' which, given the fact that he is, in my opinion, the best newspaper cartoonist there is, made sense."

Bain observed that a good cartoon has a unique quality: it casts an oblique light, both showing its subject as it really is and revealing its absurdity. "The cartoon can also expose what is poignant or horrible. But there will be in the viewer that same instant flash of recognition of a truth revealed. Duncan's cartoons are clever, but they are a lot more than that; they can also bring you up short – or they do me – with their strength as pictures.

"So – I am a Duncan fan. He does, though, have a terribly intimidating 'Well?'"

There are so few political cartoonists working in Canada these days that, although we are competitors, we generally get along. Macpherson's main competition during his years at the *Toronto Star* was Andy Donato, editorial-page cartoonist for the city's morning tabloid, the *Toronto Sun*. Still active today, Donato is the longest-working cartoonist in Canadian history.

Andy always said that Macpherson was the best political cartoonist in North America. "He simply revolutionized political cartooning. He

Duncan Macpherson made these sketches in the House of Commons in 1966, during the debates on the Gerda Munsinger scandal. John Diefenbaker leads the Conservatives on one side, Lester Pearson heads the Liberals on the other.

CARDIN
PEARSON
FAVREAU
MARTIN
PICKERSGILL
HOUSE OF COMMONS
OTTAWA

drew so bloody well," he once remarked. "He can draw someone, and you know exactly who it is. He has fantastic line control. He'll draw a line on the first try exactly as it should be drawn." Admiring Macpherson didn't mean that Donato was inclined to make life easier for his competition. Their first social interaction, which took place in 1966, is illustrative.

Just after Donato had started working for the *Toronto Telegram*, the Gerda Munsinger story broke. Munsinger was an East German prostitute and alleged Soviet spy who, in 1955, had immigrated to Canada. Unbeknownst to the Canadian public, she had affairs with two of Diefenbaker's cabinet ministers. Years later, *Toronto Star* reporter Robert Reguly found Munsinger in Munich and interviewed her. The story dominated the Canadian media for weeks, and since senior government officials were involved, the affair was taken up in Parliament.

Andy was supposed to do courtroom-style sketches in the House of Commons. Learning that Duncan was in town doing the same thing, Andy wondered whether he could spike his competitor's guns and stop Duncan's art from getting to the *Star*. He phoned the Château Laurier, got Macpherson on the line, and invited him for a drink. They arranged to meet at the hotel bar once Macpherson had sent off his drawings for the day. During the course of the evening, Macpherson asked Donato several times to remind him to phone in the waybill number for the package he had sent off. "I guaranteed him I would," said Donato, "but I was lying through my teeth." Without this number, the package would never reach the *Star* in time for publication the next day.

They eventually wound up in Hull, where the bars stayed open until 2 a.m. Donato decided it was time to leave when he saw Macpherson grabbing the piano player by the throat for playing the wrong songs. He was quite pleased with himself, however: he had prevented Macpherson from phoning the *Star*. Back in Toronto the next morning, Donato went straight to the office to see how well his cartoons looked in print. He then gleefully opened the *Star*, believing they would have no art to go with their stories. His elation was short-lived. The *Star*'s report featured two half-page Macpherson cartoons on the debate. "It was a bloody masterpiece," said Donato. Macpherson had managed to phone in the waybill number during a trip to the bathroom. No matter the circumstances, Duncan always met his deadline.

A self-portrait by Andy Donato, tiptoeing away from Duncan Macpherson's late-night boisterousness.

Duncan Macpherson experiments by drawing John Diefenbaker on a transparent screen for possible use in TV animation.

Most mornings, Duncan Macpherson would scan newspapers from Toronto, Montreal, and New York as well as a number of magazines – any publication he thought might inspire that day's drawing. After choosing several possible subjects, Macpherson would doodle on a piece of paper, trying out various ideas in thumbnail sketches. He called this process "mental acrobatics." Settling on one scenario, he would draw a larger rough sketch to work out the proportion, balance, and design. Sometimes he liked to chat while working out which idea to develop.

Stephen Wickens, a Toronto freelance writer and editor, has worked for all the Toronto newspapers at one time or another. After managing to get kicked out of high school in 1974, he began his career in journalism by taking a job as an office boy at the *Toronto Star*'s new building. During his first week, he was asked to report to Macpherson's newspaper-strewn office. He relates what happened next:

> He promptly sent me back up to the fourth-floor cafeteria for coffee, and I dutifully returned with coffees plus creams and sugars, having forgotten to ask how he liked it. He immediately dumped the cream and sugar in the garbage, along with some of the coffee in order to make room for a tot of Canadian Club … and he asked if I wanted some. I soon learned that he just sometimes liked to have someone to talk to about the news while he was working. I couldn't believe my luck, that while my schoolmates were studying calculus or chemistry or whatever, I was getting paid to hang

> *I know no such thing as genius – genius is nothing but labour and diligence.*
>
> WILLIAM HOGARTH

14

AT THE DRAWING BOARD

NDP
Broadbent
PC
TORY
TORY
FIRST
AID
Parrot
Rubber
Boots
squirrel
Trenchcoat.
SPORTY- BELLIGERENT
morning suit + running shoes
AUTOMATON
Turner track suit
GRIT
STEAM BATH
TENNIS/SPORTS

Turner: - I HAD NO OPTION
- BAY STREET
- ELECTION 84: FLYING CIRCUS (coke)
more like 8 mil - BANK(CAN) 4.8 mil. FORECLOSURE
- could be 6–8 mil by now. (lib. funds.)
fermez la PUTSCH - PUTSCH (at least 22 members.)
- NEGATIVE platform manner.
- BEER IN FRIG
- TENNIS - any one?
• Can always be POPE – says his mom.
• Chalk Talk by Chick
• Simon Reisman – 'best finance minister I ever trained.'
• Successful PUPPET of civil servants.
• Monte Cristo #3 cigars.
• Walking Filing cabinet (cards in pockets)
• YEP YEP – LOOKIN' GOOD – YOU BETCHA – NICE LEGS – TERRIFIC FOLKS – WRAP IT UP – YEAH –
• NO POLICY – NO ORGANIZATION – NO MACHINERY – NO STRATEGY – NO MONEY.
• CAMPAIGN CHAOS – THE FLYING CIRCUS
• F.T. TEAR IT UP (RAT PACK)

Macpherson's rough notes before starting a cartoon. These were made at the time of the 1984 federal election.

LEFT | The first rough sketch.

RIGHT | Squaring the dimensions.

out and have drinks with a famous newspaper guy – I'd grown up in a multiple-newspaper household and was into them. I remember that he'd have three or four cartoons on the go, not sure which one was going to be the one for the next day's paper.

He seemed to want to get a variety of people in to discuss news and politics while he worked – I think it was good for his idea-generating process. Duncan sometimes seemed like a gruff guy, but he was always nice to me. He sometimes sent me to the liquor store next to the *Star* building – or sometimes he'd send me to get sandwiches. He made an impression on me and, for a teenaged kid, it was really cool to see, in the newspaper, cartoons that I'd watched come together the previous day – or sometimes a few days earlier.

Since Macpherson's time, the technology involved in getting a cartoon from the drawing board to printed form has changed completely. Indeed, many cartoonists today have abandoned pen and ink in favour of a computer tablet and a stylus. The multi-stage process of bringing Duncan Macpherson's creations to life, however, was based on traditional methods that had been in place for decades.

The first step was to get approval of the concept from the editorial-page editor, after which Duncan would do a careful pencil sketch on an illustration board before applying brushwork, pen, and ink on top of the pencil lines. (A close look at his original drawings from that time will often reveal blue-pencil sketches under the ink; blue, because the camera didn't pick up that colour when the final drawing was photographed prior to printing.)

LEFT | Showing the idea to editorial-page editor Mark Harrison.

MIDDLE | The final brushwork …

RIGHT | … then the fine detailing with a pen.

One day in 1966, everyone was talking about Mao Tse-Tung having taken a dip in the Yangtze River – to show the world that he was still in robust health. The news item caught Duncan's fancy.

Macpherson inked the border of the cartoon first, since he preferred to draw within a contained area. At this stage, the cartoons were usually 30 to 50 per cent larger than the final reproduction, which was itself about 8 by 9 inches (roughly 20 by 23 cm.), twice the size generally allotted to an editorial-page cartoon. To render most elements of his drawings, Duncan used a brush. He would then turn to pen and ink in order to achieve the intensity of shading he wanted, adopting the cross-hatching method that was developed to a fine degree in the nineteenth century. His understanding of the etching process, which he had learned through his courses in Boston and at the Ontario College of Art, was very helpful.

It was then up to the technical experts at the newspaper to start the cartoon's transition to a finished product. A camera operator sized the drawing and then produced a film negative to be printed on a zinc pate for etching. The zinc etcher would carefully check the plate for discrepancies and make any corrections with a brush and an acid resist. Once the zinc plate was in place, the stereotyper would produce a paper mould of the whole editorial page, creating a casting of a curved lead plate.

The pressman then placed the curved lead plate on a roller, adjusting the tension before starting to print on newsprint in the actual press. This process was called "letterpress," with one machine able to print thirty thousand newspapers an hour. In the *Star*'s case, many such presses would be running at the same time.

It was a technical, exacting process, but Macpherson made a point of understanding it from start to finish. If a flaw were discovered in the reproduction of his cartoon at any point in the chain, he could correct the error before later editions of the newspaper went out that same day.

The quality of the reproduction is of paramount importance, but newspapers always had difficulty printing grey tones when using the high-speed letterpress. Macpherson experimented with an American inking process called "Flouro." This technique enabled him to achieve grey tones in print, without the dot-matrix patterns normally observed in reproduced photographs. Macpherson explained, "I mixed line and wash drawings without having to worry about wire photo limitations."

A Macpherson cartoon drawn one day might be totally different from one drawn the next. Although both would be unmistakably his, the dramatic differences in style, mood, and subject make sweeping generalizations about his cartoons

LEFT | A photograph is taken of the final artwork.

MIDDLE | A zinc plate is produced, which is then checked by an etcher for discrepancies.

RIGHT | The plate is positioned with other items on the page.

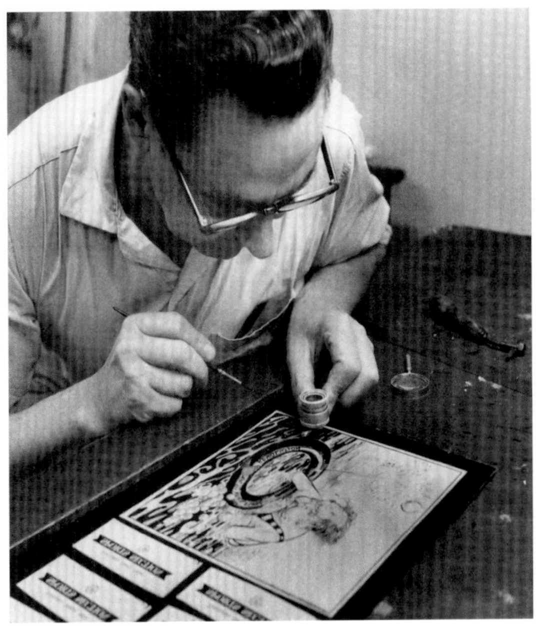

risky. Macpherson was particularly bitter on the subject of war. He objected fiercely, for example, to the possibility that American weapons with nuclear capability might be based in Canada.

When he was angry about something, he made his cartoons white-on-black – the reverse of his usual technique – and worked with a scratch-board to produce a woodcut effect. He used either the same technique or a heavy black line to produce dramatic portraits – and even Christmas cards for the *Toronto Star*.

Macpherson prized timeliness and didn't like to see a good cartoon idea go to waste. When, late one Sunday night in February 1971, he learned that American astronaut Alan Shepard had hit a golf ball on the moon, he immediately dressed and drove to work. He drew a striking cartoon of a golf ball sitting in a moon footprint; it made the Monday morning edition. "Another day," said Duncan, "there was nothing else on my mind but a man having been shot trying to crawl across the Berlin Wall. This is not a funny situation." Macpherson wanted to get the emotion and anger inside him down on paper as directly as possible. "I'll go right in and, with the brush, do a finished drawing immediately."

Caricature is the starting point and foundation of most of Macpherson's cartoons. Even a static situation can be enlivened. He once said, "If you get the proper expression on the man's face, you

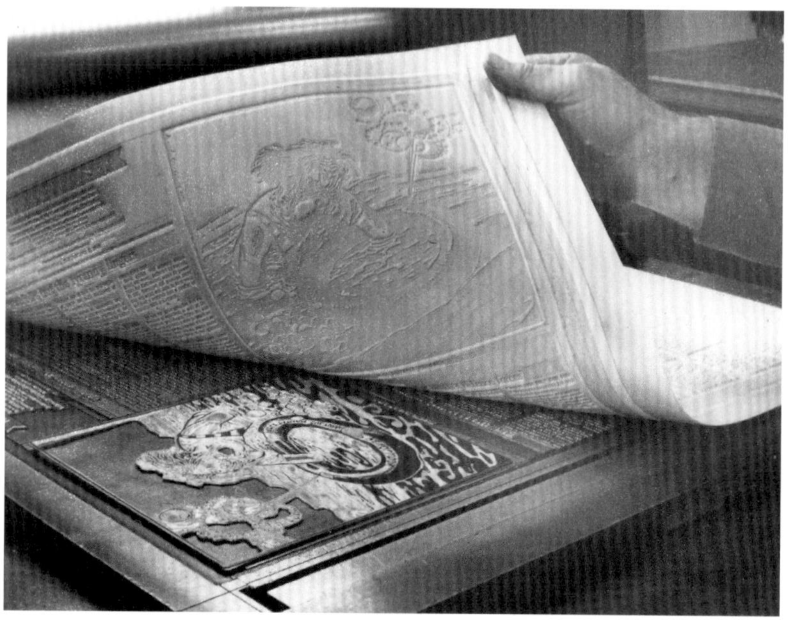

LEFT | A paper mould is made for the casting of a curved plate.

RIGHT | The curved plate is produced and placed on the press.

LEFT | A pressman adjusts the tension in order to get optimum printing results.

RIGHT | Macpherson carefully looks over the final printing.

read the sort of anti-thought or pro-thought." Duncan made good use of his dramatic drawing abilities even on the occasional off-day. He once told me that when you don't have a good cartoon idea, you can fake it with technique. "Draw a big, dramatic hairy hand or something. Readers will be so impressed with the drawing that they may not notice that it is rather a mundane idea."

In the early 1960s, Macpherson became impatient with the restrictions inherent in working within a newspaper forma, and experimented with cartooning for television. Like many other cartoonists, he believed that the small screen would be a more compatible outlet for his graphic work than the editorial page of a newspaper. As he noted in his journal, "animation as it was in those days was too time-consuming and completely out of the question. What I wanted to do was a dynamic thirty-second display for TV news. The lead-time for the delivery of the item would be four hours at best."

Macpherson devised a process to reverse-film a sheet of paper as he drew, with the camera placed below the drawing board. "The brush line as it developed was a very interesting display – rapidly growing like a plant. And then it was simply a matter of speeding up the final product, and flipping it, in order to fill the 30 seconds."

Working with the CTV network in Toronto, Macpherson constructed a special drawing board

LONG DISTANCE SWIMMER.

A MAN.

Macpherson painted this tribute to Zhou Enlai when China's first premier died in 1976. Brushing with a fluoro liquid achieved fine greyscales in the newspaper.

to make the process possible, and then patented the technique. Although the network included the display in several newscasts, it was – perhaps inevitably – a short-lived initiative. Television people, although impressed with Macpherson's approach to animation, were very nervous about him expressing a point of view that might offend viewers. This timidity angered Duncan. After all, he was used to being able to express himself freely in the newspaper every day.

Nonetheless, television was a great help to Macpherson. "In the standard news photo," he said, "you get the man's head. He's frozen. You don't know how he walks. You don't know what his mannerisms are like. There is an attitude in every person, a dumb attitude, which is very helpful in caricature. Even though you are not going to use the whole body, if you understand how the person moves, and get the man's attitude verbally, it's a big help."

There was a time when caricaturists would fill every inch of their page with pen work. Macpherson's dip into television may have influenced his thinking about white space, because he started to use it to good effect, understanding that it draws the eye to the highlighted dark spaces of the graphic.

When he travelled on assignment for the *Toronto Star*, Macpherson rarely had access to a proper studio or his usual array of drawing implements.

With all this travel, Duncan needed to come up with a light, packable drawing set. This kit included a large drawing pad, three or four pocket-sized notepads, some HB pencils, a variety of nibs, four to eight watercolour brushes, several small bottles of India ink in plastic bags, a gum eraser, a razor blade, and a ruler.

A number of Macpherson's trips abroad were to countries with totalitarian regimes, so he worked out a way to avoid having his work confiscated by border officials when he crossed out of their territory. Using a 4H pencil, he would

WHY CAIN'T WE-ALL UNDERSTAND OUR FELLOW HUMAN BEINGS?

draw only vague outlines of his subjects on hard illustration board: "It was not easily read, even by myself, but it was enough." Once he was safely on his way home, he added the funny or satirical bits and finalized the drawing.

Duncan liked to map out possible drawing scenarios, so he would know ahead of time exactly what he wanted to capture and how he would do it. He appreciated champion golfer Jack Nicklaus's thorough pre-competition preparations: "Before Nicklaus plays a tournament, he walks around the course, jotting down directions for himself on how to play each hole. He will pace off distances so he will know which clubs to select for every conceivable shot. The illustrator should follow much the same procedure."

Duncan was fascinated with what he saw of land and water from an airplane. "Looking down from the air at the puzzles and patterns of rivers, farms, forest, lake, rock, one thinks what meaningful abstracts these would make for the experimental painter. Life and death, season pursuing season; in full, the history of our life on this planet spread out for the artist to read."

The technological side of cartooning was being revolutionized by the time Macpherson retired. His friend Bob Church recalls having discussions with him in the late 1980s and early 1990s about the spate of new drawing and painting computer software. "For Macpherson, it was the 'line' that was so important, and he couldn't achieve that characteristic line with the software as it then was. Of course, the computer stylus had yet to be invented." It is intriguing to speculate about what an artist like Macpherson, who had such magnificent graphic talents, could have achieved with the array of computer drawing programs and software that is available today.

OPPOSITE | U.S. President Lyndon Johnson again.

ABOVE | An Inuit nativity scene for the *Toronto Star*'s editorial page, Christmas Eve 1976.

Macpherson clearly enjoyed experimenting in colour when he could. One example emerged from a trip to St John's. As he told the story:

> I was warned that it would be very, very difficult to see Joey [Newfoundland's storied Premier Joey Smallwood]. Even the cab driver going up there said that he was too busy and unapproachable. So, I found his office and

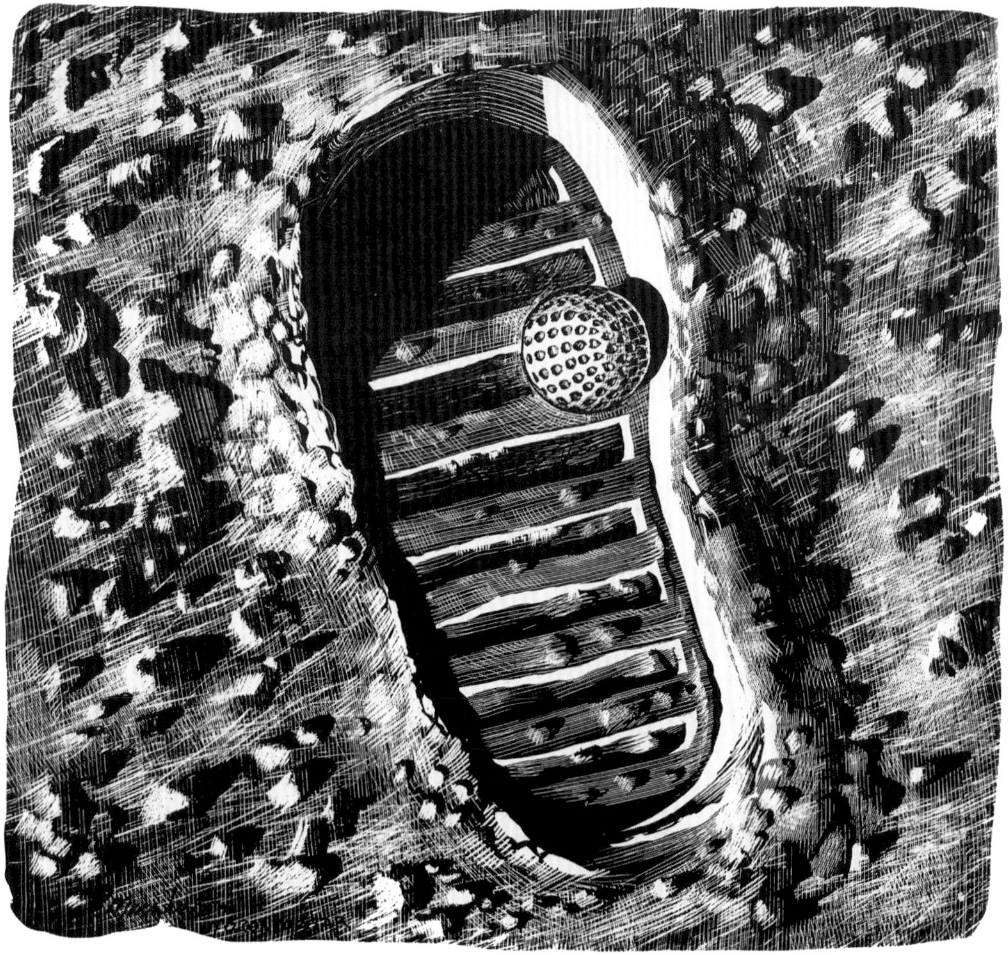

No matter the circumstances, Duncan Macpherson always met his deadlines.

simply wandered in. He was in the middle of a debate with some fellow from New York and didn't even look in my direction. So, I just sat down and started sketching. When they finished, Joey turned in my direction and asked if I was going to the state dinner with Governor-General Michener that night? I said no, that I hadn't been invited. "Well," Joey said, "You're invited now." At the dinner, Joey seemed to be taking up Mr Michener's time with an awful lot of chitchat while the Governor General, obviously a pretty good trencherman, seemed more interested in eating. I was waiting for the G.G. to stick a serviette in Joey's mouth, but he didn't.

Apart from his interest in colour, however, Duncan was a master of chiaroscuro – the contrast of dark and light. In many of his cartoons, his dramatic use of white space draws your eye to detailed tension points within the darker areas – as in this drawing of Henry Kissinger – giving both a sense of movement and gravity.

THE BERLIN WALL.

THE SITUATION IS WELL IN HAND.

Both networks CTV and CBC refused the use of an editorial cartoon on the grounds that it was just <u>That</u>. EDITORIAL COMMENT —and they didn't want editorial comment on the news.

Now I was mad. They suggested sports cartoons — and other program illustrations. My target ~~of an~~ for an editorial cartoon on TV news was my only target — and it was shot down. After all the fuss of delivering the goods and inventing a process of ~~anono~~ animation — WHY DIDN'T THEY TELL ME <u>IN THE FIRST</u> PLACE?

Macpherson's bitter thoughts on his experience of television.

Aerial view of Newfoundland's northwest coast.

Newfoundland's wily Joey Smallwood was always a Macpherson favourite to draw – almost as much as Joey himself enjoyed being caricatured.

At a state dinner in Newfoundland, Macpherson sketched Governor General Roland Michener and Premier Joey Smallwood.

Henry Kissinger's futile climb for peace.

As many children do at some point in their young lives, six-year-old Duncan Macpherson briefly ran away from home. The family was then living on Erskine Avenue in Toronto. Macpherson was proud of having made it up Yonge Street as far as Lawrence Avenue before knocking on a door and telling the woman who answered that he wanted to go home. A nice policeman gave him both a ride home – in a Model T convertible – and an ice-cream cone! Macpherson's first solo expedition had been a success.

When the family later moved to the top floor of a house on Hillsdale Avenue, Duncan's summertime bed was on the back verandah. At night, he could hear the train whistles coming up from the Don valley. He was eleven then, and as he listened to the trains, he seriously considered leaving home – just jumping on a train and going somewhere, anywhere. As an adult, he was able to make that dream a reality. Even better, someone else paid his expenses.

Macpherson travelled far and wide for the *Toronto Star*, eagerly accepting assignments that took him to the United States, Cuba, the Caribbean, Germany, northern Africa, Russia, China, and elsewhere. During these trips, Macpherson was able to return to his roots as an illustrator, except that now he was illustrating his own thoughts and words. He loved travelling, perhaps in part because it beat being confined to a studio and having to grind out a cartoon every day. It also allowed Duncan to use colour occasionally as opposed to the daily black-and-white cartoon.

What I enjoyed the most about the job at the Toronto Star was travelling to areas of the world that interested me as an artist. I couldn't see enough. It was great.

DUNCAN MACPHERSON'S PERSONAL JOURNAL

15

PEREGRINATIONS: TRAVEL SKETCHES

ABOVE | Duncan Macpherson, wearing a Russian hat, is greeted at Malton Airport by his son and his wife after his return from Russia in 1962.

BELOW | A charcoal sketch of a woman in the crowd during the queen's 1961 visit to the Caribbean.

Queen Elizabeth and Prince Philip watch a jump-up dance being performed in front of the royal yacht *Britannia* on a visit to British Guiana in 1961.

CUBA

Macpherson had always wanted to go to Cuba – in fact, had threatened to quit the *Star* partly over being denied the opportunity. Once that was sorted out, he made three trips to the island in very short order in the early 1960s.

Each of these visits revealed a nation in a state of constant transformation. Under Fidel Castro, old Cuba was disappearing.

Macpherson's first and most extensive tour of Cuba was in 1960. His assignment was to document his impressions of the country one year after Castro and his band of *barbudos* (bearded revolutionaries) had taken over. Fidel had not yet declared himself a Communist and in fact was still making desperate overtures to the Americans as the stores emptied of goods. Cuba was broke.

Macpherson was accompanied on this trip by *Toronto Star* senior reporter Jack Brehl. Upon arrival in Havana, the duo checked into Havana's historic Hotel Nacional, where the casino was still in operation – if almost empty.

Brehl thought he had an advance commitment from the Cubans for an interview with Fidel Castro. Although Brehl and Macpherson gave tracking down Castro their best shot, it was not to be. They spent fruitless hours in government anterooms and attended a baseball game where they had been told the Cuban leader would deliver a political speech. But Castro never arrived, having decided to attend a postage-stamp exhibit instead.

Brehl was supposed to check in with the *Star* by telephone as often as three times a day. This was easier said than done in Havana, and outside the capital it was completely impossible. He and Macpherson decided to avoid the obligation completely by getting on a train and exploring the countryside.

They spent a glorious few days travelling to Santiago de Cuba, taking in the beautiful views

HE'S JUST TAKING OFF TO INSPECT HIS COASTAL DEFENCES.

ABOVE | Duncan Macpherson and Jack Brehl attended a baseball game in Havana that was preceded by political speeches.

RIGHT | Transportation in Cuba.

of mountains, ocean, and beaches, and buying cigars and lunch through the open windows of the train. Later, the two men were given a tour of western Cuba, complete with an official driver and a commandeered vehicle.

On this first trip, Macpherson had no deadlines to meet. His assignment from the *Star* was just to bring back detailed drawings for a feature on Cuba. He could therefore afford the time to look around, gather his impressions, and prepare rough sketches. When he returned to Toronto, he had twenty pieces for the series the *Star* wanted to run.

On his second trip to Cuba, Macpherson sensed a very different atmosphere. In his journal, he wrote: "The early days of the happy revolution had disappeared. The Bay of Pigs invasion had been repulsed and the Russians had moved in." Indeed, they seemed to be everywhere, and as the world later discovered, were busy building rocket sites.

Macpherson believed that, with the island under Communist control, no partnership with the United States was remotely possible. "There is no doubt in my mind that the States could have patched up minor differences and

ABOVE | Three Russians in tropical shirts.

LEFT | An image from the city of Santiago de Cuba.

A Canadian prisoner in Cuba, Ronald Lippert.

kept Cuba within the American family. The U.S. chose not to and is still paying the price. Nothing worked in Havana anymore: water, plumbing, air-conditioning, elevators, the transportation system – all ceased to function."

There was no open hostility toward Macpherson and Roy Shields, the reporter accompanying him, but bureaucratic suspicion and confusion made for uneasy working conditions. "I borrowed a trick from Sir David Low," said Macpherson, recalling his New Zealand hero. "When the occasion warranted, Low would use his finger to draw on an imaginary pad in his pocket, thus registering a mental image that he could later translate to paper."

In November 1963 Macpherson made his third trip to Cuba to attend the trial of two Canadian pilots, William Milne and Ronald Lippert, who had been charged with smuggling ammunition into the country – in tins of fruit – for delivery to anti-Castro groups active in the island's eastern region. Macpherson and *Star* reporter Alan Edmonds found Havana much altered: no longer a city with an active street life, it had become a fortress, a collection of abandoned, shuttered storefronts. Macpherson was dismayed. "A few years ago, Havana was the liveliest city in the world. It was now a hollow tooth – a graveyard."

The three-day trial of the Canadian pilots was held at the Castillo de los Tres Reyes del Morro, built in 1589 to protect the port of Havana. El Morro had since been transformed into one of the city's largest prisons, and it was there that the Canadians were being held. Macpherson noticed that the members of the military tribunal seemed to particularly enjoy playing up to the CBC's cameras. They handed one pilot a ten-year sentence, while his companion received a lesser penalty, perhaps for having cooperated with the prosecution.

This time, Macpherson had a deadline to meet. He neatly avoided delays and government interference by sending his drawings to Mexico with a CBC news team. They in turn transmitted the sketches to Toronto by wire, just in time to meet the deadline for the following day's edition.

Macpherson considered his collection of drawings from Cuba to be some of the most interesting of his career, and he featured many cartoons about Cuba on the editorial page of the *Star* for years after his visits.

USSR

The *Star Weekly* arranged for Duncan Macpherson to travel to Russia in the fall of 1962 to do drawings for a full issue on the USSR. He was supposed to travel by train from Berlin to Warsaw and then on to Moscow. However, he was removed from the train in East Berlin because he was missing a specific on-again-off-again pass. After a full day of dealing with red tape – and drawing a few sketches in East Berlin – he returned to West Berlin before flying to Moscow via Copenhagen.

During his stay in Moscow, Duncan witnessed the October Revolution parade. "Officials in open cars are followed by heavy artillery, tanks and mobile rockets. The air is blue with exhaust smoke. Then hundreds of thousands of soldiers and other humans pass by. What a spectacle!"

Macpherson came to believe that the Russians didn't hate Americans. In Moscow's Pushkin Museum, he was touched to see a family staring at a bust of Benjamin Franklin. "The guide seemed to be explaining who the U.S. hero was; I could see only reverence in their faces." He visited many of the cultural highlights of Moscow, including the magnificent, pre-revolutionary Bolshoi Theatre, where he felt the Russians could dream a little.

President Kennedy set up the Business Group for Latin America in 1963; it later became the Council of the Americas. Cuba was not invited to participate.

There was little private traffic on Moscow's streets at that time except for trucks and the occasional bureaucrat's chauffeur-driven car. "But I did see this old motorcycle. A car costs about $5,000 and the average city worker earns about $65 a month. Even then, if you save for a car, it will be several years before it is delivered. But five cents will get you anywhere on public transportation."

Benjamin Franklin on display in Moscow.

"At night, I found the Twist, the Charleston, champagne, vodka, U.S. cigarettes and even U.S. hairdos in the restaurant of my Moscow hotel. Of course, it wasn't every comrade who was allowed into the place."

Travelling beyond Moscow, Duncan needed to go back and forth to Leningrad in the north and to Rostov, Volgograd, and Kiev in the south. For this, he sometimes had the use of a car, a chauffeur, and a translator. During a stop in Kiev, in Ukraine, Macpherson had a particularly interesting encounter with the locals. First, he was offered a job. He had stopped off to drink some vodka and swap cartoons with the staff of the humour publication *Pepper*. Macpherson thought the offer of employment was a joke brought on by the liberal consumption of alcohol, but the offer was repeated the next day. He would receive a monthly salary of 220 rubles, plus the use of a car and an apartment. "If I would defect, they would fly my family over, but eventually I would have to pay back the airfare." He politely declined.

LEFT | The Berlin Wall.

RIGHT | Military parade in Red Square.

ABOVE | Getting around in Moscow.

RIGHT | Inside the Bolshoi Theatre.

Nightlife (for some) in Moscow.

ABOVE | On the Don airfield in Rostov, a new jet engine – turned on to blast snow and ice from the runway – is pushed around by an ancient truck. In case anything breaks down, the truck is followed by a person with a broom.

BELOW | Mounted guns and tanks, grim reminders of the Second World War, look down on the Volga River. Industrial hydro installations dominate the background while, on the right, pre-fab apartment blocks are under construction.

UNITED STATES

A "Kennedy wins" scenario from the 1960 Democratic National Convention, with a note to the *Star*'s art director, Des English. In a pre-PhotoShop move, Macpherson also sent versions of this sketch featuring headshots of Kennedy's rivals for the nomination, Lyndon Johnson and Adlai Stevenson.

One of Macpherson's very first travel assignments for the *Star* had been to attend the Democratic National Convention in July 1960, held in Los Angeles. John F. Kennedy and Lyndon B. Johnson were chosen as the candidates for president and vice-president respectively and went on to win the November election.

On a late November day in 1963, Lee Harvey Oswald assassinated President Kennedy in Dallas. Macpherson happened to be on the way to Cuba for his third visit when he heard the news. Just two days later, while in police custody, Oswald himself was gunned down by nightclub owner Jack Ruby.

Ruby went on trial in Dallas, where he was found guilty of murder and sentenced to death. However, following a successful appeal on the basis of a questionable oral confession, a new trial venue and date were set. Before the new proceedings could take place, Ruby died of cancer.

Duncan Macpherson travelled to Dallas for the original trial with *Toronto Star* reporter Ray Timson. Photographers were not allowed into the courtroom, so Macpherson's job was to send character sketches of the participants back to the newspaper by wire-photo. "These transmissions require a clear, black and white definition as a safeguard against any aberration in the final sketch," he noted.

Ray Timson managed to arrange a meeting with sitting Judge Joe Brown, even though there were supposed to be no interviews given to the media. He pitched the session as an opportunity for the judge to sit for a portrait, which Macpherson would draw for the *Toronto Star*. Macpherson sketched very, very slowly, while the judge, a bit of a chatterbox, did a lot of talking. Timson listened in, and later filed a story using the tidbits he had picked up.

Judge Brown was very pleased with the drawing and asked Macpherson to send him the original. Thereafter, the judge gave Macpherson free rein during the trial, even allowing him to sit in the jury box for a better view. "This was

LEFT | Judge Joe Brown.

RIGHT | Spectators at Jack Ruby's trial in Dallas.

astonishing to the television network artists who were grouped in spectator seats and generally got nothing but the back of heads."

Attending Jack Ruby's trial sparked Macpherson's lifelong interest in the circumstances surrounding the John Kennedy assassination. He read everything he could find on the subject for the next twenty-five years, developing his own theories about what had actually taken place on 22 November 1963. He became convinced that three shots had been fired, and that the Mafia was behind the murder of both John and Robert Kennedy.

Among Macpherson's papers when he died were minutely illustrated maps and extensive notes on the Kennedy shootings. They make for fascinating reading. "May, 1986: I'm looking at my map now, and I will stash it away with these memoirs, so any interested party can check it out."

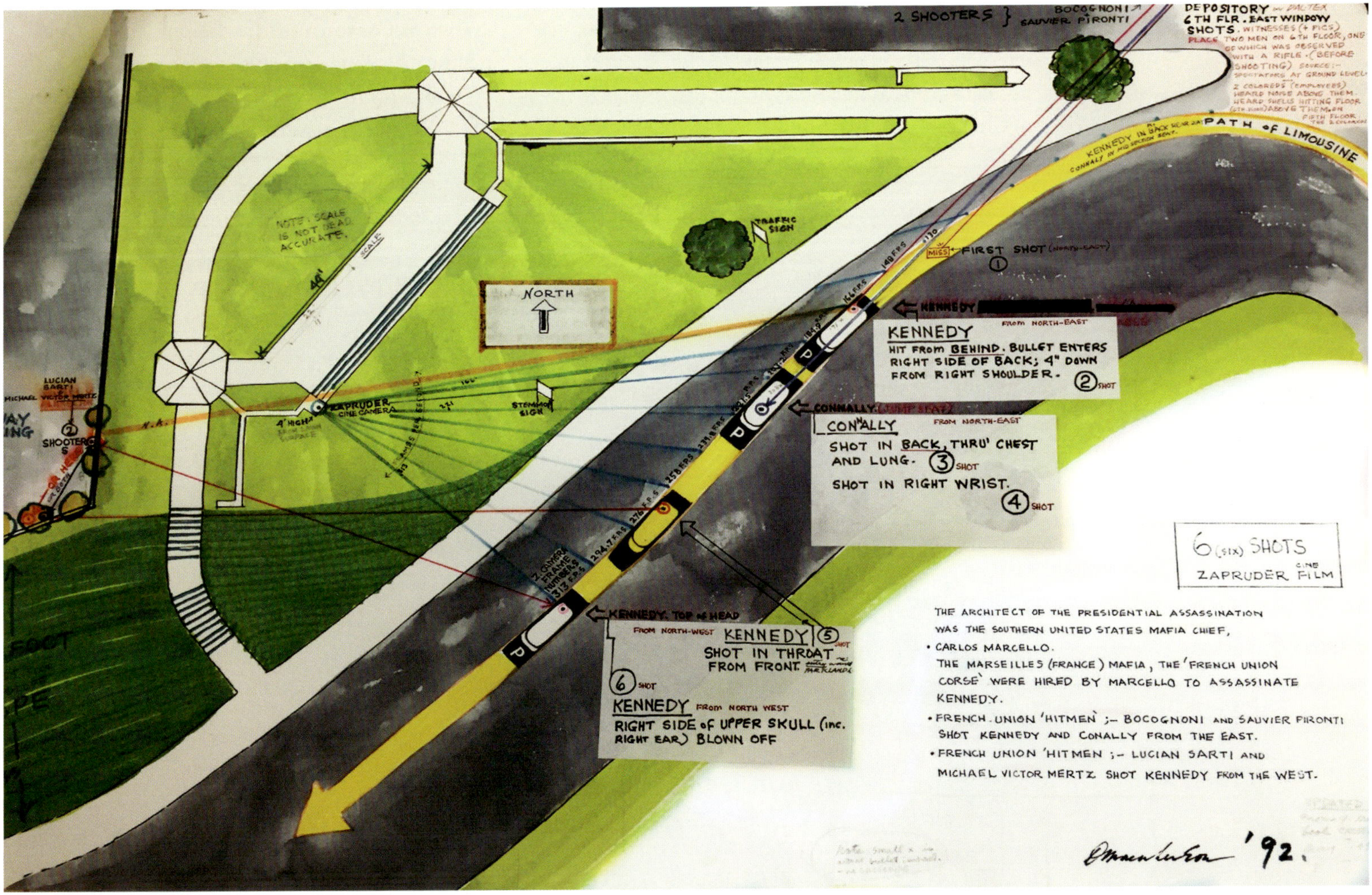

Macpherson's assassination theory, meticulously illustrated.

CHINA

Macpherson travelled to China for fifteen days in February and March 1979. This was his last major international assignment for the *Toronto Star*. Of all his many travel sketchbooks, the ones completed in China are perhaps the most representative of the people themselves. These drawings show a nation in the early stages of a profound transformation.

Macpherson journeyed from Guangzhou, then known as Canton, north to Beijing and beyond, making sketches of everyday life.

The captions below these sketches come from Macpherson's personal journal.

A Canton street scene in the evening. On the sidewalk, free-enterprise vendors sell buns and cabbages,
while a little kid chops firewood.

Beijing: An old, crowded part of the city is slowly being demolished. The man-made hill in the background is the site of a future government building.

People's Liberation Army soldiers play basketball in a courtyard of Beijing's Imperial City (the Forbidden City). The crane and the lion are imperial symbols.

The great wall of China near Beijing. The wall and the mountains cannot be described; it is a psychedelic vision. On the pill-box at the left, note the poster showing a life-size head and shoulders within concentric rings of a target – well riddled!

Children in a Shanghai "workers' school" hit ping-pong balls hanging from a string across the room. The background posters proclaim the "modernization" theme you see everywhere.

A Shanghai worker's home in a new complex for 6,000 people. Toilet facilities are mostly shared. Generally, one room for two or three people, no heating. Note the chickens in the hamper and the bamboo rig for hanging the laundry out the windows. Still, these units were far better equipped than what the average person was used to.

TOMORROW, PISTOLS AT DAWN.

In 1956, while Duncan Macpherson was working as an illustrator in Toronto, an advertising agency approached him about trying his hand at something new. One of the agency's clients, political organizer Dalton Camp, was working with the Nova Scotia Progressive Conservative Party to have its leader, Robert Stanfield, elected premier in the upcoming election. Camp commissioned Macpherson to create cartoons lampooning the province's sitting Liberal government.

"Camp was an impetuous man," wrote Macpherson in his journal, "who seemed to function best at night. I recall inking these slanderous cartoons late into the evening in some downtown office building, with Camp egging me on. Well, Dalton and I helped to oust the long-reigning Liberals and put in a Conservative government under Robert Stanfield." The routed Liberal premier later blamed his party's defeat on the muckraking campaign and those "damn cartoons!" Macpherson himself did not get caught up in the politics. "It is interesting to note that I just considered this another job, and did not see the situation as an early herald of my later occupation as an editorial cartoonist."

As for Dalton Camp, he remained a "Stanfield man." While national president of the Progressive Conservative Party, he played a key role in having John Diefenbaker voted out as party leader in 1967 in favour of Stanfield.

Stanfield had always been a progressive. During his eleven years as premier of Nova Scotia, he brought in increased educational funding, the province's first Medicare program, and a provincial parks system. As the leader of

If I was going to be upset by cartoons,
I should have retired from politics
a long time ago.

ROBERT STANFIELD,
FROM THE 1975 FILM
THE HECKLERS

16

STANFIELD AND TRUDEAU

Dalton Camp at work.

the federal Progressive Conservatives from 1967 to 1976, Stanfield was fully engaged with the issue of Canadian unity and bolstering Quebec's role within Confederation. He had the support of the west, if not always of John Diefenbaker, but never found the right political formula to defeat the very crafty Pierre Trudeau.

At one time, it was not unusual to hear Canadians say wistfully that Robert Stanfield was the best prime minister Canada never had. As much as anyone, Duncan Macpherson would have liked to see Stanfield lead the country, if only because his craggy physiognomy made him such fun to draw. Despite Macpherson's personal admiration for the politician, he often drew him as an emaciated, stumbling Ichabod Crane who never got anything right.

At the 1967 Progressive Conservative convention, Stanfield was caught by the TV cameras in the midst of eating a banana. That banana became a recurring element in Macpherson's Stanfield sketches.

Cartoonists never had any shortage of Stanfield stumbles on which to sharpen their wit. During the 1974 federal election campaign, Stanfield's plane made a quick stop in North Bay, Ontario. On the tarmac in shirt and tie, Stanfield tossed a football around, catching most of the passes. However, photographer Doug Ball just happened to capture him awkwardly fumbling one pass. The photo appeared on the front page of the *Globe and Mail.* Some say it, and the cartoons it inspired, cost Stanfield the election. Years later, Ball asked Stanfield to sign a few of the infamous pictures for posterity. Stanfield wrote: "To Doug Ball, I should have taken off my tie."

The football image endured. Five years later, Joe Clark, who had replaced Stanfield as Tory leader, was preparing for a federal election. Macpherson pictured Stanfield trying to teach the awkward Clark how not to drop a football.

This famous cartoon shows the Conservative benches in Parliament with Robert Stanfield as leader and John Diefenbaker a constant irritant.

LEFT | Robert Stanfield was one of those people who could get lost in a crowd. And did. The cutline on this Macpherson cartoon reads: "No more trains till tomorrow, stranger."

RIGHT | The Cheshire banana.

Political cartoonists had always drawn Robert Stanfield with an emphasis on his droopy left eye. It made him appear rather woeful. Speaking to a cartoonists' convention in the early 1970s, Stanfield said, "You guys haven't noticed – I had my eye operated on and corrected six months ago." Of course, we noticed. We just weren't going to let go of a good thing.

One summer in the late 1960s, Duncan Macpherson was visiting Halifax. As Parliament wasn't in session, he knew that Robert Stanfield was likely to be home, so he phoned the house and introduced himself to Mrs Stanfield. Macpherson asked if he could come over to meet with the Opposition leader. Mrs Stanfield said, "Well, why don't you come over now? He's working in the garden."

"Arriving at the house, I went down a slightly wooded section of the property, and there was Stanfield yanking out weeds, left and right. I got several sketches of him. I was very impressed with this, something Canadians possibly take for granted: the access the ordinary fellow has to leaders of society – and the response, which is generally quite human."

The image of Robert Stanfield in his garden stuck with Macpherson, inspiring him to draw an amusing cartoon in May 1969 of the Progressive Conservative leader tending some tulips on Parliament Hill.

Stanfield was once asked if he had a favourite cartoon. "I can think of one that I see quite often, because my wife put it up in the bathroom I use at Stornoway [official home of the leader of the

Opposition]. It's a cartoon by Macpherson of our family at the dining-room table. My daughter Mimi is looking at me and asking: 'Are you really a power-hungry obstructionist, Daddy?' Macpherson's message was very clear. I'm not sure what my wife's message was."

The Public Archives of Canada mounted an exhibition of Duncan Macpherson cartoons in 1980, at which the former Progressive Conservative leader was the guest of honour. He observed: "There are very few really good political cartoonists, but everyone I know believes Macpherson was one of the best. At the time that some of these cartoons of me were published, they seemed a bit savage. Seeing them again – well, they seem more humorous."

Sketches of Robert Stanfield in his garden – Halifax, Nova Scotia.

Although Duncan Macpherson drew many, many cartoons of Pierre Elliott Trudeau over the years, he seldom had any direct interaction with him. He did, however, travel once by train from Ottawa to Moncton in the prime minister's special coach – sketchbook in hand, of course.

In the spring of 1968, the federal Liberal Party held its leadership convention in Ottawa. Lester B. Pearson had recently announced his retirement, and eight high-profile candidates were vying to replace him. To most Canadians' surprise, it was the relative newcomer, Justice Minister Pierre Elliott Trudeau, who was chosen to lead the party into the June election. Trudeau was a charismatic figure whose public appearances caused such a stir that the term "Trudeaumania" was coined.

Fifteen years as prime minister and a very strong personality ensured that Pierre Elliott Trudeau was caricatured more often than any Canadian had been to that point. For Duncan Macpherson, however, it took a while to get his caricature of the man just right.

Fortunately, he had the time and the impetus to improve upon his caricature of Trudeau, whose two spells as prime minister (1968–79 and 1980–84) were marked by waves of dramatic social and political change in the country.

A staunch federalist, Trudeau had no patience with separatist sentiment in Quebec. In October 1970, on the grounds that a militant separatist faction – the Front de Libération du Québec – had kidnapped the British trade commissioner and a provincial cabinet minister, he took the nearly unprecedented step of invoking the War Measures Act. This granted military and police authorities vast powers to arrest and detain suspects. For this action he was both praised and vilified. Duncan Macpherson was not among the prime minister's supporters in this instance.

Throughout the 1970s, Trudeau continued to argue forcefully against the concept of a separate Quebec. Following the 1976 provincial election in which René Lévesque led the Parti Québécois to victory, Trudeau believed that countering the sovereignist movement was his greatest challenge and obligation – that and advancing the concept of a bilingual Canada.

Then there was Trudeau's marriage to the much younger Margaret Sinclair. Margaret demonstrated early on that she would be her own woman – she is quoted as saying, "I want to be more than a rose in my husband's lapel." She found a passion for the cause of access to clean water for the world's poor. She actively campaigned for her husband in the run-up to the 1974 federal election but came to find life as the prime minister's wife claustrophobic and stultifying. Macpherson did several cartoons featuring the high-profile couple early in their relationship but turned his gaze away when the marriage went sour. After the couple separated in 1977, Margaret Trudeau scandalized some people by her carefree and jet-setting lifestyle that was splashed for all to see across newspapers around the world.

Two issues haunted Pierre Trudeau throughout his time as prime minister: lack of political support in western Canada and inflation. His only solution to the latter problem seemed to be to spend his way through it.

ARE YOU REALLY A POWER-HUNGRY OBSTRUCTIONIST, DADDY?

Pierre Trudeau effortlessly fends off the Opposition.

QUESTION PERIOD.

Prime Minister Pierre Trudeau, on Canadian National Coach 100 from Ottawa to Moncton.

Despite "Trudeaumania" initially sweeping the globe, Pierre Trudeau was indifferent to the idea of an ongoing British Commonwealth.

With Trudeau as his subject, the intention and impact of Macpherson's cartoons had changed. Caricatures of the prime minister as Napoleon, Nero, Oliver Cromwell – and even as the first Emperor of Canada – seemed to lack the exasperation or the grudging admiration that had animated his caricatures of Diefenbaker. "Dief" as Marie Antoinette was hilarious; Trudeau as the Emperor of Canada is funny, but ominous. It is worth mentioning that by the time Trudeau came to power, it was fully ten years after Diefenbaker had been elected, a decade that Macpherson had spent in what he called a gut-wrenching job.

The 1970s brought increasing economic difficulty, inflation, and labour unrest across the country, leading to the defeat of the Trudeau Liberals in 1979. The Progressive Conservative Party under leader Joe Clark was able to form a minority government.

It was a brief interregnum. Trudeau was returned to power in the general election of February 1980, just in time to campaign against the proposition set out in Quebec's May 1980 referendum, which could have led to the province's secession from Canada. Quebecers voted – and the independence proposition failed. Trudeau then began work on his plans to reform Canada's constitution, an endeavour that many considered to be his crowning achievement.

When Macpherson began his career in political cartooning in the late 1950s, he was able to say with some justice: "I am a far superior artist due to my training than my contemporaries." However, by the 1970s, many cartoonists who had been inspired by Macpherson's work were catching up. He acknowledged as much in the 1975 film *The Hecklers*. "We have quite a fine collection of cartoonists in the Canadian papers today who use their individual creative processes and generally come up with original work."

The 1970s were sometimes referred to as the "golden age of Canadian cartooning." Major

Macpherson felt that Trudeau's two weakest points were the War Measures Act and the economy.

newspapers like the *Toronto Star* had two cartoonists on staff. Even in smaller markets across the country, editors understood that having a talented local cartoonist would boost readership. In cities like Hamilton, Windsor, Kingston, Regina, and Victoria, newspapers hired their own cartoonists rather than running syndicated material. Today that is no longer the case, even though Canadian newspapers still get brilliant work from the likes of Brian Gable at the *Globe and Mail*, Serge Chapleau at *La Presse*, Bruce Mackinnon and Michael DeAdder at the *Chronicle Herald* in Halifax, and André-Philippe Côté of *Le Soleil* in Quebec City.

By the 1980s, those in the know had begun to notice a slight chill. Newspaper owners began to reassert their influence after a very liberal period in the media. In 1982 Roy Peterson signed one of his cartoon books to me with: "Terry. Is the golden age of cartooning really over? Roy."

Margaret Trudeau demonstrates in support of safe drinking water for the world's poor.

An increase in welfare rates to fight inflation.

Pierre Trudeau loved to sneak away to Cuba on vacation and get away from it all.

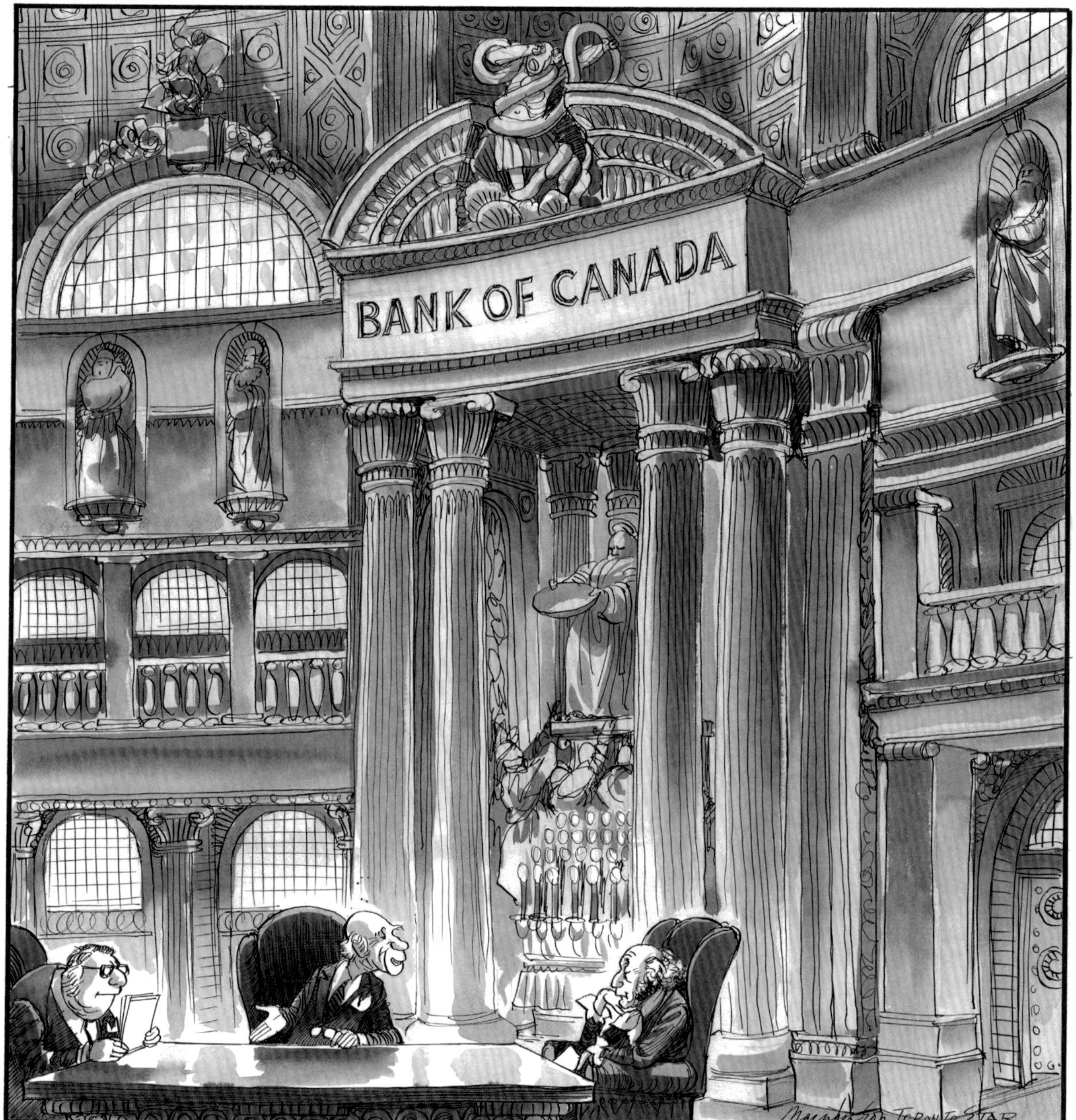

WHAT GERALD IS TRYING TO SAY, PIERRE, IS THAT INSTEAD OF NOT HAVING THE MONEY WE HAVEN'T GOT, WE HAVE TWICE AS MUCH, BUT IT IS ONLY WORTH HALF OF WHAT WE HAVEN'T GOT NOW.

MOI
THE STATE, C'EST MOI.
BAISEMENT
THE OFFICIAL SECRETS ACT:– A LAW THAT NO CITIZEN MAY HAVE A PURPOSE PREJUDICIAL TO THE INTERESTS OF THE STATE.
Macpherson TORONTO STAR

THRONE
SPEECH

Trudeau's infamous quotation, "Mangez la merde," being spelled out for the unemployed crowds below.

Joe Clark is elected prime minister, and he and Maureen McTeer move into 24 Sussex Drive.

Macpherson explains one of his FLQ trial drawings to Prime Minister Trudeau at a 1972 exhibition in Ottawa.

In one of the most significant events of the decade, President Richard Nixon visited Communist China in 1972.

Duncan Macpherson was at his most prolific during the twelve years between 1968 and 1980. He cut back significantly on the travel sketches he would normally have done for the newspaper: there was so much of significance happening at home and abroad that he felt compelled to focus on producing editorial-page cartoons. This portfolio contains the cartoons that I believe represent the best of his wide array of work during that time.

Despite stunning the world and winning plaudits for making overtures to China in 1972, U.S. President Richard Nixon was soon in the headlines again, but not for the right reasons. Nixon was implicated in a scandal ("Watergate") involving a burglary at Democratic Party headquarters followed by an attempted cover-up. He eventually chose to resign in August 1974, having been impeached and facing trial in the Senate. He was succeeded by Vice-President Gerald Ford, who lost the 1976 presidential election to Jimmy Carter, perhaps because of Ford's having granted Nixon a full and unconditional pardon. The United States brought its military involvement in Vietnam to a close; the war officially ended in April 1975, following the American pullout and North Vietnamese forces taking Saigon.

An international oil crisis began in 1973, when the Organization of Petroleum Exporting Countries (OPEC) proclaimed an embargo on exports, creating havoc in the global economy and global politics. Tensions in the Middle East remained high throughout the 1970s. India acquired nuclear weapons, while the news from Africa was dominated by horrific stories about

It is often said that a picture is worth a thousand words. A cartoon well done is worth a thousand pictures.

JOHN DIEFENBAKER,
FROM THE 1975 FILM
THE HECKLERS

17

CARTOON PORTFOLIO, 1968–80

Newly elected Toronto mayor David Crombie's first order to city council.

NO MORE "HEY, SHORTY."

the human-rights abuses perpetrated by various strongmen and despots.

As if that weren't enough to spur a cartoonist's creativity, Macpherson could easily have filled his time just cartooning people and events in Ontario and Quebec. John Robarts, one of a long line of Progressive Conservative premiers of Ontario, was an advocate of individual freedoms and opposed to centralizing initiatives from the federal government. The 1970s were boom years for development in the city of Toronto, requiring close attention from both the municipal government under new mayor David Crombie (in office from 1972 to 1978) and the provincial Progressive Conservative government under Premier Bill Davis (in office between 1971 and 1985). Down the road in Montreal, planning for the 1976 Olympic Games was in full swing under autocratic mayor Jean Drapeau; there was already a whiff of scandal and mismanagement in the air.

Despite these distractions, Macpherson's attention was most often focused on Ottawa and the federal government. A weak economy and the waning of Trudeaumania yielded a Liberal minority government following the 1972 federal election. The New Democratic Party (NDP) under David Lewis agreed to support the new government in exchange for concessions such as the creation of Petro-Canada. Although Trudeau won a majority in 1974, inflation and other economic woes proved to be nearly intractable. Meanwhile, the Royal Canadian Mounted Police

LEFT | Crombie looks at several favourite caricatures that Duncan Macpherson drew of him in the 1970s.

RIGHT | Mayor David Crombie proposed a limit on the height of all new construction.

January 25/79

LEFT | As Rosedale's new Tory MP, Crombie learned that he was not allowed to speak about the possibility of negotiating any kind of deal with the separatist government recently elected in Quebec.

RIGHT | David Crombie's friend Jean Drapeau was another mayor whom Duncan Macpherson quite enjoyed lampooning, especially on the subject of the 1976 Olympic Games. Here Drapeau lights the torch for the games, an event that had an eventual price tag of $1.4 billion.

was found to have engaged in a number of illegal actions (break-ins, thefts, and the like) targeting the Parti Québécois, the FLQ, and others.

No wonder that by 1980 Macpherson was reaching the point of exhaustion.

Christina McCall Newman wrote the introduction to Macpherson's sixteenth annual collection of cartoons. In it, she observed: "His work ranges from Jimmy Carter and Menachem Begin to Aleksandr Solzhenitsyn and Fidel Castro. But for me, as a longtime observer of Canadian politics, his most telling drawings – the ones from which I derive the greatest pleasure and insight – are always his caricatures of our own politicians."

Based on my over fifty years of cartooning, I can attest that the closer to home a cartoon's subject matter is, the more strongly the reader reacts to it. Cartoons about the goings-on at city hall evoke a more visceral response from the local reader than even the most powerful condemnation of a far-off warlord. This is something Duncan Macpherson understood very well, so he devoted lots of "ink" to municipal politicians.

In the early 1970s, *Toronto Sun* columnist Gary Dunford christened David Crombie the "Tiny Perfect Mayor." The label stuck. Crombie, who is a popular figure in his downtown neighbourhood of St Lawrence Market, is still greeted with that nickname today. I recently met with Crombie to reminisce about his time as Toronto's mayor. He remembers many of the cartoons drawn of him, but Macpherson's in particular stood out. In his view, Duncan was at his peak in the 1970s.

Macpherson was quite interested in Crombie's proposed bylaw to limit the height of new buildings to 45 feet (13.7 metres), a measure that the mayor hoped would moderate development of the city's core. Although the overall height measure was overturned, Crombie did succeed in imposing restrictions in neighbourhoods whose culture and character were acknowledged as worthy of protection.

In 1978 David Crombie announced that he was making the move to federal politics. Mayor Jean Drapeau of Montreal called Crombie to warn him that he was making a dreadful mistake: "As mayor, you are an emperor." (Drapeau tended to think of himself as a benevolent dictator.) "As a federal politician, you will always have to watch what you say – and will always have to answer to someone." Drapeau wasn't wrong. Crombie served in Parliament from 1978 to 1988 (for several of those years as a high-profile cabinet minister) and ran for the leadership of the Progressive Conservative Party in 1983. However, he never achieved the presence in Ottawa that he had had as a popular mayor of Toronto.

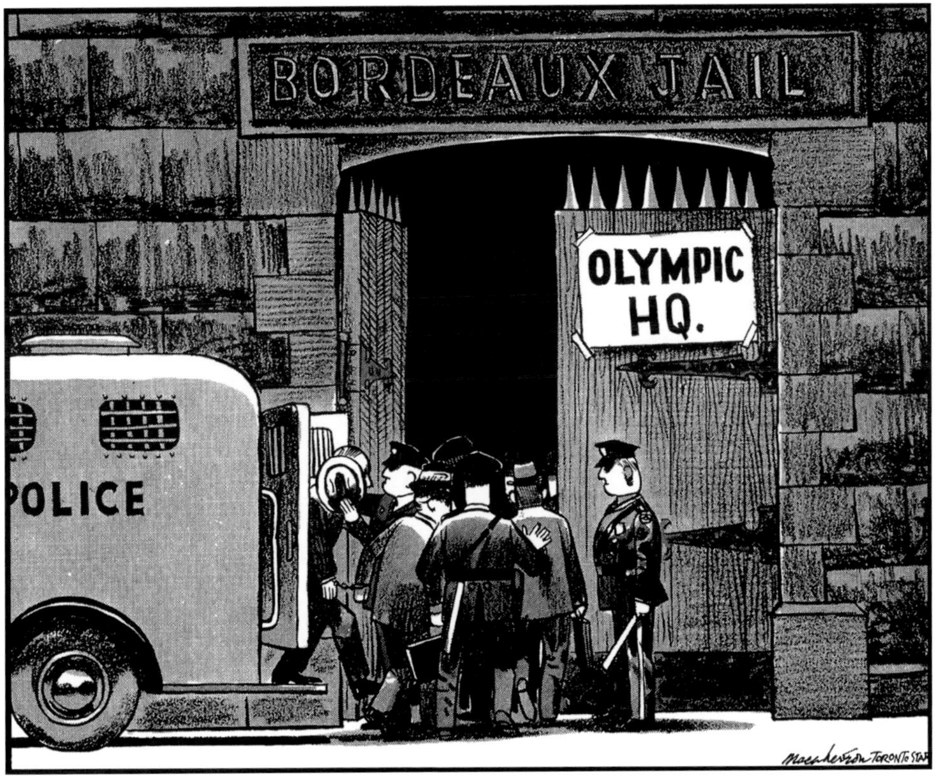

The Montreal Olympics were tarnished by a number of corruption scandals, prompting Macpherson to suggest new headquarters for the organizers.

Toronto baseball fans at a game in 1978 show what they think of "O Canada" being sung partly in French.

Macpherson felt that members of the provincial legislature didn't always take the problems of their constituents seriously.

This 1969 cartoon was Duncan Macpherson's most famous (and most cutting) on the subject of Ontario premier John Robarts, who initially opposed Medicare for the province. (He later changed his mind.)

Robarts's successor as premier was William Davis. (David Crombie told me about a conversation he had with the crafty Bill Davis in the early 1970s. Mayor Crombie wanted to move forward with a particular public-works project, but he knew that for political reasons the premier could not openly support the initiative. "Davis asked me how long it would take for me to finalize the project. 'About two years,' I said. 'OK,' Bill responded, 'I won't send anyone over to actually inspect the thing for, let's say, two years.'")

Federal NDP leader David Lewis supported the Liberals' minority government following the 1972 election. Macpherson portrays Lewis as Xaviera Hollander, the "Happy Hooker."

Mitchell Sharp – "Old Twinkletoes" – was minister of finance under Lester Pearson and secretary of state for external affairs under Pierre Trudeau. Once asked what he thought of political cartoons, Sharp responded: "They are something that is allowed in a democracy."

ROYAL CANADIAN AIR FORCE FLY-PAST.

Minister of Communications Gérard Pelletier outlines the qualifications for a new head of the CBC. Pelletier once told me that he loved all political cartoons, except for the ones in which he featured.

Even the price of food seems beyond reach.

IT BEATS HAULING WHEAT.

In 1975 Pierre Trudeau had an indoor pool and sauna installed at 24 Sussex Drive. This was particularly galling in view of the bitter postal strike over job security and technology later that year.

Always sympathetic to the plight of the everyday consumer, Macpherson imagined a group of women demonstrating over rising food prices.

THEY ATE THE MINISTER OF CONSUMER AFFAIRS!

Jean Chrétien was minister of finance from 1977 to 1979.

Trudeau's new finance minister, Donald "Thumper" Macdonald, introduced wage and price controls in the 1976 budget.

THE HALL OF FINANCE MINISTERS.

In 1976 the young Joe Clark was chosen by the Progressive Conservatives to replace Robert Stanfield as Opposition Leader.

C.L.A.R.K. ... CLAIMS TO BE THE LEADER OF THE OPPOSITION.

The Progressive Conservatives are elected in 1979 and Joe Clark becomes prime minister. What to do about those extravagant campaign promises?

Phil Esposito was key to Canada's victory in the 1972 Canada-Russia hockey series. A *Toronto Star* reader suggested to Macpherson that "Espo" could be our first "Italian" prime minister. As they were travelling home from Moscow, the *Star*'s Boris Spremo took this photo of Phil Esposito admiring Macpherson's cartoon.

European officiating seemed to favour the Soviet hockey teams.

"Black September" terrorists massacre eleven members of the Israeli delegation and a West German police officer at the 1972 Olympics in Munich.

The war in Vietnam draws to a close.

A beleaguered Richard Nixon, facing impeachment charges after his re-election to a second term in office.

HAH! MISSED!

Time was running out for Nixon. In 1974 he resigned to avoid impeachment, the only American president ever to do so.

As the United States celebrated its bicentennial, Macpherson portrayed accident-prone President Gerald Ford with his finger caught in the Liberty Bell. I love the look in Betty Ford's eyes.

U.S. President Jimmy Carter as a preacher hoping to solve the world's problems.

HEAL!

A partial meltdown at a nuclear reactor at Three Mile Island, Pennsylvania, in 1979 causes panic and mass evacuation of the area.

The insatiable American appetite.

OIL! OIL! OIL!

A joint USSR-U.S. space shuttle, docked in orbit over a divided world below.

THE WAILING WALL.

The (almost) monolithic face of world communism shows itself at a United Nations General Assembly gathering in 1977.

In 1974 there was widespread and endemic drought and starvation in Africa.

In May 1974 India tested its first nuclear weapons.

Caricatures that compare individuals to animals have always been a common tool of the trade. Here, for example, Duncan Macpherson draws Ugandan dictator Idi Amin as a big frog in a small pond.

Francisco Franco, Chiang Kai-shek, Zhou Enlai, Haile Selassie, and Mao Zedong … all these dictators see their time running out.

THE OLD SAW.

John G. McConnell (1912–74) was the president and publisher of the *Montreal Standard Magazine* for fifteen years before moving to the *Montreal Star* in 1953. He was an admirer and early supporter of Duncan Macpherson.

McConnell, a notoriously early riser, was always in his office at the *Star* by 8 a.m. One morning, he arrived to find a bedraggled Duncan Macpherson sitting in his anteroom. Macpherson explained that, after consuming too many drinks at the Toronto Press Club the night before, he had apparently made his way to Union Station and somehow managed to board the overnight train to Montreal. Awakening in his berth, Macpherson realized he had no money on his person. Could he borrow fifty dollars? McConnell obliged.

Despite being based in Toronto, Duncan eventually drew many more cartoons on the subject of Quebec politics than on the action at Queen's Park. Macpherson initially loved Quebec – Montreal in particular – and visited often, especially in the 1950s. When in Montreal, he would usually go to see his friend Dick Hersey, the *Standard*'s art director. Together they would repair to the Montreal Press Club, then housed in the centrally located Mount Royal Hotel. They could always count on finding journalist and illustrator friends there.

"There is a lot to see in Quebec, and one can see her faster than one can understand her," Macpherson wrote in his 1969 book, *Macpherson's Canada*. "I travelled by air over hundreds and hundreds of miles of virgin land; travelled by motor launch to small islands where

There is a lot to see in Quebec,
and one can see her faster
than one can understand her.

DUNCAN MACPHERSON

18

QUEBEC … AND RENÉ LÉVESQUE

communities spoke only French. I saw Indians playing lacrosse. I saw politicians, church leaders, painters, separatists, wood carvers, fishermen and bush pilots." He found it irritating to visit officials such as the premier of Quebec or the mayor of Montreal because of all the pomp and fuss. But then, on occasion, "the politician pictured in the terrible baroque frame of badly-stitched red velvet and chipped gilt turns out to be a warm and intelligent man who is actually interested in the ordinary person's welfare."

Over the course of his career, Macpherson was often assigned by his Toronto-based employers to travel to Quebec to cover cultural, political, and sporting events. During the 1965 Stanley Cup finals, *Star Weekly* magazine asked him to do some sketches in rival cities Montreal and Chicago. In the end, those drawings were published during the Stanley Cup finals the following year.

Duncan's sketches turned out to be some of the most dynamic he had ever done. In one, he captured rabid Chicago fans showering debris on the ice – including a dead fish. One woman in Chicago complained bitterly that he was drawing Canadiens goalie Gump Worsley rather than her favourite, Black Hawks goaltender Glenn Hall.

Macpherson had obtained written permission from NHL president Clarence Campbell to wander at will in both the Montreal and Chicago arenas during the finals. Hoping to enter the Habs' dressing room should they win the Cup, Macpherson showed Campbell's letter to Toe

LEFT | Wheelsman Robert Genest and Captain Émile Boelard guiding the Lévis–Quebec City ferry.

RIGHT | A Macpherson watercolour of a patron in a Lower Town tavern, Quebec City.

Blake, the gruff Canadiens' coach. Blake poked a finger into Macpherson's stomach and said that the only person who could grant him permission was the team's owner, Senator Hartland Molson. Blake then growled, "I don't think I'd let a sissy like you in the dressing room anyway!" Macpherson, who, at 210 pounds, looked a lot like heavyweight boxer Jack Dempsey, always loved that story.

But Duncan Macpherson wasn't the sort to give up. The Canadiens clinched the series at the Forum, and Macpherson saw his chance as Senator Molson escorted Prime Minister Lester Pearson through the crowd, clearly heading for the Habs' inner sanctum. "I fell into step as an uninvited and unofficial guest of the party." The guards just waved him through.

In the euphoric atmosphere of the Habs' dressing room, Macpherson found the players, "teeth out and underwear on," to be very down-to-earth men. He was struck by how quickly the bedlam in the dressing room quieted down when yesteryear's hero – Rocket Richard – walked into the room to congratulate the winners.

Macpherson had experienced quite a different mood in the province in October 1964. On a

LEFT | A watercolour sketch of Montreal mayor Jean Drapeau in his office.

RIGHT | An interpretation of 1965 Stanley Cup action between the Chicago Black Hawks and the Montreal Canadiens, an identifiable Bobby Hull in the foreground.

LEFT | Macpherson's sketch of the old Montreal Forum during the last game of the Stanley Cup finals, 1 May 1965.

RIGHT | The Habs' dressing room after their 1965 Stanley Cup victory.

visit to Canada, Queen Elizabeth had stopped in Quebec City. No one was prepared for the hostility that met her there. She was greeted by large crowds of booing separatists, who saw her as a symbol of British oppression. Many turned their back on the queen while chanting that she should go home. City police charged the crowds, nightsticks swinging. They arrested thirty-five people and injured six, including several bystanders who were there to cheer the queen. The day became known as "le samedi de la matraque," or Truncheon Saturday.

Macpherson was there, sketchbook in hand. "When the Queen appeared, there was so much speed and crowd movement, it was next to impossible to catalogue. The artist should pick out a spot illustration – as simple as a policeman with a truncheon chasing a demonstrator – to sum up the mood of the affair. The reaction, the unusual, unplanned human elements happen in the crowd."

During that same visit, Macpherson produced a series of insightful drawings of city streets, rooming houses, and amused youths watching events unfold on television. The original drawings are now held in Montreal's McCord Museum.

At the time, Macpherson had some sympathy for the demonstrators. "The young and educated French-Canadian is going about this social revolt in a different manner than say, the violence of Japanese youth, the U.S. Black Panthers or university Students for a Democratic Society. These confrontations seem constructive. I feel the youth of French Canada will be the philosophical backbone of Canada in the not too distant future."

Macpherson's prediction was borne out with the arrival in Ottawa of the newly elected "Three Wise Men" – Pierre Trudeau, Jean Marchand, and Gérard Pelletier – following the 1965 federal election. Prime Minister Lester Pearson had been concerned for some time about the growing separatist movement in Quebec, and believed these men could help stall its progress. He had helped persuade the three Quebec notables to run as Liberal candidates, and had found safe ridings for two of the three.

Macpherson's attitude began to shift subtly in 1967, Canada's centennial year. He happened to be in Rouyn, Quebec, watching television in a hotel dining room, when visiting French President Charles de Gaulle shouted, "Vive le

LEFT | Police in action against demonstrators during the queen's 1964 visit to Quebec City.

RIGHT | Quebec shows some reluctance about participating in the upcoming centenary celebrations.

THE PROBLEM IN TENDERING MY RESIGNATION IS ... I MIGHT NOT ACCEPT IT.

Québec libre!" from the balcony at Montreal City Hall.

Of all the international figures Macpherson drew, he was at his best with de Gaulle, whom he obviously disliked. In a 1970 cartoon, he showed de Gaulle in a typical haughty pose: "The problem with tendering my resignation is ... I might not accept it."

Over the next few years, Macpherson's opposition to Quebec nationalism began to harden. "A Canadian finds it difficult to describe his feelings about his own country – he really does. But they take it very hard when there is any questioning of their country. And I took the whole Quebec nationalist thing very hard." He acknowledged that nascent feelings of nationalism in Quebec may have had a legitimate basis, but he didn't believe that the way they were being expressed was rational. He felt personally affronted by the actions of the FLQ during the so-called October Crisis. Macpherson's disgust at the arrogance of the FLQ members charged in 1971 with kidnapping and murder comes through strongly in the sketches he did during the trial, and he felt great satisfaction at seeing the accused being held to account. At the same time, he had been embarrassed by Pierre Trudeau's invocation of the War Measures Act. Macpherson complained that the authorities were "arresting people without any evidence at all ... just holus-bolus, absolutely out of hand. Disgusting, with a lot of mistakes made."

Although the more violent expressions of Quebec nationalism died away, there was increased support for political action to achieve independence. One of the principal actors was René Lévesque (1922–87), a former minister in the government of Liberal Premier Jean Lesage.

Once Macpherson felt confident that he had grasped Lévesque's new political objectives as leader of the fledgling Parti Québécois, he began to draw him as a member of the 1792 Paris

NEXT!

René Lévesque defeats Robert Bourassa in the 1976 Quebec provincial election.

Commune. Lévesque's cartoon supporters wore battered top hats, tricolour rosettes, and wooden clogs. Although the historical references may have been lost on some of Macpherson's audience, they could not have misunderstood the cartoonist's view that separatism was an antiquated objective.

Just as eighteenth-century cartoonist James Gillray had expressed England's horror and incomprehension at the excesses of the French Revolution, so Macpherson conveyed the puzzlement and indignation of English Canada in the face of Quebec separatism. With the election of the Parti Québécois in 1976, he ramped up his criticism with a whole series of cartoons on the fledgling government as it flexed its separatist muscles.

Macpherson hammered away at Quebec nationalists right up until he announced his retirement from the *Toronto Star* in 1980. The debate wasn't over in Quebec, not by a long shot, but Duncan's anger had lost its edge and he wanted to move on to the pursuit of a lifelong dream.

SEPARATISM
QUEBEC
Macpherson TORONTO STAR

AIR SEPARATISTE.

Jacques Parizeau and René Lévesque plan a referendum on separation. This cartoon appeared in the *Toronto Star* on Saint-Jean-Baptiste Day, 1978.

René Lévesque delivers a speech to the National Press Club in Washington, DC, hoping for cooperation between the United States and an independent Quebec.

CANADA, NON. YANKEE DOLLARS, SI!

There were always suspicions that Radio-Canada, the French-language arm of the CBC, was sympathetic to the separatist cause.

IS THIS YOUR LITTLE BOY?

Macpherson imagined language informers at the Montreal Forum during a hockey game between the Habs and the detested Boston Bruins. Duncan's French captions were somewhat awkward – but he did his best!

This 1950s illustration for an article in *Maclean's* demonstrated Duncan Macpherson's lifelong love of boats and ships.

Even a cartoonist of Duncan Macpherson's stature eventually begins to tire. When he began his career, he had confidently described himself as belonging to the "elbow smash school of journalism." By the mid-1970s, his outlook had changed: "I'm at the stage now where I'm not a boat-rocker anymore."

"In the late seventies," he wrote, "I was getting very tired of working as an editorial cartoonist for a newspaper. It had become boring – and as far as the Canadian scene was concerned, I could not stand the repetitious meanderings of a rich dilettante named Pierre Trudeau." (After briefly being thrown out of office, Trudeau would return as prime minister.) In a telephone conversation with me at the time, Duncan said: "I can't stand drawing that goddamn Trudeau anymore. I'm quitting!"

Macpherson also attributed his decision to leave the newspaper to the appointment of George Radwanski as the *Star*'s editorial-page editor and later editor-in-chief. In his journal, Duncan wrote: "I think the decision to leave occurred when another Liberal midget, George Radwanski, a Trudeau freak and fellow traveller, became the editor of the *Star*. I couldn't stand the guy." (Radwanski later held various high-profile government posts in both Toronto and Ottawa. While serving as the federal privacy commissioner, he was involved in a controversy over his expenses. While he was cleared of criminal wrongdoing in 2009, the episode tarnished the last decade of his life.)

Given an opportunity, Macpherson had always liked to slip boats and water into his illustration

Canada, as clumsy as she is, means well.

FROM *MACPHERSON'S CANADA*

19

BOATS AND A YEARNING FOR CHANGE

REDNECK FALLS.

LEFT | A boy studies a model boat in a shop window, Saint John's, Newfoundland (from the book *Macpherson's Canada*).

work and cartoons. As his patience with the demands of editors and the pressures of cartooning wore thin, his longing to spend a lot more time actually being on the water and playing around with boats grew stronger.

By the time he was five years old, Duncan Macpherson had crossed and recrossed the Atlantic Ocean by boat. When he was an eighteen-year-old RCAF recruit, as we have seen, his passage from Halifax to Liverpool was aboard the *Louis Pasteur*, "a bathtub of a ship that rolled in absolutely calm waters." Returning from the war in Europe in 1946, he sailed on the *Queen Elizabeth* from Portsmouth to New York.

Where some people might have had enough of the sea by then, Duncan Macpherson had instead

developed a lifelong love affair with boats, ships, and open water. As a schoolboy, Duncan drew romanticized images of the sailing vessels used by early Canadian explorers. He also loved the intricate models built by a family friend. "I liked to watch Mr MacDonald building his model ships: great galleons, built to scale – and the farmhouse seemed to be full of light illuminating these ships."

Duncan Macpherson loved playing around with boats – he just didn't know how to run or maintain them properly. During his early days at the *Toronto Star*, his best friend was Bruce Palmer, the Toronto lawyer who had helped negotiate his groundbreaking contract with the newspaper. Palmer acquired a thirty-six-foot tugboat from a client in lieu of fees. Christened

LEFT | Duncan Macpherson, *Star* staffers Jack Brehl and Gerry Hall, and an unidentified acquaintance in a straw hat enjoying a day's cruise aboard the *SS Chiquita*.

RIGHT | A Macpherson sketch of the *Chiquita*.

RUB-A-DUB-DUB: THREE RUBS IN A TUB

A capital ship for a Great Lakes trip
Was Duncan's indomitable tug,
No gale that blew dismayed her crew
The three jolly rubs in a tub.
The man at the wheel was taught to feel
His way through the darkest night,
But it often appeared, when night had cleared
He had done something ~~less than~~ not quite right.

The captain sat in the cabin below
And drank what he could find
There was bubbly beer, so full of cheer
And booze to befoggle the mind.
Gerry the boatswain was apparently mad
For it was he who surrendered the wheel
And ~~he~~ who took command could scarcely stand
And knew not a Hall from a keel.

Composed of sand was the underwater land
Which claimed the tug so tight
And violent blue was the unpleasant hue
Of Duncan's speech that night.
They slept on the edge of the sandy ledge
All warmed by a glorious glow,
And the Royal ~~XXXXX~~ Yacht club rescued the tub
As the morning cock did crow.

And they all felt ill as mariners will
On a diet that's liquid and strong,
For they had no shaves on the rolling waves
As they brought no razors along.
With nautical pride they strode inside
The newsroom sharp at nine,
And with hands that shook, the news they took
(But without them the paper looked fine.)

Jack Brehl's poem about the infamous *Chiquita* incident.

the *Chiquita*, the scow had been built in 1933 by the city of Toronto and was used originally to tow garbage around the city's harbour.

Macpherson decided to become a partner in Palmer's tugboat venture so he could invite people out for cruises around the harbour and through the Toronto Islands. At one point, Macpherson even attempted to join the Royal Canadian Yacht Club. The white-clad membership committee hemmed and hawed – and then said no.

In a 1962 *Toronto Star* column, Pierre Berton described his first time stepping aboard the *Chiquita*: "a symphony of coiled ropes, half-filled crates and old beer cartons." They toured around the harbour, puttering along at eight knots, getting about two miles per gallon. Berton had some sailing experience and soon realized that Macpherson was operating with only the crudest understanding of nautical terminology, his directional vocabulary being limited to "front," "back," "left," and "right."

"It's tough enough operating this thing without learning a whole new language," Macpherson explained as he turned on the pumps. "Tugs are built to take on bilge. If you leave them alone, they'll fill right up and sink."

One morning the *Star* city desk called the police to say that Duncan Macpherson and two staffers – Gerry Hall and Jack Brehl – had gone out on the *Chiquita* the previous evening and were missing. Police quickly located the tug and the Yacht Club effected the rescue. Apparently the trio had been operating the boat for half an

The *Chiquita* plied the waters of Lake Simcoe for several more years until Macpherson tired of the novelty. He gave the boat to the owner of the Beaverton Marina in the early 1970s. As Ian Macpherson explained, "Dad liked to give things away. He didn't like to sell personal stuff." Macpherson once had a Peugeot that kept giving him trouble, so he gave that away too.

The *Chiquita* sank a few years later after running aground. Macpherson occasionally visited the site of his boat's demise.

In 1969 the *Toronto Star* published a striking book titled *Macpherson's Canada*. It was a boxed, hardcover collection of the watercolours, pastels, drawings, and notes that Duncan Macpherson had made over four consecutive summers travelling the country, through all ten provinces as well as the Yukon and Northwest Territories.

These drawings are very different from his political cartoons and reminiscent of his early

LEFT | Gigantic lock in the Trent-Severn waterway system.

BELOW | Kids gathering driftwood along the Trent River near Peterborough.

hour in the dark before realizing they hadn't moved. They were stuck on a sandbar all night.

Some years later, Duncan decided to move the tug to the family cottage at Beaverton on Lake Simcoe, north of Toronto. There was only one water route possible: east along the north shore of Lake Ontario to Trenton, then back westward through the whole Trent-Severn system and into the Kawartha region.

My God, I never saw so many kids in my life. They were all over the place in St. John's in Newfoundland, a lovely town: the artist's own caption for what would be the cover of *Macpherson's Canada*.

Donald LePan sketching schooner *Bluenose II*, Lunenburg, Nova Scotia.

magazine illustration work. Generally, he liked to sketch the everyday activities of Canadians: "sophisticates, cosmopolitans, yahoos, old craftsmen, new technologists." He was also fascinated by the landscapes he explored. Of the 200 drawings and paintings in the book, fully one-quarter depict boats, ships, and life on the water.

Macpherson's friend Jack Brehl wrote the text based on the numerous conversations they had had about the project. Some reviewers did not particularly like the book. "For all the book's charm, we were left with the impression that Macpherson the painter is not to be taken as seriously as Macpherson the cartoonist," huffed *Canadian Dimension* magazine. Nevertheless, *Macpherson's Canada* was a popular success and the collection of which Duncan seemed proudest. He had desperately wanted to get out of Toronto and to sketch the people he would meet as he travelled across Canada. "We are all contrast and all bickering, but all of us have one thing in common: this big, beautiful, lonely country."

In 1971 the *Toronto Star* moved from its old King Street building to a beautiful new waterfront location at One Yonge. Duncan Macpherson was provided with a spacious upper-floor studio with a view of his beloved Toronto Islands and Lake Ontario beyond. Right in front of the large window, he displayed a model of the Nova Scotia schooner *Bluenose*, complete with captain's spyglass, blueprints, and the chart of her final race. All of this had been furnished – in exchange for a few drawings – by a good friend, steak-house owner Harry Barberian.

Although it was some years before he made the move out of Toronto's noise and bustle, Duncan was already longing for a more tranquil, rural life. "In a cabin on the west coast of Vancouver Island," he wrote, "I found it hardest to work. It is a lotus existence that began to work on me. Many west coasters are somewhat languorous, but they do live a civilized pace and their outlook is simple and healthy."

Macpherson never lost his love of being on the water. His wife's favourite memory of her husband, even today, is her image of him sitting like a figurehead on the bow of his tugboat, as it

LEFT | Macpherson in his studio at the *Toronto Star*.

RIGHT | *Dry dock, Lévis, Quebec* (from *Macpherson's Canada*).

chugged, wheel lashed down, along the storm-tossed north shore of Lake Ontario.

Shortly after Duncan Macpherson left the *Toronto Star* in 1980, the newspaper donated 1,220 original Macpherson cartoons to the Public Archives of Canada, which mounted an exhibition in Ottawa and produced an attractive companion catalogue. At the launch, the cartoonist was swamped with people asking for his signature. "I should have brought a rubber stamp!" he laughed. In the end, though, Macpherson was not particularly pleased with either the exhibition or the catalogue. His personal copy has copious notes in which he took the editors to task for shoddy research. Furthermore, the people who had put together the exhibition and catalogue had chosen several innocuous cartoons as opposed to controversial drawings so as not to upset anyone. Even the cover drawing was of an atypically beaming Macpherson.

It may be that Duncan and Dorothy had been contemplating his retirement from the newspaper for some time. He had never relinquished the dream of becoming a "serious" artist and seems to have longed for public recognition far beyond the attention he had garnered as a cartoonist. "It had always been an ambition of mine to run an art gallery. So, with the transition out of the *Star*, I sold the family home on Blythwood and bought a two-floor building on Mount Pleasant, with an apartment upstairs for us to live in." It was a very attractive location. It also proved to be very costly.

I spoke to Duncan as he was getting ready to launch this new phase of his life. I congratulated him on the initiative and asked what sort of art he would be exhibiting. "My own, of course!" I then asked him what he would be calling the gallery. "Macpherson!" he responded, as though I were a blithering idiot for even asking.

He sold several cartoons and paintings in the first few optimistic months, then the market suddenly went flat. Sadly, Duncan was forced to close the gallery and sell the property. He and Dorothy then had another parting of the ways. The fact that Duncan had sold their house on Blythwood without consulting her may have played into her decision. This time, Dorothy stayed away for four years.

However disappointing, the failure of the gallery opened the door for Duncan to make his dream of small-town life a reality. He bought a bungalow in Beaverton, Ontario, the town in which he would spend the rest of his life. In the meantime, Dorothy Macpherson rented an

LEFT | *Toronto Star* president Martin Goodman and Duncan Macpherson look over the cartoons that were donated to the Public Archives of Canada in 1980.

RIGHT | The cover of the catalogue produced by the Public Archives in 1981.

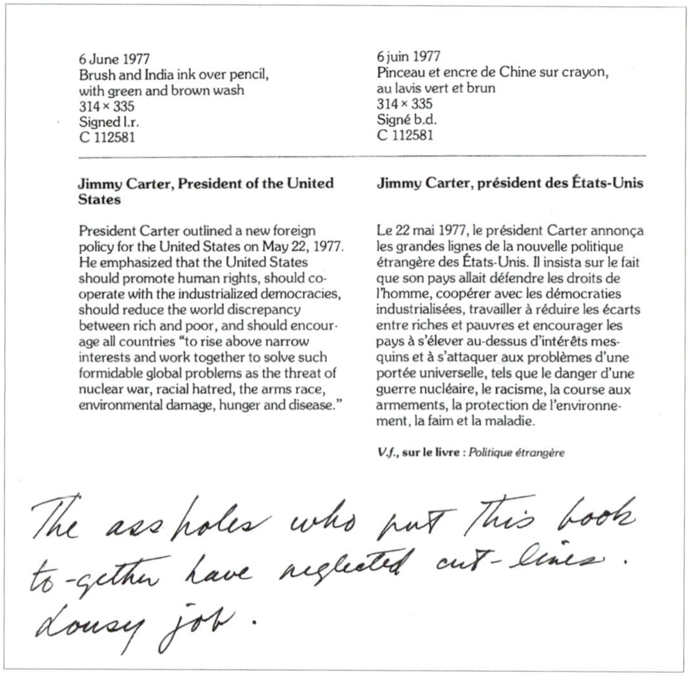
6 June 1977
Brush and India ink over pencil,
with green and brown wash
314 × 335
Signed l.r.
C 112581

6 juin 1977
Pinceau et encre de Chine sur crayon,
au lavis vert et brun
314 × 335
Signé b.d.
C 112581

Jimmy Carter, President of the United States

President Carter outlined a new foreign policy for the United States on May 22, 1977. He emphasized that the United States should promote human rights, should co-operate with the industrialized democracies, should reduce the world discrepancy between rich and poor, and should encourage all countries "to rise above narrow interests and work together to solve such formidable global problems as the threat of nuclear war, racial hatred, the arms race, environmental damage, hunger and disease."

Jimmy Carter, président des États-Unis

Le 22 mai 1977, le président Carter annonça les grandes lignes de la nouvelle politique étrangère des États-Unis. Il insista sur le fait que son pays allait défendre les droits de l'homme, coopérer avec les démocraties industrialisées, travailler à réduire les écarts entre riches et pauvres et encourager les pays à s'élever au-dessus d'intérêts mesquins et à s'attaquer aux problèmes d'une portée universelle, tels que le danger d'une guerre nucléaire, le racisme, la course aux armements, la protection de l'environnement, la faim et la maladie.

***V.f., sur le livre** : Politique étrangère*

The assholes who put this book to-gether have neglected cut-lines. Lousy job.

LEFT | A page from the catalogue. Even when being celebrated, Macpherson could be ornery.

RIGHT | *Vancouver Island* (from *Macpherson's Canada*).

apartment in downtown Toronto, across the street from Ian and his family.

The cartoonist John Larter came from the *Edmonton Journal* to the *Toronto Star* in 1982. To George Radwanski's credit, the not always popular editor hired Larter, who should have been a natural successor to Macpherson since he drew beautifully and consistently came up with clever, original ideas. Just as Macpherson was a master of drawing boats, Larter was unbeatable in his renderings of trucks, trains, and airplanes, and he produced exquisitely detailed caricatures. However, Larter was uncomfortable with life in Toronto. "I was always aware that I was way too far east for a prairie boy. In Toronto, licence plates, buses, and dirt all seemed to be the wrong colour. Homesickness took over and I headed back west to work for the *Calgary Sun* in 1989. In retrospect I should have stayed at the *Star*." He was probably right. So many Conservative-leaning newspapers got rid of talented people that the west gradually became a wasteland for cartoonists. Today, the only full-time cartoonist working west of Hamilton, Ontario, is Malcolm Mayes at the *Edmonton Journal*, traditionally a more Liberal newspaper than most out west.

Larter's only direct interaction with Macpherson was a twenty-minute chat when

Macpherson came back to the *Star* for a brief time. "I remember trying hard not to gush and blubber, what with him being the master cartoonist and me being a young nitwit. He seemed like a very friendly, nice old guy – much younger than I am today," said Larter recently.

Being the cartoonist who succeeded Macpherson was humbling in the extreme. As Larter said, "I remember sitting in the cafeteria downstairs at One Yonge Street, awaiting my interview. On the wall above the tables were hanging six-foot Macpherson cartoons. If you had any ego when you walked in, it was gone by the time you walked out. I still go limp just thinking about it."

Duncan still had to make ends meet. Within a year of closing the gallery, he was back freelancing for the *Toronto Star*. Over the next dozen years, he drew the occasional brilliant cartoon capturing the ethos of the Brian Mulroney and Bob Rae eras, but as he admitted, his heart wasn't always in it. After all, this was the period of his life in which he had imagined devoting all his energy to developing his reputation as a painter. At least he had escaped Toronto.

A watercolour by Mary Hughson of the short-lived Macpherson Art Gallery on Mount Pleasant Road in Toronto.

Aurora borealis, James Bay (from *Macpherson's Canada*).

John Larter's caricature of Macpherson fittingly shows Duncan holding a cartoonist's pen – but also a painter's brush and palette.

Macpherson watercolour of duelling clouds over Beaverton, Ontario.

20

BEAVERTON

No matter what, Dad was always an artist.

IAN MACPHERSON

Situated on the eastern shore of Lake Simcoe, Beaverton (pop. 2,822) is a little over an hour's drive north of Toronto, depending on traffic along the Don Valley Parkway. Boasting a small harbour and a yacht club, it is just a few kilometres south of the point at which the Trent-Severn waterway system connects with Lake Simcoe. The town is a friendly and popular destination for summer residents, tourists, boaters, and fishermen.

When Duncan Macpherson was courting Dorothy Blackhall in the late 1940s, he got to know the town since her family had spent summers there since the 1930s. Once they were married, the couple continued to vacation in the area. In 1971 Duncan bought a boathouse on Beaverton harbour, and it became the Macphersons' summer cottage. While Duncan painted, Dorothy got involved in community activities. Town authorities told Duncan that he couldn't use the small building as an art gallery, but he paid no attention.

Duncan also bought an A-frame building on Thorah Island, almost five kilometres across the water but within sight of Beaverton. The island had already attracted several well-known cottagers, such as Stephen Leacock and Mitchell Sharp. The problem was that Duncan's place was located on a boggy stretch, the tall grasses crawling with insects. Always inventive, he came up with a design for bird condos big enough to fit Canada geese, assuming that the birds would eat the bug-infested grasses. One local tradesman built the wooden "apartments," while another helpful resident installed the boxes on Thorah Island. Duncan even created a new logo for his gallery incorporating a Canada goose.

A summer drawing for the *Toronto Star*.

All that was left to do was sign up the avian tenants. Ian Macpherson remembers driving to the University of Guelph with his Dad to pick up half-a-dozen Canada geese. The problem was that there was no barrier to keep the birds in the back of the station wagon, so the geese pecked at their necks all the way back to Beaverton, and of course left plentiful smelly deposits on the floor. Wrangling the geese from the station wagon to the boat, and then onto the island, must have been quite an adventure. Once released, the geese took a quiet look around, and Duncan went home. When he checked on the birds the next morning, they were all gone. As is their nature, the geese had probably returned to Guelph.

"Your father was often right," Dorothy said to Ian. "But when he was wrong, he was terribly wrong!"

In 1980 Duncan moved permanently to Beaverton because he wanted a slower pace of life than he had found in Toronto. That yearning to be immersed in the rhythms of small-town life comes through particularly strongly in his 1969 book *Macpherson's Canada*.

John Stabback, a long-time Beaverton resident and retired general contractor, describes his hometown this way: "Beaverton is your basic, average, no-nonsense Canadian town with an arena, a curling rink, a small library, a pub, and more recently a Tim Horton's. That's about it." When Stabback was a very young man, he travelled the world, but by the time he was twenty-six, he was back in Beaverton, trying to figure out how to make a living. In 1981 he bought a small harbour restaurant called "Skippers Snack Bar." He recalls his first encounters with Duncan Macpherson. "A big fellow started dropping in every afternoon. He'd sit by himself with his newspaper. Coffee was forty cents. He'd leave fifty. After a while, we got to chatting about places I'd travelled to in the world. Because I was so

young, I don't think he quite believed me at first, so he really grilled me about my travels. It turned out that we had been to many of the same places."

"For the longest time," said Stabback, "I didn't know who this guy was, until someone said that he drew cartoons for the *Toronto Star*. He just seemed like a nice guy who knew a lot about the world. He may even have liked me because John Diefenbaker and I shared the same birthday, if not the same birth year!"

Stabback did occasional work at Macpherson's home on Riverdale Drive and helped Duncan in other ways too. "He was having an exhibition somewhere out of town, and asked if I would help load his car. He offered me money, but I wouldn't take it. Later, Duncan showed up at the restaurant with a tube, insisting that I take it. Inside was a great colour painting of Pierre Trudeau on a trip out west somewhere, dancing with a woman, while a Mountie looked on. I framed the painting and still have it today."

John Stabback takes some pride in the fact that Beaverton is home to the Strand Theatre, one of the first cinemas to be established in rural Ontario. For the town's sesquicentennial celebrations in 2009, the theatre displayed large images of famous residents, including NHL broadcaster Foster Hewitt and Duncan Macpherson.

The Hewitts and the Macphersons were not on the best of terms after Dorothy's father, Chester Blackhall, and Foster Hewitt got into a

LEFT | A new Macpherson logo.

RIGHT | The Boathouse Gallery.

"disagreement." The notoriously grumpy Foster Hewitt, then a summer resident, had loudly complained once too often about local children running across his property. Chester, a physically imposing figure, gave Foster a bit of a shellacking in a scene right out of a Stephen Leacock story.

By the time he moved to Beaverton, Duncan was finding it more and more difficult to get around. He eventually got a hip replacement in Toronto in 1985. True to form, he convinced a fellow patient to sneak off with him to the Press Club for a drink or three before surgery. Since he wouldn't be able to manage on his own during convalescence, Dorothy agreed to move to Beaverton to look after him. She would remain with him for the rest of his life. Duncan bought a larger house with a backyard that Dorothy loved because its lawn stretched down to the Beaver River.

In Beaverton, Macpherson found the time and the motivation to get more organized. He arranged for a large collection of his cartoons to be properly housed in one accessible location by selling a number of his originals to the Public Archives of Canada, adding to the 1,220 Macpherson drawings the *Toronto Star* had already donated.

Out of financial necessity, Macpherson had returned to drawing a cartoon or two a week for the *Toronto Star*. One other project held out great promise. CTV started a personality-focused television show that would display gigantic Macpherson caricatures of the invited guests.

LEFT | Macpherson's boathouse studio with a view of Thorah Island in the distance.

RIGHT | John Stabback, outside the harbourfront restaurant he once owned, proudly displaying his Duncan Macpherson cartoon.

For this, he would be paid the unheard-of sum of $2,000 per caricature. Unfortunately, after several broadcasts, the show folded.

The move to Beaverton also finally provided Macpherson with the right environment to explore his talents as a painter and to indulge his love of local subject matter. He did a series on the old steamboats of Lake Simcoe, which had been locally built in the 1830s.

Other subjects included the rolling hills of the Kawarthas, the Trent Canal, and Lake Dalrymple. Duncan also painted six large acrylics of mythological Scottish heroes. These paintings, as noted earlier, now hang in Beaverton's public library.

Although Duncan was by now well established in Beaverton, many of the locals were still not sure what to make of him. An unnamed reporter for the local *Express Gleaner Sun* was asked to write a story on the local celebrity in 1985: "When I phoned Duncan Macpherson, I was a little nervous. Whenever I asked people in Beaverton about him, they tended to fret over their words and come up with something like: 'Well, he's a very private man.' I found these halting responses puzzling, and I was never sure if they were guarding his privacy or trying to tell me that one of the world's most respected editorial cartoonists also happened to be an axe murderer."

Duncan told the reporter that he could see why an interview might be good for the newspaper. "Why don't you come over for coffee and we'll talk about it?" he suggested. In the end, the reporter got a very good interview, including some unique observations from Duncan on his cartoon work.

The homemade studio behind the Macpherson home where Duncan did most of his work during the 1980s.

"Verbally, I'll speechify all over the map," said Macpherson, "but when I draw, I edit it right down to the bone. It's a completely different process. I sit up in the stands and give them all the raspberry. I sure as hell don't come up with any constructive solutions. Look at Joe Clark. He can't use a knife and fork properly. If he uses a spoon, he misses his mouth. If you're a cartoonist, you have to use that."

As a young man, Duncan was mesmerized by a large portrait that hung in the home of his model-boat-building neighbour, Mr MacDonald.

A wall of fame in Beaverton, Ontario.

(The portrait showed MacDonald's wife.) Duncan spent hours studying the brush strokes. Through all his years as an illustrator and caricaturist, he never lost sight of his dream of becoming a successful painter and portraitist.

In the late 1980s, Macpherson was commissioned to paint formal portraits of Canada's sitting Supreme Court judges. All the portraits contained some element of caricature – Duncan just couldn't help himself. In the case of Justice Bertha Wilson, he added an Adam and Eve teapot, a reference to her status as a feminist. While it was reported that Bertha Wilson thoroughly enjoyed her portrait, other justices reserved judgment, at least publicly.

Bob Church was a newsman at radio stations CFRB and CHUM in Toronto in the 1970s. He got to know Macpherson fairly well since they both frequented the Press Club. Church was quite interested in art and in learning how to draw. Macpherson saw some of his work and encouraged him to attend the Ontario College of Art. He also had some of Church's art in his possession. In 1988 Church moved to North Street in Beaverton and was delighted to discover that he was living just around the corner from the Macphersons. When Duncan and Dorothy moved to another home on Riverdale Road that backed on the Beaver River, Church considered buying the house they had left behind. "Instead, Macpherson sold the place to the nice Greek lady who owned the fish-and-chips shop in town, while I found another location on the lake very close to Foster Hewitt's place. It was in the old house, in the studio out back, that I first saw Duncan's portrait of Prime Minister Trudeau – a large acrylic – hanging upside down, as it hadn't been officially commissioned. That was Duncan's humour." The portrait finally found a home in the law library of the University of Toronto.

As Macpherson continued to develop his skills as a portraitist, he experimented with strong colours, setting his subjects in arresting compositions. A fine example is his painting of Margaret Atwood, in which he gave his subject gleaming Asiatic eyes. Atwood had agreed to sit for him at a studio in the Ontario College of Art – in return, she asked for one of his watercolours. As *Toronto Star* journalist Peter Goddard observed after Macpherson's death: "His large-scale portrait of Margaret Atwood is overwhelmed with colour, as if he couldn't resist going chromatically over-the-top after all the fine line work in black ink." Bob Church said that he first saw the Atwood portrait in the basement of the Macphersons' house on Riverdale. "I won't forget his telling me he had trouble painting the hands, until it hit upon him to paint them larger – and it worked."

Macpherson also did a portrait of his grandson, Andrew, who was the delight of Duncan's later years. (He was given strict instructions by Dorothy and Ian that he was not to drink when Andrew was visiting. For once, Duncan listened.) I can see an intriguing combination of influences in the face in the portrait: hints of both Norman Rockwell and the Dutch master Pieter Bruegel. (Although Duncan admired the work of Leonardo da Vinci, he preferred the impishness of Bruegel.) When I examine the lower section of the painting, I see that Duncan has given the child the stretched-out hands of El Greco.

While Duncan Macpherson was everywhere praised as a brilliant cartoonist, he was generally dismissed as only a passable painter, a "mere illustrator." I believe that judgment should be re-examined.

Bob Church remembers the entrance hall of Macpherson's house in Beaverton being lined with cloud studies: "bright, cheerful oil paintings, as I recall." Indeed, during the last years of his life, Duncan closely studied clouds with his painter's eye and gave them a prominent place in many of his paintings. In his 2008 article for the *Toronto Star*, Peter Goddard observed of Macpherson: "When not toiling away for the *Star* – where one hallway is lined with better-known Macpherson cartoons – he painted around the Lake Simcoe area in an almost naïf manner, bringing to his boat harbours an almost toy-like quality, perhaps as a reflection of his never-ending delight in sailing. Whenever Duncan disappeared from his studio, he would inevitably end up in his backyard, just sitting and looking – not talking."

All the cartoonists I know – the good ones anyway – are able to disappear into themselves to focus only on what is right in front of them. Most cartoonists' partners get used to it: the silent introspection when the wheels are turning. This blocking out of the world is probably true of many creative people, but I've certainly heard a number of cartoonists' spouses and partners share anecdotes about "the absent look." Ian Macpherson says that his mother never really got used to these mental absences, and found her husband a bit of a puzzle.

Caricature studies of Marshall McLuhan for CTV.

The historic Lake Simcoe steamboat, *Ogemah*.

In late 1992 Macpherson went to the doctor, complaining of pain in the hip that hadn't been replaced. The doctor ordered a battery of tests. When he and Dorothy returned to get the results, they were told Duncan had terminal pancreatic cancer. There was a long silence. Then Duncan said, "OK – but what about the hip?"

Lynn Johnston, creator of the internationally distributed comic strip *For Better or for Worse*, is Canada's best-known comic-strip artist. When Johnston lived in North Bay, Ontario, she became friends with Inez Ross, who was a family friend of the Macphersons. Johnston had always admired Macpherson's work, and when she heard from Inez that he was ill, she sent him a hand-drawn caricature of himself to wish him well. It was one of the last things Macpherson saw before he died. He had always admired *For Better or for Worse* and respected Johnston for having stayed in Canada rather than moving to the United States when she became successful. He told his sister that the drawing was quite a good likeness but that his front teeth were too big. She said that was a bit rich, coming from the master of exaggerated noses and ears. Macpherson just smiled.

Duncan Macpherson died in his sleep, at home in Beaverton, on 3 May 1993, with his wife and son by his side. He was sixty-eight years old.

The day after Duncan died, Peter Gzowski, the host of CBC's *Morningside*, recalled a day in October 1978 when the two men had researched topless bars in the seedy west side of downtown Toronto, research that resulted in a Macpherson cartoon. "He was as much an artist as a cartoonist," Gzowski told his listeners, "and his death at sixty-eight from cancer leaves a void."

Duncan's funeral was held at the historic Old Stone Church in Beaverton, five days after his death. His friend, the *Star*'s Tom Harpur – who was an ordained Anglican priest though a very unorthodox Christian – seemed the right person to speak at the funeral. Duncan was cremated and his ashes scattered off the point of his beloved Thorah Island.

A wake attended by Macpherson's friends and associates was held by the Toronto Press Club on 14 May 1993. According to reports, there were no fights.

A painting of the Kawartha Hills.

A careful portrait of Pierre Trudeau.

Macpherson's caricatured portraits of Canada's Supreme Court judges.

A striking portrait of author Margaret Atwood.

Portrait of grandson Andrew Macpherson, with pencil (and amazing hands).

"For Better or For Worse" cartoonist Lynn Johnston was in touch with Duncan Macpherson just before his death.

A final painting of water by Duncan Macpherson.

A photo of Duncan Macpherson, still laughing – and still defiantly smoking.

Ronald Reagan proposed fast-tracking free-trade negotiations.

The 1980s were marked by momentous shifts in the international world order. U.S. President Ronald Reagan (in office from 1981 to 1989) dominated the decade, changing his country and the world. His sweeping new domestic initiatives (like so-called "Reaganomics" and the war on drugs) were key elements of his first term. He also followed a policy of "peace through strength" on the international stage, which led to confrontations with Russian Premier Leonid Brezhnev, who died early in Reagan's presidency. (Brezhnev was quickly succeeded by Yuri Andropov, who lasted in office until 1985, when Mikhail Gorbachev came to power.) Re-elected for a second term, the fervently anti-Communist Reagan oversaw a massive build-up of the U.S. military, the invasion of Grenada, and the Iran-Contra affair. He eventually sought to establish closer relations with Soviet leader Mikhail Gorbachev, whose policies of *perestroika* and *glasnost* offered hope of a safer world. The Berlin Wall came down ten months after the end of Reagan's second term. Reagan's successor, George H.W. Bush (in office from 1989 to 1993), pursued more aggressive policies in the Middle East, leading to war with Iraq (the "Gulf War").

Meanwhile, federal-provincial affairs remained high on the agenda for Canadian politicians – and cartoonists.

In 1985 Ottawa cartoonist Guy Badeaux (whose pen name is Bado) published the first *Portfoolio*, an annual collection of Canadian cartoons. For the inaugural issue, Guy showcased the work of forty-two popular and talented

Let's hope Macpherson will soon be back on the battlefield.

ROBERT LAPALME

21

CARTOON PORTFOLIO, 1981–92

ABOVE | Macpherson's work was included in this book, along with drawings by many other cartoonists he had influenced.

RIGHT | This May 1985 Macpherson cartoon posited that René Lévesque's political career was coming to an end. Lévesque resigned as leader of the Parti Québécois just one month later.

cartoonists from across the country. In part thanks to Duncan Macpherson, it was a boom time for cartooning in Canada. (The decades since have not been so kind.) The forward to the 1985 *Portfoolio* was written by René Lévesque, who had retired from politics earlier that year.

Lévesque appreciated the power of a "properly targeted" caricature. He wrote that "a well-aimed cartoon is easily worth more than its weight in editorials, whose authors, to quote André Laurendeau [editor-in-chief of *Le Devoir*], all too often force us 'to drink their prose to the dregs.'"

Gerald Bouey, the governor of the Bank of Canada, guided the country's monetary policy through the difficult inflationary period of the early 1980s.

Pre-eminent Quebec cartoonist Robert LaPalme, who had long considered Macpherson to be one of the best cartoonists in the world, was surprised and disappointed when Duncan announced his retirement from the *Toronto Star* in 1980. LaPalme expressed himself rather sarcastically: "Macpherson, fed up with glory, retired in February to become Miss Rosalie Tuttlebolt, competitor in the daisy field of watercolor painting. Let's hope he will soon be back on the battlefield."

LaPalme got his wish. Just a year after Duncan's retirement, the *Toronto Star* trumpeted his return. "Canada's best editorial cartoonist is back! Effective immediately, Duncan will produce two editorial cartoons per week." And that is exactly what he did for the next eleven years.

Macpherson was happily living in semi-retirement in Beaverton, away from the stimulation of the newsroom – and secretly longing to paint rather than cartoon – but he could still drill a fastball at a deserving target. Two of his favourite subjects from the 1970s – René Lévesque and Pierre Trudeau – left political life in the mid-1980s. They were replaced in office, and on Macpherson's drawing board, by Robert Bourassa and Brian Mulroney. Duncan's lampooning of Mulroney was especially powerful when he attacked elements of the Progressive Conservative platform, such as the free-trade agreement with the United States and the Meech Lake Accord.

Robert Bourassa had been defeated in dramatic fashion in Quebec's 1976 general election, losing to Lévesque's Parti Québécois. The only person to call him to commiserate was Brian Mulroney, who had lost his bid to become leader of the federal Progressive Conservatives earlier that year. Bourassa never forgot the gesture, and the two developed a close personal friendship. Mulroney became prime minister in 1984, and Bourassa Quebec's premier in 1985. Together they dominated the Canadian political landscape for the next eight years.

This third portfolio of Macpherson cartoons contains my selection of the most striking and effective examples of Duncan's work during his final eleven years as a caricaturist.

The Canadian government stepped up its presence in London as negotiations over the patriation of the British North America Act intensified.

Most of Canada's premiers were delighted with Pierre Trudeau's 1982 patriation of the constitution.

Although the Charter of Rights and Freedoms came into force in 1982, there were still pressing rights issues to be addressed, especially among the First Nations.

The Tories boldly promised change in government but were a little vague on actual policy.

Canada was hungry for change. Wherever they travelled, fluently bilingual Brian Mulroney and his wife, Mila, charmed Canadians. Mulroney was elected prime minister in 1984 with the largest majority in Canadian history.

The wily Dalton Camp came back, acting as Brian Mulroney's backroom strategist. Mulroney once said of Camp that he was witty, thoughtful, and someone who could make Mulroney feel better just by the sound of his voice.

Liberal leader John Turner dances up a storm with Liberal stalwart Iona Campagnolo at a rally in British Columbia.

Brian Mulroney appointed senior civil servant Simon Reisman to be Canada's chief negotiator during the Canada-U.S. free-trade talks.

The Yukon and Northwest Territories were largely shut out of free-trade negotiations.

Mulroney's free-trade deal with the Americans went against long-standing Conservative values.

Many Canadians worried that Canada had lost its cultural sovereignty as a result of the Free Trade Agreement with the United States.

Mulroney's best efforts to bring the provincial premiers into line over the Meech Lake Accord ultimately failed. Surprisingly, it was Newfoundland and Manitoba that scuttled the deal, not Quebec.

Mulroney also had a hard time "selling" his proposed 9 per cent goods and services tax. Eventually the GST was imposed, but at a reduced rate of 7 per cent. While the move was highly unpopular at the time, it probably saved the country from bankruptcy.

Several unpopular policy initiatives, combined with a scandal or two, sent Mulroney's popularity plummeting. A cabinet shuffle failed to reverse the trend. Mulroney resigned in February 1993.

Macpherson drew this cover for the *Maclean's* issue of 16 March 1981, the week of an Ontario provincial election. NDP leader Michael Cassidy, Liberal leader Stuart Smith, and long-time Tory leader Bill Davis were caricatured. No surprises – Davis won. Again.

Indeed, Bill Davis seemed to have the safest political sinecure in all of Canada.

After Davis's retirement, Ontario voted in Liberal David Peterson, followed, astonishingly enough, by NDP leader Bob Rae.

The recession forced Rae's government to backtrack on several campaign promises. The NDP began to sink perilously low in the polls.

Despite sterling leadership from Ed Broadbent, the national New Democratic Party was stuck in a distant third place in the polls through most of the 1980s.

Ronald Reagan, the fortieth president of the United States, as seen by Duncan Macpherson. Tension was high as the key players bluffed and postured their way through the Cold War.

Tensions eased after Mikhail Gorbachev took charge of the Soviet Union. This is Macpherson's take on *glasnost* and the likely reaction by the Soviet Politburo.

The Western world grew increasingly excited at the possibility that the Cold War might be over.

Macpherson's prediction as to the first victim of the Gulf War (Operation Desert Storm). The campaign quickly became a propaganda-driven media circus.

In 1988, during his run for the U.S. presidency, George H.W. Bush had famously said, "Read my lips. No new taxes." Of course, he eventually did raise taxes. Macpherson used the same visual image to comment on other American policy quagmires.

The Library and Archives Canada Preservation Centre in Gatineau is home to over 2,500 Duncan Macpherson originals.

Writing a book is an adventure. To begin with it is a toy and an amusement. Then it becomes a mistress, then it becomes a master, then it becomes a tyrant. The last phase is that just as you are about to be reconciled to your servitude, you kill the monster and fling him to the public.

WINSTON CHURCHILL

22

ACKNOWLEDGMENTS

In this day and age, why write a book? Well, I suspect that a hundred years from now, electronic versions of images as we presently store them – jpegs, tiffs, and so on – may no longer even exist. I would hope, though, that on a dusty shelf somewhere, this actual book might be available to someone curious about twentieth-century satire in general, and Duncan Macpherson in particular.

The truth is, I simply wanted to write this book and, as it turns out, many others were hoping for the same. Of the several hundred people with whom I talked about Duncan, all were keen to see me do this. Therefore, some acknowledgments are called for.

THE FAMILY

After Duncan's death, Dorothy Macpherson stayed on in Beaverton, volunteering with a wide range of organizations dedicated to the betterment of the community. One resident described Dorothy as "going above and beyond ... a common fixture at many public events as a volunteer, participant or spectator. She has an unmistakable laugh and energy that make most everyone she meets take note of her opinion, her presence, and her generosity."

Dorothy was the driving force behind the restoration and relocation of the historic Beaverton Jail, a project that had not found favour with local authorities because of its cost. Dorothy was persistent and raised the money needed. It seems Duncan wasn't the only Macpherson who could ruffle feathers. In 2010 she was presented with the Harold Lodwick Citizenship award at the

The idea for this book was hatched over a lunch at the Belsize Public House in Toronto on 12 May 2018. In attendance were Christian Vachon of Montreal's McCord Museum, Ian Macpherson, Dorothy Macpherson, Terry Mosher, and the president of the Association of Canadian Editorial Cartoonists, Wes Tyrell.

opening ceremonies of the village's Canada Day celebrations.

The following year, Dorothy Macpherson moved to a retirement home in the Davisville Village section of Toronto, where she still resides as of this writing. She held onto a great deal of Macphersonalia in the form of drawings and paintings, as well as business and personal papers. Dorothy and her son, Ian, generously allowed me to delve into the personal papers. They were absolutely invaluable in helping me to understand – and write about – Duncan in a way that would otherwise have been impossible.

Ian Macpherson inherited his father's athletic and artistic abilities – and his lack of enthusiasm for school. The 6'4" Ian was an all-star football player for the University of Ottawa and played for a year with the Hamilton Tiger Cats. He taught art for nineteen years at Central Technical School in Toronto. Semi-retired today, Ian keeps fit through his work as a personal trainer. He studies classical drawing and painting techniques, just as his father had always urged.

Ian Macpherson is proud of his father's achievements and was enormously helpful as I was conducting research for this book. Looking through the material with me often prompted Ian to relate stories about his father, which he did in a very candid way. Together we also visited many of Duncan's haunts in Toronto, Bolton, Uxbridge, and Beaverton. Ian and I will continue to collaborate on finding a suitable home for Duncan Macpherson's remaining memorabilia – and establishing more of a Macpherson cartoon presence online. Ian plans to monitor a website showcasing his father's immense talent at www.macphersoncartoons.ca

Ian and I visited with Fiona Williams in December 2018. After several hours of conversation, I came away with a deeper understanding

of Duncan's childhood and the early years of his career. I also realized that a wicked sense of humour and a keen satirical eye were traits shared by brother and sister. I was grateful for the brief time I had with her; Fiona passed away in July 2019.

Inez Ross, now of North Bay, was a good friend of Fiona's, and she was able to help me understand the Macphersons' post-war lives. Inez had boarded with "Mrs Mac," Duncan's mother, for a year or so. She told me wonderful stories of the goings-on in the girls' group of friends. It was also Inez who made me aware of the letter and drawing that Lynn Johnston sent Duncan just before his death.

THE TEAM

Going through all the information on Duncan was like sorting out the pieces of a gigantic jigsaw puzzle. I couldn't have done this major sifting of material without the help and advice of my wife, Mary Hughson, and her sister, Janet Hughson. As with all my recent books – this is my fifty-first – Mary, who is an excellent graphic designer, prepared the images for the entire project before I handed it to the publisher.

Janet Hughson, an exceptional editor, is a retired civil servant living in Ottawa. She has edited almost all my written material over the past dozen years, including my own memoir, published in 2017, *From Trudeau to Trudeau: Fifty Years of Aislin Cartoons*. I sometimes say I ask her to blue-pencil my to-do lists. Janet reviewed and polished the first draft of this book before it was passed to McGill-Queen's University Press.

I have crossed paths with publisher and author Anna Porter at several key points in my professional life. It was Anna who, in 1979, greenlighted the publication by McClelland and Stewart of *The Hecklers*, a history of Canadian political cartooning co-authored by Peter Desbarats and me. (There is a plan afoot to update that history to

LEFT | Ian Macpherson accepts his father's posthumous election to the Canadian Cartoonists' Hall of Fame in 2018.

ABOVE | Fiona Williams, Duncan Macpherson's sister, proudly displays the original of her brother's most famous cartoon.

ABOVE | Mary and Janet Hughson.

RIGHT | Jean Chrétien, Anna Porter, and Terry Mosher.

include the many talented Canadian cartoonists working today.)

In the autumn of 2018, Anna Porter and I appeared at a literary event in Montreal with former Prime Minister Jean Chrétien, each of us promoting a new book. When we had a moment to chat, I mentioned to Anna that I had intentions of producing a biography of Duncan Macpherson. She insisted – as she is wont to do – that I get in touch with Philip Cercone at McGill-Queen's University Press (MQUP). So I did. At our very first meeting, Philip agreed to publish the book and suggested that we fast-track the project and complete it within ten months – hypersonic speed for an academic publisher.

Cercone asked me which editor at MQUP should oversee the project. Without hesitation, I asked for the brilliant poet and author Mark Abley, since we had worked together for years at the *Montreal Gazette*. (While at the *Gazette*, Abley produced the best books section in Canada.) Thank you, Philip, for making Mark available.

THE *TORONTO STAR*

My association with John Honderich, former publisher, editor, and chief bottlewasher at the *Toronto Star*, goes way back. We often refer to our small group of old newspapermen as the Last of the Mohicans. John was the first person to whom I spoke after confirming my agreement with MQUP. It was obvious to me that without the cooperation of the *Toronto Star*, which holds the rights to so much Macpherson material, the book could never become a reality.

Fortunately, Honderich is the chair of the *Toronto Star*'s Board of Directors, and a real Macpherson fan. He offered me any material that I might need from the *Star*, without asking to exercise any control over the content of the book. I truly appreciate his confidence in me. (I know that the lunch I bought him – on behalf of MQUP – at Biff's restaurant on Front Street had nothing to do with it.)

On 25 April 1993 the *Toronto Star* published a special piece by Jack Brehl to celebrate Duncan Macpherson's retirement after thirty-five years. Duncan died barely a week later. It is a wonderful tribute, an amalgam of so much that had been written about Duncan by many other writers over the years.

Of all Duncan's associates at the *Star*, Brehl seemed to be his closest ally. The seven Brehl children remember Duncan and Dorothy coming to visit their parents quite often. As noted earlier, Brehl wrote copy for Duncan's books and travel pieces; they shared a love of a drink or three while on the road.

Brehl was born in Washington, Pennsylvania, and attended Notre Dame before moving full-time to Toronto in 1948. He often recalled that Duncan would gleefully introduce him as a Yankee during their trip to Cuba. Brehl got even. The unilingual Duncan wanted to learn a proper Spanish "hello," so Jack summoned up his schoolboy phrases and taught Duncan a greeting that referred impolitely to the hearer's mother. The first time he used it, Macpherson got a punch in the nose. It was that kind of friendship.

LEFT | A 1991 Aislin caricature of *Toronto Starr* editor John Honderich.

ABOVE | *Toronto Star* writer and Duncan Macpherson pal, John "Jack" Brehl.

ABOVE | A photo of George Gamester back in the day. Is it any wonder that he was always being carded?

BELOW | Astrid Lange, head librarian at the *Toronto Star*.

RIGHT | Andrew Phillips makes an interesting discovery.

Of course, Duncan knew and worked with many other people at the *Star*. Where possible, they have been mentioned in the appropriate chapters. George Gamester, who wrote for the *Star* from the mid-1960s through to 2005, seems to have the clearest memories of Macpherson's time at the newspaper. I showed him a lot of my material and am grateful for his anecdotes and fact checking. It occurs to me that George's excellent recall may be due to the fact that he didn't drink quite as much as the others – and he always held the coats.

I must also thank Astrid Lange at the *Toronto Star* library for her extraordinary efforts in chasing down material on Duncan and his time at the paper. Astrid's determination led to a wonderful discovery. Andrew Phillips, an old friend of mine, is the current editorial-page editor at the *Star*. One day, he overheard Astrid and me talking earnestly about some aspect of the Macpherson cartoons that still hang on the walls of the *Toronto Star*. Andrew asked, "Are you familiar with the closet?"

"What closet?" Astrid and I asked.

Here's the "secret" Andrew knew: off a little-known men's washroom on the fifth floor of the building is a small, unlocked room in which were stored hundreds of Duncan Macpherson originals!

Astrid didn't really want to poke around in the men's bathroom, but she immediately made arrangements with the maintenance department, as well as Ed Cassavoy and the good folks at the Toronto Star Syndicate, to have the drawings removed and safely stored in an air-controlled room. All that remains to be done is to find a worthy institution to which the *Star* and the Macpherson family can donate these five hundred cartoons. Several dozen of the cartoons reproduced in this book were discovered in that loo. Thank you, Andrew and Astrid.

SPECIAL MENTIONS

Toronto editor and publisher Douglas Gibson was an enthusiastic endorser of this Macpherson book right from the beginning. His insight on Duncan was very keen since he worked closely

LEFT | Toronto editor Doug Gibson.

RIGHT | Susan Dewar at a cartoon convention in Quebec City in 2003 amidst several of her Canadian cartoonist admirers. From top left: Terry Mosher, Serge Chapleau, Michael De Adder, Graeme MacKay, Tim Dolighan, and Pascal Élie.

with Macpherson on a number of books. Furthermore, Doug made important contributions to the early chapter on Duncan's time as a child spent in Scotland.

Bob Church and John Stabback proved very helpful on helping me to understand how Duncan spent his later years in Beaverton. Gary LeDrew did much the same in describing Uxbridge in the 1950s, at a time when Duncan, Dorothy, and Ian Macpherson lived there. Speaking of that, thanks to Greg Latremoille for allowing us to reproduce the beautiful David Milne painting of Uxbridge.

Andrew Caddell, author and Ottawa-based entrepreneur, previously worked as a broadcaster, political adviser, United Nations staffer, and diplomat. I thank him for his input on Lester Pearson. In this regard, I also extend my gratitude to Michael Pearson, the former prime minister's grandson.

THE CARTOONISTS

I would be remiss in not acknowledging the many Canadian cartoonists who were highly supportive of this project. Many of their entertaining anecdotes about Duncan Macpherson are sprinkled throughout the book.

There are no family photographs to document Duncan Macpherson's boyhood years in Scotland. Three contemporary cartoonists – all Macpherson fans – volunteered some memorable work to make

The Duncan Macpherson Award, the year it was given to Stan Roach.

that chapter come alive visually: Bruce MacKinnon of the *Halifax Chronicle Herald* is obviously of Scottish origin. The family of the *Globe and Mail*'s Brian Gable is technically English, but as they originated in Cumbria, right on the Scottish border, I consider it to be close enough.

Susan Dewar was for many years the only full-time female editorial cartoonist in Canada. Over the course of her career, Sue's thought-provoking drawings have appeared in all the newspapers of the Sun Media chain. Both a talented artist and incisive social commentator, Dewar is affectionately referred as the den mother to the rest of the country's political cartoonists. When she was growing up in Toronto, a stone's throw from the Macpherson home on Blythwood Avenue, her mother used to organize Saturday night parlour games for friends and neighbours. "She would pin Duncan Macpherson cartoons from the *Star* all over the wall, with the cutlines clipped off. She would then quiz people as to which cutlines belonged to particular cartoons. It was great fun! I really enjoyed that, as did all the guests. I believe that it was just about then I decided I wanted to become a cartoonist."

Cartoonists aren't always the best organizers. However, following Duncan's death, several admirable attempts were made to keep his memory alive.

In 1999 the annual Duncan Macpherson Scholarship of Excellence Award was created, with $500 (now $1,000) being presented to the most deserving third-year student at the Ontario College of Art and Design. Dorothy Macpherson, along with Brian Gable (*Globe and Mail*) and Patrick Corrigan (*Toronto Star*), served as initial advisers. The *Toronto Star* was the principal sponsor of the award.

Several years earlier, the Association of Canadian Editorial Cartoonists had created an annual award of $500 in Macpherson's name that was to be presented to the most deserving young Canadian cartoonist, as judged by the members. Andy Donato of the *Toronto Sun* and Blaine MacDonald of the Hamilton *Spectator* were the

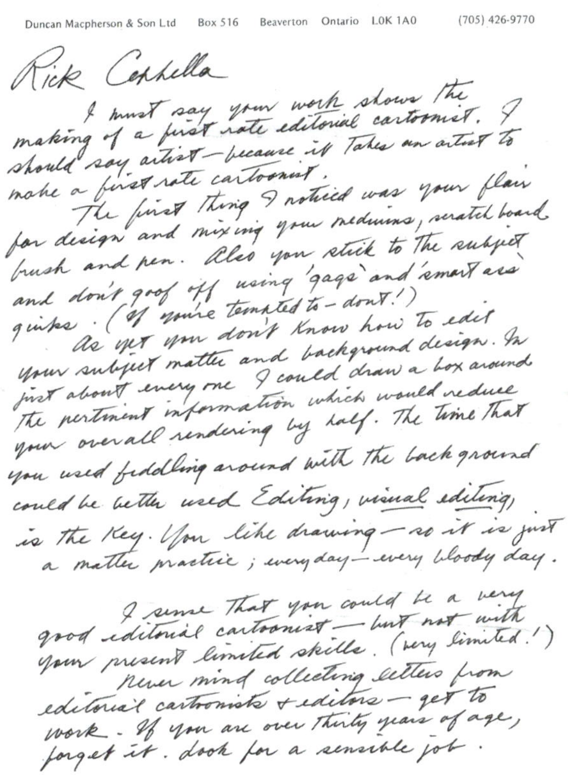

Duncan Macpherson & Son Ltd Box 516 Beaverton Ontario L0K 1A0 (705) 426-9770

Rick Cepplella

I must say your work shows the making of a first rate editorial cartoonist. I should say artist — because it takes an artist to make a first rate cartoonist.

The first thing I noticed was your flair for design and mixing your mediums, scratch board brush and pen. Also you stick to the subject and don't goof off using 'gags' and 'smart ass' quips. (If you're tempted to – don't!)

As yet you don't know how to edit your subject matter and background design. In just about every one I could draw a box around the pertinent information which would reduce your overall rendering by half. The time that you used fiddling around with the background could be better used Editing, visual editing, is the key. You like drawing — so it is just a matter practice; everyday — every bloody day.

I sense that you could be a very good editorial cartoonist — but not with your present limited skills. (very limited!)

Never mind collecting letters from editorial cartoonists & editors — get to work. If you are over thirty years of age, forget it. Look for a sensible job.

chief organizers. Blaine created a personalized plaque for presentation to the award's recipient.

Ferg Gadzala, a Montreal caricaturist and member of the Quebec cartoon group 1001 Visages, was also directly involved. Ferg was the *Westmount Examiner*'s cartoonist for twenty-two years before the newspaper folded in 2015. As a child in Toronto, Ferg had admired Duncan Macpherson. "I used to hunt down packs of bundled up *Toronto Stars* on garbage day to take home and cut out Macpherson's cartoons and Ripley's Believe-It-or-Not, for their brushwork. This was in the early 1960s, when good drawing was king, and Macpherson was right at the top!" For each of the five years of the award's existence, Gadzala created a small sculpture of Macpherson's "Little Guy" to be presented to the ACEC award winner.

Winning the award conferred a great deal of prestige in the cartoon community. The first winner was British Columbia's Rick Cepella, who had actually corresponded with Macpherson in the mid-1980s. The second recipient was Stan Roach, a cartoonist for several Montreal weekly publications. Stan told Gadzala that every drawing he did after hearing about the award was with the intention of winning it, which he did in 1996.

The award was discontinued after five years, perhaps because of feuding over responsibilities or because the organizers ran out of young cartoonists to recognize. Nonetheless, the five statuettes created by Gadzala are considered today to be collectors' items.

INSTITUTIONS

Library and Archives Canada

From the beginning, Mary Margaret Johnston-Miller at Library and Archives Canada has been helpful beyond the call of duty. The Archives has thousands of Macpherson's original drawings in storage at its Preservation Centre in Gatineau, Quebec. Together we spent days going through that material, coming across many

LEFT | A note of advice from Duncan to Rick Cepella. In his initial note, Rick had misspelled Macpherson's name – just as Duncan misspelled Cepella in his response.

ABOVE | A statuette of Macpherson's little guy, designed by Ferg Gadzala. Photo credit: Nancy Roach.

Dorothy and Duncan Macpherson always enjoyed visiting the McCord Museum on trips to Montreal. The museum is now home to 45,000 political cartoons, including 800 original drawings by Duncan Macpherson.

forgotten gems. We also enjoyed leafing through hard copies of the old *Montreal Standard* from the 1940s and 1950s. What a magic time that was for Canadian illustrators! That would make for a handsome volume alone.

Toronto Reference Library

Thanks to Alan Walker at the Special Collections Department of the Toronto Reference Library for expediting access to the *Toronto Star* photo archives. Also, I appreciated Alan chasing down rare hard copies of the old *Star Weekly* magazine in the library's collection.

McCord Museum

Montreal's McCord Museum is in possession of another important collection of Canadian political cartoons. The museum, which is devoted to Canadian history, was a latecomer to Duncan Macpherson's work but is now an enthusiastic follower and collector.

I'll let Christian Vachon, the museum's curator of paintings, prints, and drawings, tell the story:

> C'est Terry Mosher qui m'a introduit à l'œuvre satirique de Duncan Macpherson. Quelle révélation! Je n'avais jamais rien vu de si puissant, de si élégant et de si futé publié en sol canadien. Je savais que la caricature canadienne avait atteint un degré de maturité qui lui conférait une place certaine au sein de la communauté internationale du dessin de presse. Il me restait à apprendre que Macpherson était l'un des caricaturistes qui ont contribué de manière significative à lui faire gagner ses lettres de noblesse. Et je l'ai appris du meilleur professeur qui soit.
>
> J'ai fait la connaissance de Terry dans le cadre de la réalisation de l'exposition Aislin & Chapleau, Caricatures présentée au Musée McCord en 1997. J'ai été nommé ensuite le conservateur responsable de la collection de caricatures éditoriales. Terry, qui connaît tous les caricaturistes vivants ou décédés du Canada, a plus d'une fois judicieusement conseillé le musée en matière de développement de cette collection, la troisième en importance

au pays. Il a d'ailleurs été instrumental dans l'achat d'une collection de près de 800 dessins de Macpherson en nous aidant à obtenir l'aide financière du Toronto Star et de la Fondation R. Howard Webster.

Rapatriée d'un établissement d'enseignement de la ville de New York, où elle avait mystérieusement échoué, cette étonnante sélection de caricatures, d'illustrations, d'esquisses et d'aquarelles couvre l'ensemble de la carrière de Macpherson. À partir d'illustrations réalisées pour Maclean's au cours des années 1950, elle remonte jusqu'aux dernières caricatures publiées dans le Toronto Star en 1993. À titre d'exemple, cette collection extrêmement variée comprend de fascinantes illustrations de reportages réalisées à Québec en 1964 ou en Chine en 1979, ainsi qu'un abondant corpus d'aquarelles et de dessins exécutés dans le contexte de la préparation de son livre Macpherson's Canada publié en 1969.

Le Musée McCord est enchanté que plusieurs œuvres provenant de cette collection soient reproduites dans cet ouvrage et de contribuer ainsi à mieux faire connaître ce géant de la caricature et de l'illustration canadienne. Grâce au généreux soutien de nos deux commanditaires, tous ces dessins ont été numérisés et sont accessibles sur le site web du musée. Ne restait plus à Terry Mosher d'achever cette méticuleuse étude de la carrière de Duncan Macpherson pour nous aider à contextualiser le cadre de leur production. Je lui en serai éternellement reconnaissant.

THE POLITICIANS

I am grateful to David Crombie and Paul Hellyer for allowing me to interview them. Their insights helped me to understand better the context of Duncan Macpherson's earlier years as a cartoonist. Many of Macpherson's targets have passed on, but I gathered some wonderful quotes from previously published articles on the subject of political cartooning in Canada. I also drew on transcripts of interviews from the film *The Hecklers*, with comments and insights from such important Macpherson targets as John Diefenbaker, Robert Stanfield, and Joey Smallwood.

Not that every politician – past or present – wanted to be interviewed. Pierre Trudeau, when asked about cartoons of himself, used to simply change the subject with a clever bit of misdirection. And Joe Clark, one of Macpherson's favourite subjects, very politely declined to provide commentary for this book:

> Dear Terry – apologies for this late reply. Maureen forwarded your message. I've noted before that, for the person on the dart board, cartoonists are the most disconcerting of critics, because the best of your caricatures are based on characteristics that are true … I admire the insights and the skill – and am grateful that you've hardened my hide – but, as I enter my eighties, I am not inclined to add to your reflections. But you can be sure I'll read the book.
>
> Best wishes, Joe.

When the general public tired of Pierre Trudeau, Joe Clark was knocking at the door.

OTHER ACKNOWLEDGMENTS

Special thanks also to Gerry Mamone, Dominic Hardy, Charley Gordon, Jaleen Grove, Allan Dickie, Carol Lindsay (for her memories of the Silver Rail), Sigrid McFarland, Mel Morris, Graham Fraser, Ian McLaren, Warren Creates, Dawn Martin, Ted Michener, Alan King, Doug Ball, Lynn Johnston, Queenie Curnoe, Max Newton, Mel Morris, Christopher Varley, Paul Berton, Linda Sergiades, Michael Enright, Marjorie Harris, Stephen Wickens, and, at McGill-Queen's University Press, Mark Abley, Curtis Fahey, Neil Erickson, and the rest of the gang.

Books

Cartoons of Duncan Macpherson. 1961. *Toronto Star*

Cartoons by Macpherson. Volume 2: 1962. *Toronto Star*

Cartoons by Macpherson. Volume 3: 1963. *Toronto Star*

Cartoons by Macpherson. Volume 4: 1963. *Toronto Star*

Cartoons by Macpherson. Volume 5: 1964. *Toronto Star*

Cartoons by Macpherson. Volume 6: 1966. *Toronto Star*

Cartoons by Macpherson. Volume 7: 1967. *Toronto Star*

Macpherson's Canada, with Jack Brehl. 1969. *Toronto Star*

Editorial Cartoons Macpherson. 1970. *Toronto Star*

Macpherson Cartoons. 1971. Star Reader Services

Macpherson Editorial Cartoons. 1972. Star Reader Services

Macpherson Editorial Cartoons. 1973. Star Reader Services

Macpherson Editorial Cartoons. 1974. Star Reader Services

Macpherson Editorial Cartoons. 1975. Star Reader Services

Macpherson Editorial Cartoons. 1976. Star Reader Services

Macpherson Editorial Cartoons. 1977. Star Reader Services

Macpherson Editorial Cartoons. 1978. Macmillan Canada

Macpherson Editorial Cartoons. 1979. Macmillan Canada

Daily Smile. 1980. Public Archives Canada

The Hecklers, by Peter Desbarats and Terry Mosher: 1979. McClelland and Stewart

Articles

Canadian Weekly: 6 February 1965. "The Artist with a Devil in His Pen."

Canadian Art Magazine: January–February 1965

Canada Month: April 1962. Anonymous, "Macpherson: Satire to Drink By."

Toronto Life Magazine: June 1973. John Gault, "What a Friend We Have in Duncan."

Miscellaneous doodles and sketches by Duncan Macpherson.

CREDITS

The author thanks the individuals and institutions listed below for permission to reproduce the images included in this book. Those used with permission from and courtesy of the family of Duncan Macpherson are not included; nor are those that are the property of the author. The location of each image is noted by page number.

Duncan Macpherson's original captions appear in capital letters.

INDIVIDUALS

Guy Badeaux: 346 (left).

Doug Ball, Canadian Press: 249 (left).

Rick Cepella: 381 (left).

Bob Church: 332 (left).

Patrick Corrigan: 179.

Andy Donato: 201.

Brian Gable: 16 (left).

Graham Harrop: 136.

Mary Hughson: 17, 326, 374, 376 (right), 379 (right).

Lynn Johnston: 341.

John Larter: 327.

Greg Latremoille: 59.

Bruce Mackinnon: 16 (right).

Brad McKay: 375 (left).

Ian McLaren: 6, 7 (left), 7 (right).

Gerry Mamone: 5 (right).

Nancy Roach: 381 (right).

INSTITUTIONS

Canadian Dimension Magazine: 11, 175 (right).

Canadian Illustrated News: 133.

Canadian War Museum: 35 (top), 35 (bottom), 36.

Estate of Pierre Berton: 80 (left), 80 (right), 83.

Estate of Lewis Parker: 73 (middle).

Grip: 131.

Library and Archives Canada: 5 (top left), 5 (bottom left), 33, 323 (right).

Library and Archives Canada and the *Toronto Star:* 12, 14, 22, 38, 39, 40, 54, 55 (left), 55 (right), 82 (left), 96, 99 (top), 99 (bottom), 102, 103, 104 (right), 105, 106, 107, 108 (right), 112 (right), 119, 123, 125, 128, 134, 135, 138, 141, 144, 145, 146, 147, 148, 149, 151, 153, 154, 155, 156 (left), 157, 158, 159, 160, 161, 162, 166 (left), 166 (right), 171, 172, 173, 182 (right), 184 (right), 188, 191, 193, 194, 196, 197, 210, 211, 213, 215, 219, 221, 225, 244, 246, 248 (left), 248 (right), 252, 254, 256, 257 (left), 257 (right), 258, 259, 260, 262, 264, 266, 267, 269, 271, 272, 276, 277, 278, 279, 280, 282, 283, 284, 285, 287 (right), 288, 289, 290 (left), 290 (right), 291, 292, 294 (left), 294 (right), 295, 296, 297 (right), 300, 307, 309 (left), 309 (right), 313, 316 (right), 330, 349, 363.

Maclean's magazine: 23, 51 (right), 70, 71 (top), 73 (left), 77, 78, 314, 362.

McCord Museum: 68, 71 (bottom), 73 (right), 74 (left), 74 (right), 76 (top), 76 (bottom), 190 (right), 192 (right), 308 (left), 308 (right), 316 (left), 319, 324 (right), 328, 342, 352, 354, 382.

McCord Museum and the *Toronto Star*: 230, 231 (left), China sketchbook (from page 238 to 243), 305 (left), 344, 351, 355, 357, 359, 360, 365, 370, 371.

(Montreal) *Standard Magazine*: 48, 49 (top left), 49 (top right), 49 (bottom left), 49 (bottom right), 50.

The Toronto Public Library: 19 (right), 45 (bottom right), 47 (right), 87, 101, 143, 178, 183, 378 (top left).

The *Toronto Star*: indd. 2, 6, 10, 21, 29, 41, 75 (left), 75 (right), 84, 85, 86 (left), 86 (right), 89, 90, 91, 92, 93, 94, 104 (left), 108 (left), 109, 110, 112 (left), 113, 114, 115, 116, 117, 118, 120, 121, 122 (left), 122 (right), 124, 126, 127, 129, 130, 132, 137, 140, 142, 150, 152, 156 (right), 164 (left), 164 (right), 165, 167 (left), 167 (right), 168, 169, 170, 174, 175 (left), 176, 180, 185, 186, 198, 199, 202, photo essay from page 205 through to page 209, 212, 214, 216, 222, 224 (top left), 224 (bottom left), 224 (right), Cuban sketchbook from page 226 to 229, 231 (left), 231 (right), 232 (left), 232 (right), 233, 234 (top), 234 (bottom), 235, 238 (left), 238 (right), 247, 249 (right), 251 (left), 251 (right), 255 (left), 255 (right), 261, 263, 268 (left), 268 (right), 270, 273, 274, 275, 281, 286, 287, (left), 293, 297 (left), 298, 299, 305 (right), 306, 310, 311, 312, 322 (left), 323 (left), 343, 347, 348, 350, 353, 356, 358, 361, 364, 366, 367, 368, 369, 377 (right), 378 (bottom left), 384.

Tate, London: 37, *Tube Shelter Perspective*, 1941, Henry Moore OM, CH (1898–1986), Presented by the War Artists' Advisory Committee 1946; TATE N05709.

Weekend Magazine: 51 (left), 52, 63, 64, 65, 66 (left), 66 (right).